INTERNATIONAL POLITICS

IN THE ATOMIC AGE

International Politics

in the Atomic Age

JOHN H. HERZ

COLUMBIA UNIVERSITY PRESS

New York and London

Preface

This is an old-fashioned kind of book. It is the result neither of teamwork nor of any similar type of group study or collective research. It is not the product of a seminar, nor that of a study conference for which the author acted as reporter. It has not issued from a lecture series, and it is not based on a field trip or any wide traveling whatsoever. The author has not used a single IBM facility in the book's preparation, nor has he conducted any interviews for it, whether in depth or otherwise. There has not been any polling, nor have questionnaires been distributed. As a matter of fact, the book does not contain a single chart, graph, map, diagram, table, or statistical figure. It is simply the product of the application to problems and subject matter at hand of whatever intelligence was available.

However, in this age of the vanishing "free scholar" (that is, one who lives and works on his own means or is subsidized by family or friends), even the type of writer who operates alone has to be supported if he wants to be free, for a while, from the toils of teaching undergraduates or selling insurance. The author therefore gladly acknowledges the assistance of one of those beneficial institutions to which scholarship is so greatly indebted these days. His thanks go to the Rockefeller Foundation, which, in 1954-55, made a research grant enabling him to write the first draft of this study.

Not a word will be said here about the book itself. Either it speaks for itself or it is a failure.

Acknowledgments are gratefully made to the following publishers for permission to quote: Harcourt, Brace and Co., for the use of Bernard Brodie (ed.), *The Absolute Weapon* (copyright, 1946); Harper & Brothers, for the use of Henry A. Kissinger, *Nuclear Weapons and Foreign Policy* (copyright, 1957). I further wish to thank the editors and publishers of *World Politics* for permission to reproduce passages from my article entitled "Rise and Demise of the Territorial State," which appeared in the issue of July, 1957.

Last but not least, I wish to express my deeply felt gratitude for stimulation and unceasing encouragement to one whose spiritual comradeship-in-arms I greatly cherish: Kenneth W. Thompson.

JOHN H. HERZ

Scarsdale, New York
July 4, 1958

Note to Paperback Edition

This edition reprints without change the original text published some years ago. I do not think that this renders it outdated, even though we live in a world of rapid change. Some references, not so obvious then as they are now, may seem superfluous (e.g., remarks on summit conferences) ; others may appear dated (e.g., references to African colonialism) ; in still other instances, the reader may miss reference to later events and developments (e.g., the Sino-Soviet conflict). But, I believe that the essence of the book—its theses on nature and changes of statehood and on the impact of nuclear weapons on international systems—still stands, and that new developments have served to corroborate my theory. The current-affairs-conscious reader, knowing so much more today than the author knew when he wrote the book, may even enjoy testing its theses against subsequent developments.   *Spring, 1962*

Contents

INTERNATIONAL POLITICS

IN THE ATOMIC AGE

Introduction

I tell you these are great times. Man has mounted science, and is now run away with it. The engines he will have invented will be beyond his strength to control. Some day science may have the existence of mankind in its power, and the human race commit suicide by blowing up the world. HENRY ADAMS, 1862

In our present predicament, which the young Henry Adams predicted with such amazing perspicuity almost a hundred years ago, it is tempting to apply to scholarly enterprise the Latin saying "primo vivere deinde philosophari" by freely translating it into, "Let us think first of all about how to survive, thereafter about everything else." But thinking about how to survive means thinking about international politics. While a past is not remote in which other matters, such as economic affairs or domestic politics, loomed larger in the daily concerns of people than those which then were perhaps fittingly called "foreign" affairs, today the latter's impact on the well-being and, indeed, survival of every one of us has become only too patent in an age in which the black threat of nuclear annihilation hovers over all. In the field of international politics, where events now govern the very basis of everything else—namely, the survival of mankind in the literal, physical sense of the term—studying facts, explanations, and solutions is no longer mere "philosophizing" but an essential part of that "life" which is at stake.

How, then, is it that "theory of international politics," in the sense of the study of the basic data, conditions, trends, and systems of international life, is so recent a phenomenon in the universe of scholarship? How is it that even in recent days that study is often assigned a rather modest back seat in the general field of international relations studies? Though consideration of the more specific and topical areas of foreign affairs, such as investigations into foreign policies of particular powers, is abundant, serious studies of what makes all such policy "tick," what are the underlying causes of events, are still few and far between.

One reason for neglect may lie in what seemingly is a general characteristic of international relations: the absence of regularity of situations and events. Social sciences, in their attempt to imitate the natural sciences in order to substantiate their claim to being "sciences," have grown in stature and respectability in proportion to their being able to indicate probabilities of events and to deal with predictable situations on the basis of "like" relationships and repeatable sequences of events. Thus, "political science," of which "international politics" is a part, has attained respectability as a discipline where large numbers of similar phenomena and comparable data, such as behavior patterns of voters, or motivations of "decision makers," can be assembled, tested, and made the objects of—ideally—statistical findings. The trouble with international politics was—and is—that in international affairs most relationships and sequences of events seem to be unique, connected as they are with the particular character, needs, and consequently policies of a relatively small number of entities and agents.

International politics therefore was for a long time descriptive of untypical events, that is, part and parcel of history-writing ("diplomatic history"). Or it was that field of study where wishes for a better world were expressed by builders of models for the future, who believed that the actual world of international affairs was hardly worth considering because it was doomed sooner or later to yield to a more perfect world. The latter approach was typical of nineteenth-century optimism. The hopes of that century were shattered by the upheavals of the twentieth.

If needs give rise to policies, they also have their impact on theory. So it is easy to see why the thirties witnessed pioneering attempts to analyze those factors which seemed to underlie the more specific events and conditions in the international arena and which all seemed to relate to "power." They grew out of the rise to prominence of totalitarian and aggressive regimes, which destroyed the chances of isolation as well as the hopes placed (or misplaced) in leagues of nations and trends toward peace. International politics was thus studied as "the struggle for power and influence among nations," [1] and the foreign policies of nations emerged as policies concerned with the "national interest." Then came the dawn of the atomic age, and with it the dusk of the era when nations were uncontested and not-to-be-doubted "power units." When, as this study will show, the very foundation of the traditional power holders' coherence, strength, and therewith "power," their territorial impermeability, is vanishing, a reappraisal of concepts and assumptions of the "traditional" approach (recent though it is) is clearly called for. And it may well turn out to be an "agonizing reappraisal" where so much of that which is connected with the future of nations, of statehood, of international relations, and of military technology is indeterminate, multifaceted, and subject to often contradictory and mutually exclusive interpretation.

WAYS TO STUDY INTERNATIONAL POLITICS

How shall we approach the deeper problem of theory in international politics? Here we are faced with the question

[1] See Kenneth W. Thompson, "The Study of International Politics," *The Review of Politics*, 14: 441 (1952).

of method.   Questions of methodology may seem frustrating or even useless to doers who crave to delve into *medias res*. But the approach—that is, the method—may well determine the object.   This is particularly so in a field such as international politics, where so much is still unexplored and where the object itself, or core of study, is still somewhat indeterminate.   It is therefore incumbent upon students in this discipline to clarify for themselves and their readers the ways in which they propose to approach international politics as an area of investigation.

Let us distinguish two opposite methods of analyzing phenomena in this area.   We do this for reasons of clarification and better understanding and not to imply that these extremes occur frequently in actual study.   One may be characterized as "abstract," the other as "ultraconcrete."   The latter is close to the "historical" approach to which we referred before as the one that identifies international politics more or less with the history of foreign affairs—either past history or, more often in the case of international politics, current history.   It perceives in international politics nothing but the flux of changing concrete situations and constellations and is inclined to deny the possibility or usefulness of generalizing and systematizing in this connection.   The other approach considers what is going on in international affairs as a sort of raw material from which to abstract types of power patterns, models of all kinds of possible relationships, or, in the behaviorist manner, types of attitudes, such as behavior patterns in foreign policy decision making.   Theory in international politics is here reduced to typology or phenomenology.   At the one pole, everything in international affairs is always new and incomparable, and nothing whatsoever repeats itself.   At the other, events and actions fall into immutable patterns.

It is clear that if students of international politics are to distinguish themselves from historians and their discipline

from diplomatic history, they must be able to show that some
amount of abstraction, that is, generalization, is feasible in
their area.   Thus the reaction against overconcreteness—even
though it seems occasionally to have gone too far in the direction of abstraction—was all to the good.   It showed that a
generalizing approach is possible in a field apparently characterized by its dearth of "like" data and its abundance of
"unique" ones.   But the question, where may subject matter
be found that is repetitive and thus open to generalization,
remains.

I believe that in international politics it is relationships
among basic units of international affairs, rather than behavior patterns of agents, that lend themselves most properly
to theoretical investigation.   I suggest, therefore, that the
primary method of studying international politics should be
one that deals with the "structures" and "systems" of international relations as the basic data.

Structure, in what follows, refers to the basic features which
characterize the given units of international politics at or
within a particular period; system indicates the ways in which
these units organize their relationships (formally, or infor-
mally) on the basis of such structure.   This constitutes a middle way of regarding situations which develop and change in
history and yet are more stable than mere fleeting events as
the primary object of research in international politics.   It
implies—and here some historians may disagree—the possibility of generalizing to some extent from the historically
given concrete phenomena, that is, of distinguishing in the
flux of historical development recurring situations, relatively
stable general patterns of relationships, and systems of policies
which emerge and are describable for broader periods.   It can
be seen, for instance, that for a considerable period in the
history of foreign relations nation-states existed together in a
"balance," or equilibrium, which, although always en-

dangered, was also restorable and restored. This system of relationships was based on an international structure characterized by what on the following pages will be described as the "territoriality" of its units, the so-called "sovereign," independent states. It was this structure, and the framework of relationships resulting from it, with which policy makers and others whose attitudes bear on foreign policy, had to reckon. Therefore—and here some behaviorists may disagree —the study of international politics cannot exhaust itself in a study of the motives and actions of those who are responsible for the making of such politics. Policy makers do not act in a void; they are confronted with conditions (partly man-made, to be sure, but once made, *faits accomplis*) which form the framework in which they have to place their activities, even though they may wish to change the conditions.[2]

This is not to deny that attitude study has its legitimate place in the study of foreign affairs; attitudes and institutions are obviously interactive. It is merely to say that, while others, for instance, psychology or sociology, may be better equipped to deal with the former, there are no disciplines outside political science that are peculiarly fitted to treat of the relationship patterns of political entities, and of the related political procedures and institutions. And it is supposed that international politics is part of political science. Thus the approach favored here comes closest to the one which distills "models" of international systems from international phenomena,[3] provided these models are not products of abstract speculation but distillates from life.

[2] See the discussion of these and related problems by David Easton, *The Political System* (New York, 1953), in particular chs. 7 and 8, dealing with the "Structure of the Situation."

[3] See, for instance, Morton A. Kaplan, "Balance of Power, Bipolarity, and Other Models of International Systems," *American Political Science Review*, 51: 684 ff. (1957); and also his *System and Process in International Politics* (New York, 1957), ch. 2.

Assuming, then, that generalizations are feasible, and structures and systems observable, we must beware of looking at them in too static a light. Especially if we wish to study and evaluate concepts which spring from and apply to them, there is a danger that what has been referred to as "preoccupation of contemporary political research with stationary conditions" will impede our endeavors.[4] Concepts in international relations, though possibly applicable to broad periods of time and large parts of the globe, still reflect changing conditions. They cease to be applicable where structures change fundamentally, but they have a tendency to linger in the minds of those reared in their tradition and to obscure the necessity for reevaluating the conceptual framework once its material basis has changed. Since the latter changes continually, reevaluation of some kind is constantly necessary. And this applies to the "doers," too, who, in their decisions and actions, cannot help but be influenced by the universe of concepts and ideas that forms their environment.

It follows that the efforts of those who do engage in the study of structures and systems of international relations are sometimes in danger of being vitiated because factors are considered constant and concepts permanently valid. Thus, we may be told, "international politics has always been, and will always be, concerned with power relations among nation-states"; or, "there is always some kind of a power balance among these states." From this it is inferred that standards for action can be obtained by comparing two seemingly similar situations and drawing "parallels" from the earlier one. But such parallels can be deadly. Together with the similarities there may be (in fact, always are) dissimilarities in the compared constellations, and it is easy to neglect the latter, or give them too little weight, where situations are considered as basically unchanging. One of the crucial problems, for in-

[4] Easton, *The Political System,* p. 43.

stance, with which present Western policy is confronted, concerns the question whether or not the situation at the time of the Nazi-Fascist expansionism and aggressiveness can be considered fundamentally similar to that of present Communist attempts at foreign penetration. To find an answer it is necessary to compare two sets of circumstances: one, the international one, involves comparing the present international structure and system with conditions of twenty years ago; the other refers to the general character and structure of the respective political regimes at home and their relevance to the respective foreign policies. We may then arrive at the conclusion that, despite outward parallelisms, there is a basic dissimilarity between the warlike aggressiveness of fascist-type totalitarian regimes and the expansionism of Communism, especially the post-Stalinist version. For that expansionism (possibly even more dangerous than the warlike type) operates through revolution from within or through domestic developments in the nontotalitarian countries of the world. We might further discover that means to oppose the earlier expansionism—for instance, a system of genuine "collective security"—have, because of fundamental changes in the international structure, become inapplicable, and that attempts to cope with the situation through different means are, therefore, not necessarily "appeasement." [5]

Lastly, in addition to factors of a foreign policy nature or those referring to internal (domestic) structures and regimes, factors dealing with the general culture (civilization) out of which international systems have arisen must be taken into consideration. A conscious equilibrium policy, for instance, as distinguished from the mere *de facto* presence of some balance, was coeval with the age of rationalism in which the

---

[5] On the danger of "forming a distorted picture of the nature of a negotiated settlement" because of drawing the wrong parallel see Hans J. Morgenthau, *In Defense of the National Interest* (New York, 1952), p. 140.

modern European state system and its peculiar diplomacy arose. A state system which in many other respects was similar to this one—where, for instance, for certain periods power balances did exist among "independent" units of international relations—namely, that of Antiquity in the Hellenistic and early Roman period, never knew such a policy *qua* conscious policy.[6] And a policy of that kind may encounter difficulties in our age, where not only do power relations proceed from quite a different basis but where, in addition, international relations are comprised of units of widely varying cultures and civilizations, in fact, all civilizations in the world.

It is the objective of this study to find out to what extent the traditional concepts of international politics are still applicable and at what points they must be reevaluated in the light of changed conditions. It will be the main thesis of this study that some of the factors which underlay the "modern state system" as it emerged about three hundred years ago and which determined rather stably its structure and relationships have now, in our century and even within the lifetime of many of us, undergone such fundamental changes that the structure of international relations itself is different, or in the process of becoming different, and can no longer be interpreted exclusively in traditional terms. To this might be leveled the objection that the apparently "fundamental" nature of recent or present changes is merely a subjective impression; that changes have forever been occurring in history; and that those who are affected by them are naturally inclined to lend them more significance than future generations will be willing to grant from hindsight. Therefore, in claiming that the advent of the atomic age has initiated something radically new, we must show in some detail the special nature

6 For references see my *Political Realism and Political Idealism* (Chicago, 1951), pp. 208-10.

of this newness, before proceeding to that comparison between the traditional and the new in international politics which will constitute a major part of this study.

THE NEWNESS OF THE NEW AGE

During the Second World War a skeptical observer of the flood of plans for a "new" postwar world asked doubtingly how new the better world would be.[7] More appropriately (if he could have foreseen what would happen), he might have asked how much better or worse *even* the new world would be. Nobody at that time could so much as faintly visualize the dimension of the change which was about to occur—whether for better or worse—in the aftermath of the war. I do not, of course, refer to that change regarding which Carl Becker and others were skeptical: a change, as the idealists hoped for, of human nature or, at least, in human arrangements of domestic and international affairs; I refer to the change which has affected the "material" or power basis of any and all such arrangements.

The change which the advent of the "atomic" or "nuclear age" has wrought is not simply a matter of the invention of one or another specific weapon. It is the accumulated and accumulating impact of a process which can be termed truly revolutionary: the process of scientific invention and technological discovery which not only has "perfected" the fission and fusion weapons themselves, but in its wake so far has brought jet aircraft with intercontinental range and supersonic speed, missiles with nuclear warheads, and the prospect of nuclear-powered planes and submarines with unlimited range, and rockets with equally unlimited range and with guidance to specific targets anywhere in the world. It may be that experts could add to this list equally or more significant achievements and prospects (such as the ones connected with

7 Carl Becker, *How New Will the Better World Be?* (New York, 1944).

earth satellites and space stations). To the lay observer the foregoing is enough, because it seems to add up to an almost uncanny absoluteness in the effect the new process produces. This in itself involves something entirely new. I refer to its effect—far beyond the area of the military and its usual implications—on the structure and function of that unit, or entity, which thus far has proved to be the decisive organization in the lives of human beings: the unit of protection. This unit, whether tribe or township, nation-state or empire, whatever its additional functions, has always had as its most elementary objectives the pacification of a certain area or group to establish peace within it and the defense of this area or group to ensure security from outside danger. Previous "revolutionary" innovations in military technology and similar fields could certainly affect it, but their effect was relative. They might, as in the case of the "gunpowder revolution" of the later Middle Ages in Europe, render particular power units, such as castles or walled cities, obsolete *qua* units of protection, but this did not mean doing away with protective units as such. It usually, and merely, led to an extension of the realm of a defensible entity, for instance, from city-state to territorial state, or from territorial state to empire. The new process of our age, on the other hand, seems to have a more fundamental effect. When not even half the globe remains defensible against the all-out onslaught of the new weapons, it is no longer a question of enlargement of basic area and of substitution of one unit for another. The power of protection, on which political authority was based in the past, seems to be in jeopardy for any imaginable entity.

Since we are inhabitants of a planet of limited (and, so it now seems, insufficient) size, we have reached those limits within which the effect of the means of destruction has become absolute. Formerly, a new weapon might mean the

destruction in war of a limited circle of people and their
civilization: of a city, even of an entire region. But there still
remained the seemingly inexhaustible reservoir of mankind,
of other civilizations. Now the universal destruction—extensively and intensively—which the new age presages, does
not seem to leave any imaginable way out.

The dilemma thus reached is obvious. J. Robert Oppenheimer summed it up several years ago in a now famous
simile:

We may anticipate a state of affairs in which the two Great Powers
will each be in a position to put an end to the civilization and life
of the other, though not without risking its own. We may be
likened to two scorpions in a bottle, each capable of killing the
other, but only at the risk of his own life.[8]

It is this impression of a situation which defies rational approaches and has somehow become unmanageable which has,
perhaps, been the most striking immediate effect of the
"new." Even the most "realistic" and detached persons have
confessed to such a reaction. Thus Churchill has spoken of
"the immense gulf between the atomic and the hydrogen
bomb":

The atomic bomb, with all its terror, did not carry us outside the
scope of human control and manageable events in thought or
action, peace or war. But when Mr. Sterling Cole, the chairman
of the United States Congressional Committee, gave out a year ago
—17 February 1954—the first comprehensive review of the hydrogen
bomb, the entire foundation of human affairs was revolutionized
and mankind placed in a situation both measureless and laden
with doom.[9]

More recently, a report on the discussions of a group of experts in defense and international affairs revealed that in their
minds the loss and destruction incurred through nuclear war

[8] "Atomic Weapons and American Policy," *Foreign Affairs*, 31: 529
(1952–53).
[9] Speech in Commons, March 1, 1955 (New York *Times*, March 2, 1955).

would be "beyond comprehension. The world would be incredibly changed." [10] Such references could, of course, be easily multiplied.

But perhaps the impression thus gained is exaggerated. Has not, we may ask, every "revolutionizing" event in history first so stunned contemporaries that many would predict the "end of everything"? Perhaps, therefore, it is advisable to be cautious in assessing the newness of the new. We may be warned, in particular, by the fate of predictions made previously at times when technological innovations seemed to presage immediate and fundamental changes in warfare, strategy, and human relations in general. Thus, prior to the First World War, the invention of the machine gun and other developments in warcraft seemed so revolutionary that they induced one famous student of military affairs and world relations to make this prediction:

The very development that has taken place in the mechanism of war has rendered war an impracticable operation. The dimensions of modern armaments and the organization of society have rendered its prosecution an economic impossibility. It is impossible for the modern state to carry on war under modern conditions with any prospect of being able to carry that war to a conclusion by defeating its adversary by force of arms on the battle-field. Neither is any war possible that will not entail, even upon the victorious Power, the destruction of its resources and the breakup of society. War therefore has become impossible, except at the price of suicide.[11]

This statement sounds familiar today and may, indeed, fit

[10] *NATO: A Critical Appraisal,* report prepared by Gardner Patterson and Edgar S. Furniss, Jr., on Princeton University Conference on NATO, Princeton, June 19–June 29, 1957, p. 30.

[11] Jean Bloch, as quoted in Frank M. Russell, *Theories of International Relations* (New York, 1936), p. 307. We may also recall a story about Clemenceau, who is said to have asked an officer to explain to him the strategic importance of the machine gun. This too was before the First World War. The officer declared: "Faced with the machine gun, every strategy ceases."

the conditions of the atomic age, but it was clearly premature at the end of the nineteenth century and proved to be so even in the two world wars of the twentieth. The prematureness of statements such as this might lend credence to the assertions of those who, in the face of similarly dire (or, if you wish, hopeful) predictions regarding war in the atomic age, point out that prophets of doom have so far always been disproved by the seemingly unlimited stamina of human beings under adverse conditions and their equally unlimited capacity to organize resources, as well as the continuation of life in society even under catastrophic conditions.

There are other precedents for similar faulty prophecy. We may, for instance, remember the forecast and conclusions of those who, in the interwar period, developed theories of air power according to which any future war between big powers would be decided in the initial stages through bombardments from the air.[12] One might be inclined to compare such earlier predictions concerning the effects of what now appears to be "conventional" air war with forecasts of the effects of the original atom bomb. Those forecasts, in which the bomb appeared to be "the absolute weapon," found expression in statements like this:

Even the most revolutionary developments of the past seem by contrast with the atomic bomb to have been minor steps in a many-sided evolutionary process. . . . With the introduction, however, of an explosive agent which is several million times more potent on a pound-for-pound basis than the most powerful explosives previously known, we have a change of quite another character.[13]

[12] According to Douhet, in case of war it would be "sufficient to conquer the command of the air." On the Douhet-Mitchell-Seversky prophesies see Edward M. Earle (ed.), *Makers of Modern Strategy* (Princeton, 1943), pp. 485 ff. See also B. Brodie, "Some Notes on the Evolution of Air Doctrine," *World Politics*, 7: 349 ff. (1954–55).

[13] B. Brodie, *The Absolute Weapon* (New York, 1946), p. 34. Similar statements are mentioned in Louis J. Halle, *Choice for Survival* (New York, 1958), pp. 17 ff.

It is surely significant that a tremendous new weapon like the atomic bomb of 1945, whose glare cast the gloom of doom over the entire world, has now come to seem almost "conventional" among the weapons since developed. In fact, it is sometimes cheerfully referred to as the "baby bomb," or "nominal" atomic weapon. Experts have indeed found in the meantime that there might have been ways to accommodate oneself even to the impact of that weapon. B. H. Liddell Hart told us in 1947 that "past experience has shown that no development is ever quite so overwhelmingly potent as it appears in anticipation, or even on the promise of its first performance." [14]

But there may be as much danger in underestimating as there is in overestimating the newness and impact of new developments. If a prior history of exaggeration warns us not to be duped by the effects of the new and unaccustomed and thus tempts us to play it down as repetitious, as "one more of the same" in a steady stream of evolution, history also shows that reliance on "repetition" can be shattered by genuinely "unprecedented" happenings. For an example from a quite different field, we may refer to Charles E. Merriam, surely no unrealistic observer of things political, who once wrote: "The persistence of the Jewish group is a striking evidence of the futility of persecution as a means of destruction of a determined and cohesive society defiant of the power group." [15] This was written in 1934, when that "power group" had already attained power which a few years later managed to exterminate one half of all the Jews on earth, comprising practically the entire group under its control. Instead of indicating "futility of persecution as a means of destruction," this event proved that new methods, combined with new policies, can

---

[14] *The Revolution in Warfare* (New Haven, 1947), p. 97.
[15] *Political Power,* as republished in *A Study of Power* (Glencoe, Ill., 1950), p. 167.

attain entirely novel results. Can this also be true of the new scientific-technological developments which have followed upon the original atomic explosions?

Let us then return to these developments and ask what are the chief factors that can be said to account for the seemingly unprecedented nature of the new developments in the nuclear field. A first one would appear to be the unpredictability of discoveries and similar events which have been and still are following each other in such dizzyingly swift sequence that the mind—and, consequently, policy planning—cannot keep pace. To this it is that Oppenheimer referred when he said:

One thing that is new is the prevalence of newness, the changing scale and scope of change itself, so that the world alters as we walk in it, so that the years of man's life measure not some small growth or rearrangement or moderation (sic; modification?) of what he learned in childhood, but a great upheaval.[16]

Thus in the field of military planning the rapid sequence of innovations has meant that "efforts at adaptation are hardly begun before they must be scrapped"[17] and that it renders "almost impossible the task of military men whose responsibility it is to anticipate the future. Military planning cannot make the facts of this future stay long enough to analyze them."[18] What this entails for foreign policies and international systems built on them will be discussed at a later point; suffice it to recall here the rapidity with which military bases are being established only to become doubtful shortly

[16] From his address on "Prospects in the Arts and Sciences," in *The Open Mind* (New York, 1955), p. 141. And from a different vantage point Reinhold Niebuhr wrote thus: "The pace of history in our era is so swift that only the most agile can adjust their imagination to the rapidly changing scene" ("Yesterday's Anticipations and Today's Realities," *Christianity and Crisis*, June 25, 1956, p. 81).

[17] Roger Hilsman, "Strategic Doctrines for Nuclear War," in William W. Kaufmann (ed.), *Military Policy and National Security* (Princeton, 1956), p. 42.

[18] Thomas K. Finletter, *Power and Policy: US Foreign Policy and Military Power in the Hydrogen Age* (New York, 1954), p. 256.

thereafter in their usefulness, together with the political alignments they imply. Thus, in addition to their impact on the
structure of statehood itself, the new weapons developments
seem to affect the system of international relations in novel
fashion: where formerly innovations, even radical ones, would
permit the emergence of more or less stable new systems of
some durability, the dynamic of the present is such as to fore-
close any kind of stability.

A second factor is the apparent absence of an effective defense against the new weapon. Even though a considerable
percentage of attacking planes or missiles may be prevented
from getting through, it is in the nature of weapons of which
the fall-out alone, for just one of them, can blanket the famous
cigar-shaped area of thousands of square miles, dusting it with
lethal radioactivity, that a few of them not so coped with are
enough. This again would be unprecedented. The assertion
that for each new means of attack a defense will sooner or later
be found is familiar, as is the fact that previous history would
seem to confirm its correctness. But the near-unanimity with
which recent observers, and the experts in particular, have
been inclined to draw the pessimistic conclusion [19] makes one
doubt that assertion's validity for the present and the future.
If these observers be called "prophets of doom" and their
voices Cassandra voices, one should remember that Cassandra,
after all, predicted the doom correctly.

Closely related to the factor of defenselessness is the decisive-

[19] The following quotations may serve to illustrate numerous similar
attitudes: "No modern system of air-warning and air-interception can
deal completely with modern attacking bombers and rocket missiles"
(Asher Lee, "Trends in Aerial Defense," *World Politics*, 7: 247 [1954–55]).
"We must assume that SAC will get through to its targets now . . . but
we must also assume that the Soviet strategic air force will be able to
retaliate against us with equal devastation. . . . we will be likely to suffer
costs as great as those we inflict" (Kaufmann [ed.], *Military Policy and
National Security*, p. 21). And see the more recent elaborate argument
by Henry A. Kissinger in his *Nuclear Weapons and Foreign Policy* (New
York, 1957), pp. 65 ff.

ness of initial attack. While initial attack may not exclude instant retaliation with countermeasures held in readiness, its effect on cities, economy, and society in general is likely to be such as to prevent that recuperation of defensive power which previously gave those surprised a chance. As one observer put it in the early period of the atomic age, "The essential change introduced by the atomic bomb is not primarily that it will make war more violent . . . but that it will concentrate the violence in terms of time." [20] And so far as retaliation is concerned, it is now "a matter of minutes." [21] Should other nuclear powers rise beyond the present two blocs, it may even prove impossible to determine the attacker.

Third, and perhaps most important of all factors, nuclear developments are bound to lead to a stage (which may or may not yet have been reached at this point) where military "superiority" loses its meaning because even the—in traditional parlance—"inferior" power has become capable of "saturating" its opponent. Once this point of saturation, or "nuclear plenty," has been attained, it does not make any difference whether A has 200 ICBM's, while B has "only" 100, provided that 100 are enough to destroy what is worth destroying in A. What kind of conclusions must be drawn from this factor of "stalemate" so far as policies are concerned—whether, for instance, it is liable to instigate a policy and a system of "mutual deterrence"—will be a matter for subsequent discussion. What matters here is to realize that one of the chief functions of "power," namely, its effectiveness as military force which can be applied to attain foreign policy ends "in defense of the national interest," becomes dubious when total nuclear saturation is possible. There certainly is unprecedented newness in a situation in which traditional means of achieving national security and protecting national interests are no longer avail-

[20] Brodie, *The Absolute Weapon*, p. 71.
[21] *NATO*, report on Princeton University Conference, p. 38.

able. Where formerly even minor nations, through temporary superiority in armed forces or alignment with superior
nations, could hope to achieve policy objectives, now nations
with more concentrated power than any units ever before
possessed are open to total destruction and, in this sense, more
impotent than smaller ones have ever been.

Thus there is what the military expert of the New York
Times calls "a vicious circle" of equipping "armed forces with
more and more atomic arms, which in time are bound to produce less and less security." [22]   Unlimited war, in other words,
can no longer bestow on any power waging it in the form of
nuclear war that which used to be the fruit of "superiority"
and thus of "victory": the attainment of war aims, whether
security or any others.   Victory, in the classical sense of
obtaining policy objectives by constraining an opponent's will
through force of arms, becomes meaningless where it involves
total destruction of the enemy's territory and possessions, and
this at the risk of one's own similar destruction.   It would not
be sensible to risk one's own "national substance" to conquer
an atomic wasteland.   Nuclear war, in now almost trite words,
involves the "danger of mutual suicide." [23]

[22] Hanson W. Baldwin in *New York Times*, August 10, 1954; that which
the same expert has recently referred to as "over-kill capability" in the
United States atomic armory (see New York *Times*, February 3, 1958).

[23] It seems hardly necessary to refer to the large number of persons
who, in more or less colorful terms, have drawn attention to the fact
that all-out use of nuclear means of defense is likely to leave nothing to
defend.   For instance, all-out war between the two blocs "might not end
with *one* Rome but with two Carthages" (Harold D. Lasswell, *Power
and Personality* [New York, 1948], p. 180); or there are those who have
asked, "What difference will it make whether it was country A which had
its cities destroyed at 9 A.M. and country B which had its cities destroyed
at 12 A.M., or the other way round?"   (Jacob Viner, "The Implications of
the Atomic Bomb for International Relations," in *Proceedings of the
American Philosophical Society*, 90: 54 [January 29, 1946]).   The absurdity
of a mutually and simultaneously destructive war had been pointed out
long before the advent of the nuclear age by a prophetic philosopher:
"A war of extermination, in which destruction would come to both
parties at the same time . . . would allow eternal peace only on the

Summing up, there has now occurred, or is occurring, the most radical change in the nature of power and the characteristics of power units since the beginning of the modern state system or, perhaps, since the beginnings of mankind. Even the most highly organized and most strongly armed country or group of countries can now be destroyed without the necessity of first breaking the traditional "hard shell" of surrounding defense. The power to go "vertically" in *medias res*, which had gradually built up in the preatomic age through air war and similar developments, has now reached its culmination. Permeability presages the end of the traditional protective function of state power and territorial sovereignty. The chief external function of the modern state therefore seems to have vanished. Utmost power in the possession of one state goes hand in hand with utmost impotence to counter the like power that others have. In a symbolic way (in addition to their possible practical use for hostile purposes) satellites circling the globe and penetrating the space above any territory of the globe, regardless of "sovereign" rights over air spaces and duties of "nonintervention," serve to emphasize the new openness and penetrability of everything to everybody.

From such mutual penetrability of units and from the existence, within one and the same entity, of extreme power together with utmost vulnerability, it is even possible to construe the outlines of an ultimate situation in which each of the atomic powers in respect to their strategic and defense preparations splits up into two unequal portions: One, comprising most of the territory, the population, and the resources would be left "permeable." The public at large would thus become

---

graveyard of the whole human race. Such a war, therefore, as well as the use of the means which might be employed in it, is wholly forbidden" (Immanuel Kant, *On Eternal Peace*, translated by Carl J. Friedrich in his *Inevitable Peace* [Cambridge, Mass., 1948], p. 248 f.). The term "forbidden," as used by Kant, was not, of course, employed in any legal sense but to indicate such a war's immorality.

"expendable." But there would remain another portion, consisting of a strategic air force, or missile force, with its complementary bases, supplies, resources, and so forth, which might have a chance to survive and inflict defeat upon the enemy (again, with the exception of *his* strategic air or missile force).[24] Especially when automatic missiles replace manned planes, coping with them seems impossible because of the difficulty of hitting all or even most of the dispersed, underground, concealed, or mobile launching sites.[25] Once this stage is reached, unlimited power to destroy would protect nothing except, possibly, itself *qua* machine of destruction. This reduces a world of penetrable "powers" *ad absurdum*. With bombs and missiles of unlimited range and power, control of extended territories, systems of bases, and allies would become unnecessary, indeed, liabilities because of their vulnerability. In principle, then, it would be sufficient for each power unit (of which by then there might be an unlimited number) to have one or a few points from which to launch its weapons. Compared with the extent of territorial states such points of ultimate concentration of power would be of infinitely small dimension. "Mass" is transformed into "energy." Everything beyond the "energy" would remain uncovered by protective power, a no-man's (or every-man's) land. Add to this model-picture threats of chemical and biological warfare, as well as the impact of improved techniques of economic and psychological strategies, and the picture is one of unmitigated and unrelieved doom.

We should not, however, jump to conclusions, "throw in the sponge," and consider that "all is lost and the world is going

[24] See, for instance, the implications of a report on missile defense by Richard Witkin in the New York *Times,* October 28, 1957.

[25] Cf. Kissinger, *Nuclear Weapons and Foreign Policy,* p. 124. Kissinger concludes: "Even the maximum of surprise could at best destroy the opponent's national substance; it would not eliminate his ability to inflict a retaliatory blow of similar power."

to pieces." While it cannot be denied that the situation created by the nuclear threat is not only radically new but also extremely foreboding, we must keep in mind that possibility is not certainty, that we can attempt to cope with a threat in order to avoid its realization, and, last, that the nuclear situation is only one among several factors which all have an impact on the present and may influence the shape of the future. So far we have isolated one single factor, the nuclear one, and its potential effect in case of all-out war. Trying to distinguish what makes for the "newness" of the new age, we had to single out what appeared to be most obviously and most significantly new.

We must also remember that the technological developments outlined are far from finished, and we cannot know with certainty what they will look like when, and if, they arrive at some kind of durable termination. As we have already pointed out, the changeability and rate of change of these developments is one of the factors making the situation inherently incalculable. Moreover, the effects of technology on strategy, policy, and general developments are potentially multiple and indeterminate rather than uniform and definitive. Thus, possession of territory, allies, and "power" in the traditional sense, even traditional "sovereignty," while seemingly losing their usual meaning and importance under the "gloomy" assumptions we have made, may retain some meaning, or their importance may merely change under different sets of assumptions, if, for instance, avoidance, or avoidability, of nuclear war is supposed as one possibility. And finally, since this is an age of transition, there are still in existence those factors and trends which derive from preatomic or non-atomic conditions. Their interaction with each other, as well as with the atomic trends, constitutes the chief reason why the discussion of international politics in the atomic age is so complicated and the drawing of clear-cut and unequivocal conclusions all but impossible. For instance, almost simultaneously with the emergence of the atomic age a development took place in the traditional power world which substituted a bipolar distribution of power for a world of multiple powers. It is easily understood that the combined effect of bipolarity and nuclear discoveries—factors which are in part contradictory—may be complicated and possibly self-contradictory also.

This is why it would be wrong to rush to definite conclusions from the nuclear trends alone, such as that "no security is obtainable any more," or that the concept of "power" has now lost its meaning. We cannot draw these conclusions because the nuclear trend is one among others, and because the partly contradictory factors underlying these other trends render the entire situation indefinite. It is to the indefiniteness of the new age and what follows from it that we must now turn our attention.

THE INDEFINITENESS OF THE NEW AGE

Had there been a clear-cut substitution of the new for the old in the postwar international structure, it would be much easier to develop concepts and policies to take the place of the those to which we are accustomed. But, as anyone who is acquainted with present-day international politics realizes, there has been no such unilinear changeover. On the contrary, the most striking feature of foreign affairs today is the juxtaposition of the old and the new on several levels, a strange and less than "peaceful" coexistence in theory and practice of conventional and new concepts, of traditional and new policies. In Churchill's words, "We have entered a period of transition in which the past and the future will overlap." [26] Among statesmen, as well as among the general public, all over the world, the very suddenness and rapidity

26 Speech in Commons, March 1, 1955, New York *Times,* March 2, 1955.

with which the new developments have occurred and are still occurring at first seem to produce a lag in consciousness and awareness of what the new situation entails and what the new trends necessitate.[27] Discussion frequently proceeds on an "as if" basis. This is illustrated, for instance, when certain territorial or strategic problems are argued over as if power politics were still the same as before the war and strategy unaffected by atomic developments. On the other hand, we may encounter discussion of atomic or similar new problems, which remain unrelated to the traditional approach.[28] In this way policy on two levels may be produced, without relation of one level to the other, and with each of them proceeding on an "as if" basis. An army department may plan chiefly on the basis of preatomic assumptions while a strategic air force is preparing for a preponderantly atomic contest.[29] One foreign policy approach may be predicated upon traditional expecta-

[27] "American political thought came to be affected, in the postwar era, by a sort of schizophrenia. It operated on two different planes. . . . We found ourselves living in two different worlds: one world a sane and rational one, in which we felt comfortable . . . ; the other world a nightmarish one. . . . In one of these worlds the old traditional concepts still applied; in the other, there was only the law of the jungle" (George F. Kennan, *Realities of American Foreign Policy* [Princeton, 1954], p. 29).

[28] One typical example of such counting out of the atomic factor occurred in an editorial of the German newspaper *Frankfurter Allgemeine Zeitung* (October 11, 1954) dealing with the problem of European defense in case of Soviet attack. After a discussion of various political and strategic details, the following proviso was made: "To be sure, predicting how such a war would develop should atom or H-bombs be used would demand an apocalyptic imagination which we do not possess. What has been stated above is only valid provided that such a war is fought according to classical' standards." Stated or not, such a "proviso" is inherent in a good deal of present foreign policy discussion, and the trouble is not that this is just an omission but that it is not safe to proceed exclusively either on the one or on the other assumption.

[29] This is not to imply that we are objecting to planning for "limited" as well as unlimited, "conventional" as well as nuclear war. As subsequent discussion will show, such planning is, on the contrary, of greatest importance. What we are referring to here is uncoordinated, isolated, and therefore probably contradictory proceeding on the part of unintegrated agencies without common policy guidance.

tions, for example, the standing together of allies who have a common interest in joint defense, while another approach discounts alliances because of the possible impact of atomic war on allies. Great importance may be placed upon the control of some "outpost," possession, or area because of conventional calculations concerning its strategic or general political value, while, simultaneously, control over some interoceanic canal, thus far considered of supreme importance, is given up because it no longer appears vital (or defendable) in the hydrogen age. On one hand, there exists a more than usual sensitivity with regard to even the most minute frontier violation at the same time it is known that entire areas, colonies, and possessions can no longer be held in case of major war.

This dichotomy between traditional and atomic concepts and policies is perhaps the most conspicuous illustration of the different levels on which ideas and policies operate. But there are others. Especially if the United States is taken as an example, the contrast between a situation we were accustomed to and a variety of new factors we were suddenly confronted with is enormous. What one recent author has stated generally, namely, that "contemporary international relations would be difficult at best, but they take on a special urgency because never have so many different revolutions occurred simultaneously" [30] applies in particularly striking fashion to this country. America at the dawn of the atomic era was hardly even used to "power politics" in the traditional sense, tied as it was—in attitude and, in part, even in policy—to its old isolationism. This rendered it difficult for her to engage even in those policies to which the older powers had been accustomed for a long time, such as building up alliances and, something more demanding, taking on responsibilities as a leading power in such alignments. Even now we

[30] Kissinger, *Nuclear Weapons and Foreign Policy*, p. 5.

can see how much American policy, and therewith the cause of the entire Western bloc, is hampered by American inexperience in such novel and unaccustomed policy as building up and leading NATO.

But the world in which countries like America were to play their major part was no longer the traditional power world of the older world powers. At the very time America was ready for "power politics," new factors affected the ways in which powers engaged in international politics. Two things in particular are said to constitute "world revolutions" of our time: one, the rise to world eminence of a movement and a regime which has proclaimed "world revolution" in the form of Communism as its objective; the other, the global expansion of nationalism that has substituted a world of now close to a hundred nations for the accustomed and intimate world of a few dozen generally long-established units, used to each other and to the traditional ways and habits of diplomacy. These two new factors, to be sure, must affect international relations profoundly in many respects. But *per se* they would not necessarily have affected international structure and system had there not occurred at the same time other changes that did have such an effect. There was, for instance, the rise of attitudes and concepts of "internationalism," based in turn upon a long-term process under which "independent" territorial states had become ever more interdependent economically and in many other respects. At the end of the Second World War the trend toward international organization and international integration had reasserted itself, and a world-wide security organization such as the United Nations, it was supposed by many, would become the new center of international politics. Power politics now appeared old-fashioned, but there inevitably arose the problem of how to reconcile the new, internationalist level of concepts and attitudes (or expectations) with what soon reappeared as the still valid concepts and demands of power politics.

Power politics, however, itself appeared in a new mold: that of "bipolarity," the concentration of most of the world's power (military, industrial, and otherwise) in two "superpowers," which, in contrast to the multipower world of the past, now emerged as the major determinants of world politics. In a world where—a strange paradox—power was ever more concentrated in the face of an ever-increasing number of formally independent "powers," a country like the United States had to adapt concepts and policies not merely to involvement in power politics as such but to a new status as one of the superpowers, and the one leading the ideological fight against world-revolutionary Communism to boot.

By itself, the rise of bipolarity was as unexpected as the rise of the atomic age. Forecasts and expectations had been different. To be sure, there was an awareness in the Second World War that victory for the Allies would lead to a rearrangement in power relations, exactly as the First World War had meant a reshuffling of power and powers. But most postwar plans had nevertheless been based on the expected emergence (or rather, continuance) of a multipower world, that is, a system in which, as before, there would be more than two or three "big" powers. Moreover, it was expected that the big powers would continue to be surrounded by a host of middle and small powers which, at least in combination, would still constitute a certain weight in the total power balance. Concentration of overwhelming strength in only two of the victor nations was something which, at least in the case of one of them, occurred quite unexpectedly and almost against the inclinations and policies of that country.[31]

31 The unpreparedness of the United States for her postwar role is evidenced by her rapid demobilization, her initial unwillingness to play the role of chief opponent of the Soviets, and her readiness rather to let Britain play that role. The fact that she had to assume this role eventually illustrates the part "objective" underlying trends and developments can play in international affairs, regardless of the policies of the decision makers.

This bipolar distribution of power played havoc with older concepts and policies. Thus the "founding fathers" of the United Nations devised a charter for an organization of what in essence was to be a "concert" of the Big Three. But bipolarity runs counter to the idea and practice of a concert of several big powers. Whether it allows for anything but a perfunctory role on the part of an international organization will be discussed at a later point,[32] as will the relationship between bipolarity on the one hand and "collective security" on the other.

If it was already difficult to adapt habitual ways of thought and policy to the conditions of bipolarity, the simultaneous emergence of nuclear power with its implications described before could not fail to complicate the picture. There now arose the dual task of adapting traditional thought and approach to bipolarism and adapting the old-fashioned as well as the new bipolar approach to an atomic one. In other words, new bipolar thinking, unconventional when contrasted with prewar thought and procedure, now became relatively conventional, as contrasted with the peculiar new thinking the atomic age with its new developments demanded.

Thus, in view of the various trends and developments in technology and in the power sphere, concepts, approaches, and policies are bound to be bifurcated or trifurcated. This accounts for the indefiniteness of the age and the uncertainties of the future. The uncertainties are of two different kinds: they may be connected with our lack of knowing what turn developments themselves will take, for instance, what kind of

[32] The outdatedness of the Charter at the very time of its inauguration was stressed by John Foster Dulles (although with an emphasis on the atomic factor rather than on bipolarity) in his address to the American Bar Association, August 27, 1953: "When we were in San Francisco in the spring of 1945, none of us knew of the atomic bomb which was to fall on Hiroshima on August 6, 1945. The Charter is thus a pre-Atomic Age charter. In this sense it was obsolete before it actually came into force."

intercontinental missile or space weapon will have what kind of military effect; or they are caused by the fact that even on the basis of certain conditions (e.g., the availability of such-and-such military equipment), objectives, intentions, and policies may differ and thus are not clearly predictable. Nobody knows, for instance, whether certain "all-out" weapons will be used or not. It is above all this latter uncertainty which renders all calculation and policy planning so enormously complicated. Even if one knows his own mind, he cannot fully know that of his opponent. If we take the present (or impending) nuclear stalemate between the two superpowers as an illustration, there are so many possibilities for anticipating events that what actually will happen depends largely on one or the other side's or both sides' ideas of what is and will be. There is one assumption, for instance, according to which the stalemate in the nuclear armaments race will assure an indefinite peace through mutual deterrence, that is, through the continuance of the present "balance of terror." But the same all-out race makes others believe that all-out war is bound to occur sooner or later. Or, there is a multiple divergence of expectation between anticipation of all-out nuclear war, nonatomic wars which will be fought with conventional weapons, and "limited" nuclear war of "graduated deterrence," of mere tactical use of nuclear weapons, or of "counter-force strategy," that is, one where nuclear power will strike primarily at enemy military power, and not at the civilian populations in cities, and so forth. Some of the problems involved in this will be taken up elsewhere. What concerns us here is the fact that in almost every one of these instances the consequences for international systems and national policies will be different, and often diametrically so. And since the assumption may determine the event, whether or not one of the various possibilities will materialize may well depend on what the leading powers, and leading power groups and persons in power, think about these problems. Thus, taking an illustration from a long drawn-out American "great debate" on military and foreign policy, if the United States has assumed that any future war with the other side will be an all-out nuclear war, she may, by planning for this eventuality and therefore staking everything on the "Sunday punch" power of her Strategic Air Command, increase the likelihood that that is what will materialize. This example shows that policy, military and foreign, can no longer be monoemphatic in the nuclear age, that is, concerned with one chief aim and one chief strategy only, as policy could be in the preatomic age. Then, a country like Britain could rely on naval superiority and the European power balance as the props of her security, or France on an army strong enough to defend her Eastern frontier. This is no longer possible, without running grave risks for one's own country and the world, in an age in which power has lost its unequivocal meaning and effect. It is only through multilevel concepts and policies that one can prepare for all or at least several eventualities in an environment of such indeterminateness. Hence, the tragic urgency for making up one's mind.

Nor is it only the present—or rather, what is new in the present—that is equivocal. The past, or rather what reaches from the past into the present, is likewise so, and since the old extends in its effects into the present in many ways, confusion is bound to be more compounded. In the face of both bipolar and nuclear developments, the old system of plural powers, with their concepts and systems of "balances" and the like, is to some extent still effective, and this not only in the mind and concepts of acting man, but in the "things" themselves, as it were. Since nobody can know with certainty whether nuclear war, all-out or limited, will ever materialize, the comparative power status of nations will in some respects continue to be based on evaluation of the conventional power factors (location, industrial capacities, etc.). To some extent, therefore, the actual weight and influence of a given country in foreign affairs still results from these "old-fashioned" appraisals, but when the possibility of nuclear war is taken into consideration, they will yield to quite different, and possibly contradictory, evaluations. A factor effective in one respect may be deprived of its effectiveness in another context. Events themselves become "mixed" and possibly contradictory in their impact and effect. Somewhere, a "conventional" war may be in progress, with tensions, alignments, and policies of various sorts resulting among countries of the region in the traditional manner; simultaneously, however, these same countries may be aligned on one or the other side or as neutrals in the overall world condition of a "cold war," with its ideological conflicts, its atomic and conventional armaments race, and so forth. Regional power politics, in particular, may align or divide units in a given region as of yore, at the same time the all-pervasive impact of bipolarity cuts through the alignments and divides the world into two giant blocs.

Thus the "old," or traditional, is now confronted with the two new factors and levels—the bipolar and the nuclear—which have emerged as the most significant ones among what is new. And it is important to realize that the two, in nature and impact, really have nothing to do with each other, and that only by historical accident, as it were, did the conditions that caused each materialize at about the same time, so that the old was faced by two new sets of circumstances simultaneously. Bipolarity alone would have posed highly complex problems for traditional international politics. The scientific-technological revolution of the atomic age, with its novel and, in relation to bipolar power concentration, in part conflicting implications, piled one set of gigantic problems on the other.

It is not only the past but also the future that bears on the present, rendering assumptions even more indefinite. No sooner has one's mind become adjusted to some understanding of the currently new than the rapid developments of our time already presage its obsolescence. The new has just come upon us, still mixed and struggling with the old, when something still newer looms on the horizon, confusing even the most "ultramodern" inferences drawn from the existing new. To what extent this is true in regard to the nuclear factor has already been remarked upon and must, indeed, be clear to every newspaper reader. It is less obvious, although equally important, in relation to bipolarity. For bipolarity, which stamped its imprint on the post—Second World War era, may already be passing, and, with the rise of countries like China, West Germany, and possibly Japan and India, its disintegration into a new multipower system may be in the offing. There are indeed some who claim that a new system of plural powers is already in existence.[33] To a realistic observer of what actually is, this seems premature. But assuming that the observation is correct *qua* anticipation of things to come, we shall then have the final confluence of these so-far separate sets of circumstances: the ones that refer to the distribution of power and the ones relating to nuclear technology. For any new multipower system will be fundamentally different from the "classical" one; it will be based not, or not merely, on a change in the traditional power factors (such as the growing industrial strength of China and, possibly, India, the re-militarization of Germany and, possibly, Japan, and so forth), but also on a new development looming on the *atomic* horizon: the rise of additional nuclear powers. If, or when, in addition to the present two atomic powers or power blocs, an indefinite number of other countries possess atomic capabilities, any new multipower system thus arising will have

[33] See, for instance, Kennan, *Realities of American Foreign Policy*, p. 100. According to a newspaper report (New York *Times*, June 17, 1956), Justice Douglas believes that there are now six "big" powers in the world, which will form a new Big Six system.

aspects vastly different from what those who talk in terms of a "return" to a five-power or six-power system are envisaging. It would be radically new in the sense that it would add to the present two nuclear blocs an indefinite number of units which, whether "big," "medium," or "small" in traditional terms, would all exist on a basis of fundamental "equality" as possessors of the new weapon. "Multipolarity" (on the pattern of the term "bipolarity"), or "polycentrism," might be terms better fitting a situation, or system, in which each unit constitutes a center or pole of absolute power. This is something utterly different from the classical constellation of a "multinational" or "multipower" system with its graduated power of comparable "powers." [34] Military scientists have been referring for quite some time to the present superpowers' problem of providing nuclear arms aid to allies, which may consist not only in supplying them with the end-products but also with the knowledge of how to make them.[35] They have also been referring to the necessity felt by countries which desire to maintain their "uncommitted" or "neutral" station between the present two blocs to possess nuclear weapons to be able to back up their neutrality.[36] Supposing that this is the way the future shapes up, it almost staggers the imagination to envision the consequences for international politics. Will a to some extent rational policy remain possible at all? Or will it imply, as one author pessimistically predicts, that "atomic power, haphazardly distributed among a number of nations, is bound to be a source of unprecedented insecurity, if not panic," and that, "compared with the anarchy and limitless violence which then will reign, the first decade of the atomic

34 If I understand him correctly, this is the system Mr. Kaplan has in mind when he calls one of his "models" the "unit-veto system" (see his "Balance of Power, Bipolarity, and Other Models of International Systems," *American Political Science Review,* 51: 684 ff. [1957]).

35 Roger Hilsman, "Coalition and Alliances," in Kaufmann (ed.), *Military Policy and National Security,* pp. 189 ff.

36 *Ibid.*

era might well appear in retrospect as a kind of golden age in which the atomic stalemate between two nations guaranteed an uneasy atomic peace"? [37]

We have not gone that far, and, as a matter of fact, conceivably we may never go that far. For that element of uncertainty in estimating what is or will be—whose impact on the course of what actually happens we have commented upon before—may well apply to the trend of events in this connection also. Whether or not a "polycentered" or "multipolar" world will emerge may depend on what present nuclear powers think now and on how they are going to act on the basis of their present thinking. It may be, for instance, that, realizing the danger and chaos such nuclear polycentrism would mean for all, the present nuclear "monopolists" will yet be moved to do something to prevent it from arising, possibly even something which would solve the atomic problem more radically, the creation of a world authority to deal with it. In this instance, too, the future depends on what the present anticipates. It would seem, however, that the powers, if they wish to act, would better act quickly, because the time seems to be imminent (if it is not already here) when other powers will be able to produce nuclear weapons independently. Here, as has happened before in nuclear affairs, an important opportunity may escape the undecided, never to return.

Such is the picture of radical newness and indeterminateness that the present age presents. Before we undertake to study in more detail how the principal new factors affect the structure of statehood and the system of international relations, we must glance back at where we have come from: at what now appears as a golden age of relative certainty and stability, the era of territoriality.

[37] Hans J. Morgenthau, "Has Atomic War Really Become Impossible?", *Bulletin of the Atomic Scientists,* 12: 8 (1956).

1

RISE AND CHARACTERISTICS

OF THE MODERN STATE SYSTEM

This is the Generation of that great Leviathan . . . to which we owe our peace and defense. HOBBES

Dig deeper your moats; build higher your walls; guard them along with your people. MENCIUS

The Basic Features
of the Modern State System

Traditionally and customarily, the "classical" system of international relations, or "modern state system," has been regarded as a paradox. On the one hand, it has been referred to as a "society," or a "community," or even a "family" of nations, equally independent and mutually respecting each other. On the other hand, it has been considered "anarchic," because it was based on unequally distributed power and was devoid of higher, that is, supernational, authority. The units in this system, the "independent" and "sovereign" nation-states, precariously survived, but they were forever threatened in their interests and in their very existence by superior power. They were protected to some extent, legally, by mutual recognition of "rights" (such as "fundamental rights" to existence) and "duties" (for instance, duty of nonintervention), and politically, through the functioning of the balance of power system. In fact, however, insecurity ("international anarchy") ruled supreme, because of the actual inequality in power and the permissibility (even in a legal sense, namely, through the process known as war) to use superior power to destroy the inferior. This has been the traditional view, and it does not matter here whether in this view the system appeared as "good" or "bad," desirable or not. Customarily, then, the modern state system has been contrasted on the one hand with the medieval system, where units of international relations were under higher law and higher authority, and, on the other hand, with those more recent international trends which seemed to point toward a greater ("collective") security of nations and toward a "rule of law" that would protect them from the indiscriminate use of force and war characteristic of the age of power politics.

From the vantage point of the atomic age, however, things appear in a new light. It appears that "international anarchy" and "collective security" have something in common which did not exist in the particular form we know it prior to the rise of the modern state, something which is now vanishing. What is it, ultimately, that accounted for the peculiar unity, coherence, or compactness of the modern nation-state, setting it off from other nation-states as a separate unit and permitting us to characterize it as "independent," "sovereign," a "power"? It would seem that this underlying something is to be found neither in the sphere of law, nor even in that of politics, but rather in the ultimate, and lowest, substratum where the state unit confronts us, in, as it were, its physical, corporeal capacity: as an expanse of territory, encircled for its identification and defense by tangible, military expressions of statehood, like fortifications and fortresses. In this lies what, for lack of a better term, I shall refer to as the "impermeability," or "impenetrability," or simply the "territoriality" of the modern state. These terms are meant to indicate the peculiar nature of the modern territorial state as it was surrounded with what may be called its "hard shell" which protected it from foreign penetration. It is this factor which rendered it defensible and, at least to some extent, secure in its relations with other units. It thus made the state the ultimate unit of protection for those living within its boundaries. For, throughout history, we notice that the basic political unit has been that which actually was in a position to afford protection and security to human beings, i.e., peace within, through the pacification of individual and group relationships, and security from outside interference or control. People, in the long run, will recognize that authority, any authority, which possesses this power of protection.

In the absence of superior authority over and above nation-states it could only be the comparatively high degree of territorial impermeability which constituted the material basis of whatever independence, external power, sovereign jurisdiction, rights and claims such units could practically possess. There is perhaps some similarity between an international structure consisting of impenetrable elemental units with an ensuing measurability of power and comparability of power relations, and the system of classical physics with its measurable forces and the (formerly impenetrable) atom as its basic unit. And as the system of physics so conceived has given way to relativity and what nuclear science has uncovered, so the impenetrability of the political atom, the nation-state, is giving way to a permeability which tends to obliterate the very meaning of unit and unity, power and power relations, sovereignty and independence. The possibility of "hydrogenization" represents merely the culmination of a development which has rendered the "hard shell," the traditional defense structure of nations, obsolete through the power to by-pass the shell protecting a two-dimensional "territory" and thus to destroy— vertically, as it were—even the most powerful ones. And paradoxically, the most powerful powers, which now possess, or are in the process of acquiring, the extreme power to destroy even the most powerful opponent, are exactly the ones which, as the most dangerous opponents of their opponents, become the natural targets for destruction on their part. Thus utmost strength now coincides in the same unit with utmost vulnerability.

It is clear that concurrence in the same unit of unlimited power and utmost dependency renders the traditional power concept—power as a standard of comparison between equal, or superior, or inferior powers—ambiguous. Power, once measurable to some extent, graded, and calculable, becomes a doubtful standard when in some connection it indicates impotence. Considering power units as politically independent and legally sovereign units, units which would recognize fellow units as equal, as possessing certain rights, all this made sense so long as these units could be described as "impermeable." Under "classical" conditions, then, "power" may be said to have indicated the strategic aspect, "independence" the political aspect, and "sovereignty" the legal aspect of this selfsame impermeability. With the passing of the age of territoriality the usefulness of all these concepts must now be questioned.

Thus the "great divide" does not separate international anarchy, or balance of power, or power politics from incipient international interdependence, or from collective security. All of these are within the realm of the "territorial" structure of states and can therefore be considered as trends or stages within the traditional system of hard-shell power units. Collective security, for instance, appears simply as an attempt to "legalize" their relations in certain ways and through certain processes, in order to raise their security above the previous, more precarious level. But such a system is still based on the existence of separate, defensible units comparable in power.[1] Rather, the "divide" occurs where the basis of territorial power and defensibility as such vanishes. That is, it is here and now. A system which was never "eternal" or "permanent" or even static, but which grew gradually until it came to full flower in the latter part of the seventeenth century, now, three hundred years later, seems to be withering. But to understand what is happening in the present, we must study more closely the origin and nature of the classical system itself.

[1] For details see below, ch. 5.

2

The Rise of the Territorial State

On the face of it there is hardly a historical process which has been better understood and more fully described than the rise of the modern, centralized territorial state out of the socio-economic and political conditions of the late Middle Ages. Within individual countries the anarchy of feudal jurisdictions and continual contest and strife over them yielded to the ordered centralism of absolute monarchy, which ruled over a pacified area with the aid of a civil service, a professional army, and the power to levy taxes. In their foreign relations, however, these states, with their newly gained sovereign independence, now had to exchange permanent insecurity for the settled hierarchy of power and authority which had bound them together in the Middle Ages. The new condition found expression in a diplomacy of power and power shifts, alliances and counteralliances, in short, in a disorder that was only slightly attenuated by a power balance that was forever being threatened, disturbed, and then restored. Such has been the usual interpretation.[1]

It is possible to view these developments in a somewhat different light. Instead of contrasting the security of groups and individuals within the sovereign territorial state with conditions of external insecurity, one may interpret them as

[1] Recent historiography does not always agree with the traditional view on medieval "international order," which it tends to regard as the ideology of order and authority concealing a good deal of actual disorder and power conflict (see, for instance, Geoffrey Barraclough, *History in a Changing World* [Norman, Okla., 1956], pp. 97 ff.). However, it is not with this aspect of the question that the present study is concerned.

the process whereby the establishment of territorial independence was at least a partially successful attempt to render
the territorial group secure in its outward relations as well.
Especially when contrasted with the age of anarchy and insecurity which immediately preceded it, the age of fully established territorial states appears to be one of relative order and
safety. The states' very reliance on military power, usually
referred to as evidence of the disordered and anarchical nature
of their foreign relations, served in the first place to establish
their structure of impermeability, which, in turn, was the
basis of their security from outside intervention.[2]

As it is usually described, modern sovereignty arose out of
the triangular contest between emperors and popes, popes and
kings, and kings and emperors. This struggle gave the territorial rulers a chance to establish their freedom from higher
authority. When the lawyers of Philip the Fair propounded
the dual maxim according to which the king was to be "emperor in his realm" (*rex est imperator in regno suo*) and was
no longer to "recognize any superior" (*superiorem non recog-
noscens*), it was the beginning of a development in the course
of which, in McIlwain's words, "independence *de facto* was
ultimately translated into a sovereignty *de jure*." [3] But the
transition from medieval hierarchism to modern compart-
mentalized sovereignties was neither easy, nor straight, nor
short. Centuries of disturbance and real anarchy ensued during which the problems of rulership and security remained

[2] This connection between the power or might of the modern state and
protection from external threats is sometimes, but rarely, noticed by
modern, in contrast to earlier, writers. Thus, for instance, does R. M.
McIver (*The Modern State* [London, 1926], p. 240), but even here it is
more with reference to recent trends. See also the brief and not fully
explained references to a synonymity of power, *qua* "felt power," and
"security" in M. A. Ash, "An Analysis of Power," *World Politics*, 3: 218 ff.
(1950–51).

[3] Charles H. McIlwain, *The Growth of Political Thought in the West*
(New York, 1932), p. 268.

unsettled. The relative protection which the sway of certain moral standards and the absence of destructive weapons had afforded groups and individuals in the earlier Middle Ages gave way to total insecurity under the dual impact of the breakdown of common standards and the invention of gunpowder. It was out of the subsequent internal and external turmoil during the era of religious and civil wars that a "neutralist" central power eventually managed to establish itself in and for each of the different territories like so many *rochers de bronze*.

The idea that a territorial coexistence of states, based on the power of the territorial princes, might afford a better guarantee of peace than the Empire was already widespread at the height of the Middle Ages when the emperor proved incapable of enforcing the peace (*Landfrieden*).[4] Even then it was increasingly felt that it was up to the territorial princes to establish protection through their own power. They could hardly do so as long as the knight in his castle, that medieval unit of impermeability, was relatively immune from attack, as was the medieval city within its walls. Only with a developing money economy were overlords able to free themselves from their dependence on vassals and to lay the foundations of their own power through the establishment of professional armies. Infantry and artillery now proved superior to old-style cavalry, firearms prevailed over the old weapons.

All this at first, however, wrought frightening disorder in the established social, political, and "international" relations, and a feeling of insecurity swept over Europe. As in all cases of radically new developments in military technology, such as the invention of the horse-drawn battle wagon (chariot) in earlier civilizations, or that of the longbow in medieval Europe, the gunpowder revolution caused a real revolution in

[4] See F. A. von der Heydte, *Die Geburtsstunde des souveränen Staates* (Regensburg, 1952), pp. 103 ff., 277, 293 ff.

the "superstructure" of economic, social, and political relationships because of its impact on the units of protection and security. Ariosto expressed the feeling of despair which invaded the "old powers" of chivalry when gunpowder destroyed the foundations of their system, in terms reminiscent of present-day despair in the face of the new destructive forces loosed upon our own world:

> Oh! curs'd device! base implement of death!
> Framed in the black Tartarean realms beneath!
> By Beelzebub's malicious art design'd
> To ruin all the race of human kind.[5]

Eventually, the French invasion of Italy, as observed by Machiavelli, demonstrated to everybody the implications of the new weapons, the new warfare, and the new power derived from them. But still there followed more than a century of unregulated and, in addition, "ideological" warfare both inside and among the various countries before it was clearly established which would be the new units of power. The new powers had first to establish their identity before a new type of international relationships could develop. That is, it first had to be determined how far, on the basis of their new military power, rulers, new or old, were able to extend their control geographically before they could claim to be recognized as rulers of large areas. Though a Machiavelli might establish new rules on how to gain and maintain power, these were set forth long before a period of strife and "total wars" had determined with some finality which rulers and countries would emerge as members of a more stable system of international relations.[6]

---

[5] As quoted from *Orlando Furioso* by F. Gilbert, in Edward M. Earle (ed.), *Makers of Modern Strategy* (Princeton, 1943), p. 4.

[6] On the relation between power systems and early diplomatic institutions in this period, as well as on that between new power and the actual extent of controlled area, see the lucid treatment and the abundant

It may be said that such a condition was achieved approximately at the time of, and partly through, the Peace of Westphalia. From then on the large area-state started to occupy the place that the castle or fortified town, now obsolete, had previously held as a unit of impenetrability. Not before fortified cities, castles, and all other "independent" fortifications inside the new units had disappeared, and in their place fortresses lining the circumference of the country had been built by the central power and manned by its armed forces, could the new units be considered consolidated.[7] If we compare our present systems of bases and similar outposts surrounding entire continents or world-regions with the fortifications of what today are small-scale nation-states, perhaps we can envision what the frontier defenses consolidating the then large-scale territorial states meant by way of expanding the units of power in the age of absolutism. They became, in the words of Frederick the Great, "mighty nails which hold a ruler's provinces together."[8] There now was peace and protection within and some amount of protection against interference from without. For war now became limited in its function, a regularized and to some extent formalized military procedure, in which only the breaking of the shell permitted interference with what had become the "internal" affairs of another country. A certain amount of security was inherent in the very fact that only through such formalized procedure was territorial sovereignty now destructible or transferable.[9]

---

illustrations in Garrett Mattingly, *Renaissance Diplomacy* (Boston, 1955), pp. 59 ff., 121 ff., 205 ff.

[7] See Friedrich Meinecke, *Die Idee der Staatsraison in der neueren Geschichte* (Munich and Berlin, 1925), pp. 241 ff.

[8] Earle (ed.), *Makers of Modern Strategy*, p. 59.

[9] The impact of the actuality of hard-shell fortification on the development of new rules of warfare and, consequently, on the emerging "international law" was expressed by Grotius: "Only that territory will be regarded as captured which is so surrounded by permanent fortifica-

In this way the basic structure of the territorial state which was to last throughout the classical period of the modern state system was established.   Upon this foundation a new system of international relations could and did arise.   Its characteristics are indicated by terms such as "independence," "sovereignty," "nonintervention," "equality," and "international law."

---

tions that the other party will have no access to it openly unless these have first been taken" (*De Jure Belli ac Pacis*, as translated in J. B. Scott [ed.], *Classics of International Law* [Oxford, 1913], 2: 667).   "Capture" here means definite acquisition of territory through conquest, as distinguished from mere military occupation of enemy territory *durante bello*.

3

The Nature of Territoriality

In modern times concepts and terms like "sovereignty," "independence," and "power" have commonly been used without realizing that they are intimately connected with that peculiar trait of the modern state which sets it off as a particular unit from like units: its territoriality. This neglect has often meant taking what is derived for the substance, what in reality is a secondary, produced factor for the primary factor that produces it. Thus "power," in the territorial system, derives from the underlying territorial unit on which it is based. It is a force expressive of the territorial unit's effect in and on the outside world, the sum-total of that strength which radiates from one unit toward the others, aggressively or defensively as the case may be. Power—in one current definition which may stand for all other similar ones—is "the total capabilities of a state to gain desired ends vis-à-vis other states." [1] But these capabilities can be made use of in international politics only because of something pre-existing, namely, the territorial state itself, consolidated within its shell of defensibility. It may be that, at the height of territoriality, this was so well understood that it did not have to be emphasized or even stated expressly. As territoriality vanishes, however, the connection of power with what is (or was) the essence of the modern state must be reemphasized.

So it is with "sovereignty." Sovereignty, too, is a resultant of underlying territoriality, but, again, this vital connection

[1] H. and M. Sprout, *Foundations of National Power* (rev. ed.; New York, 1951), p. 40.

has not often been clearly perceived. If sovereignty, in the sense of "external sovereignty," is defined as "exclusive territorial jurisdiction," it is only the state unit's real impermeability that has enabled its rulers to claim such legal impenetrability. But even a Grotius failed to make this clear. For instance, when he calls that power sovereign "whose acts are not subject to the legal control of another, so that they cannot be rendered void by the act of another human will," [2] this still leaves us searching for the "existential" basis of such a jurisdiction. Moreover, it leaves unsolved the question as to the nature of those "controls," rights, jurisdictions which are said to affect, or not to affect, the "sovereignty" of the unit over which they are exercized.[3] Where one modern author seemingly comes closer to connecting sovereignty with the underlying territorial structure of the modern state by actually applying the term "impenetrability" to it, the term still remains synonymous with legal sovereignty and is not used to indicate the latter's factual basis.[4] Legal "impenetrability" must be seen in its connection with the actual territorial impermeability of the modern state; otherwise sovereignty is taken for an absolute, a concept which then is easily misused as a political slogan in the service of a political ideology, for instance, that of nationalism, as has often happened in modern history.

The connection, now so rarely realized, between sovereignty

[2] De Jure Belli ac Pacis, as translated in J. B. Scott (ed.), Classics of International Law (Oxford, 1913), 1: 102.

[3] The problem becomes acute in cases of dependencies, federal structures, etc., where jurisdictions may overlap or not coincide with actual controls as, for instance, in certain types of protectorates or in satellite regimes.

[4] "This [i.e., talking about 'impenetrability'] is another way of saying that on a given territory only one state can have sovereignty—supreme authority—and that no other state has the right to perform governmental acts on its territory without its consent": Hans J. Morgenthau, Politics among Nations (rev. ed.; New York, 1954), p. 289.

and territoriality was actually established at an early point in the development of modern political concepts, and by one of Europe's foremost minds. It was hardly a coincidence that this happened shortly after the end of the Thirty Years War, when formal sanction had been given to territorial sovereignty in the Peace of Westphalia. For here was the turning point, the "great divide," between what were still partly medieval situations, reflecting a certain permeability of the rising nation-state (when, for instance, outside powers could still ally themselves with *frondes* within a country against that country's sovereign), and the full-fledged modern era of clear-cut, hard-shell, "closed" units no longer brooking such interference. This transition from premodern to modern concepts, in relation to what actually happened in the course of the seventeenth century, is illustrated by the emergence of the legal concept of "nonintervention." Nonintervention is a duty directly derived from the "independent" status of the modern state. It is this independence which rendered nation-states legally "sovereign equals," or "equal sovereigns." A complete change of attitude toward intervention occurred in the brief interval between the time when Grotius wrote and that of Pufendorf. Grotius, writing during the last phases of the premodern era of religious and "international civil" wars and still thinking in terms of "just" and "unjust" wars, considered a ruler entitled to intervene in the affairs of another if it was necessary to defend oppressed subjects of the latter. Pufendorf, writing barely fifty years later, rejected such interference in the "domestic affairs" of another sovereign as a violation of the sovereign's exclusive jurisdiction over his territory and all it contained.[5]

5 For references see Walter Schiffer, *The Legal Community of Mankind* (New York, 1954), pp. 34 f., 56; see also *ibid.*, p. 65, regarding Christian Wolff.

Yet it was rather in connection with the problem of sovereignty (in its external aspect) that the clarification of the nature of territoriality actually occurred. The elaboration of the new conceptual framework is contained in a short and little-known essay by Leibniz.[6] The purpose of the essay was entirely pragmatic. It was writen to prove the right of legation of one of the territorial rulers of the time, the Duke of Hanover, in whose service Leibniz was then employed. On this modest basis Leibniz erected a theory which contained a restatement of some fundamental concepts of international politics of his time.

Leibniz's problem derived directly from the situation created by the Peace of Westphalia. This was first among those great all-embracing European settlements which punctuate the era of modern nation-states. For all practical purposes it had conferred sovereign independence upon those princes who formally still were included in the Holy Roman Empire; yet it had not abolished the long-established, essentially feudal structure of the Empire itself, with its allegiances and jurisdictions, the corresponding duties of its members, and even its clumsy and scarcely workable framework of government. Thus some of the now factually sovereign territorial rulers in Europe were still in some manner under a higher authority. Were they now "sovereign" or not? What accounted for sovereignty?

Leibniz's contemporaries failed to see the problem in this light. This muddled state of affairs was as if made to order for those, jurists and others, who argued fine points perennially on the basis of sterile or obsolete concepts. Leibniz, instead of engaging in further discussion of the applicability of Aristotelian categories of government to the modern states of Europe, proceeded to study "what actually happens in the

[6] "Entretiens de Philarète et d'Eugène sur le droit d'Ambassade," quoted in the following from *Werke*, 1st series, 3 (Hanover, 1864), 331 ff.

world today," and as a result he could boast of being "the first to have found the valid definition of sovereignty." [7]

His first problem was to distinguish from sovereign units those—at that time still abundant—minuscule principalities which were not able to defend themselves against foreign attack. Rulers of such units might well possess certain rights and jurisdictions over inhabitants of the territory in question; but they could not claim to be on a par with those that recognized each other as equally sovereign in respect to peace and war, alliances, and the general affairs of Europe, because, not possessing sufficient territory, they could at best only maintain internal order.[8] Leibniz thus arrived at a first definition of sovereignty or, rather, of "sovereign": "A Sovereign, or Potentate, is he who can make himself recognized as such in peace and war in Europe by way of treaties, arms, and alliances." [9]

In this way Leibniz established the basic condition for sovereignty: the requirement that there be that minimum of territory without which, in the age of modern "territoriality," there could be no defensibility. How a minimal capacity for defense is connected with modern concepts of sovereignty and, consequently, nonintervention, is made clear not only from instances where the sovereignty of "pigmy states" (San Marino, Liechtenstein, etc.) has been questioned. It is also demonstrated in the occasional diplomatic and military incidents

[7] *Ibid.*, pp. 340, 342.

[8] *Ibid.*, p. 349: "Si le territoire est petit, comme celuy du Royaume imaginaire d'Ivetot, ou de la petite Républicelle de S.Marin, le Seigneur ou le Sénat de ce territoire pourra sans doute entretenir une garnison pour se maintenir contre les désordres domestiques, ou contre les surprises des ennemis, mais il ne pourra pas se faire considérer par dehors, pour ce qui regarde la paix, la guerre et les alliances des étrangers et le cours des affaires générales de l'Europe. Car cela est réservé à ceux qui sont maistres d'un territoire assez considérable pour être appellés Souverains."

[9] *Ibid.*, p. 350: "Souverain ou Potentat est celuy qui se peut faire considérer en Europe en temps de paix et en temps de guerre par traités, armes et alliances."

which showed that temporary inability of larger states to defend themselves made them seem a threat to the security of
other states exactly because it rendered them "permeable" and
thus a temptation to stronger states.   Third countries, in disregard of the principle of nonintervention, might then take it
upon themselves to incorporate the "open" unit or region into
its own area in order to prevent the "other fellow" from taking over.   Cases in point are the capture of the Danish fleet at
Copenhagen by the British in 1807, when Denmark (allegedly)
was unable to defend herself against Napoleon, or that of the
French fleet at Oran after the French surrender in 1940.[10]

Establishing a minimum condition, however, was not
enough.   There still remained the chief problem: how to define the status of those territorial rulers who, because of their
membership in the Empire, were supposed to be "subjects" of
the emperor.   These rulers, many of whom possessed considerable territory, seemed hardly different in power and status
from those outside the Empire whose sovereign independence
was no longer questioned.   Could one be sovereign and subject at the same time?   If not, what was the status of these
subject-rulers as compared with that of their unquestionably
sovereign European brethren outside the Empire?   If so, what
did their membership in the Empire and their subjection to
the emperor amount to?   These questions were further complicated by the fact that at every court of Europe, including
those in the Empire, there were high dignitaries, often called
"princes," "dukes," etc., who customarily still held the rank
of "Sovereigns."   It was through this maze of relationships that
Leibniz arrived at his definition of sovereignty.

He elaborated his concept of sovereignty by distinguishing it

[10] See also German allegations as to Belgian unwillingness to defend
herself against the Allies in 1914 and to Norwegian unwillingness to
defend herself against British invasion in 1940.   These cases, of course,
show also that in an "anarchic" international system situations may serve
as pretexts for high-handed intervention or as justification for aggression.

from that of "majesty" (*Majesté*). Majesty, the authority which the emperor had *qua* emperor over the members (rulers of territorial states, free cities, etc.) of the Empire, consisted in a number of jurisdictions which conferred the right to demand obedience and involved duties of fealty, but it was not Sovereignty. Why not? Simply because, with all its supreme authority, majesty did not involve an "actual and present power to constrain" subjects "on their own territories." Their territory, in other words, was impermeable. The "subject," on the other hand, if he was a territorial ruler, was "sovereign," because he had the power to constrain *his* subjects while not being so constrainable by superior power. Thus the decisive criterion of sovereignty was the actual, i.e., in the final resort, the military, control of territory, the pacification of one's "estates" by one's own military power. Contrariwise, the absence of such force of his own in his "subjects'" territories accounted for the absence of sovereignty in the emperor's majesty. If he wanted to enforce his superior rights or authority, he could do so only by applying his own or other "sovereigns'" forces from the outside, that is, "by means of war." He would have to break the hard shell of his "subjects'" territorial possessions, and in this his condition would not be different from that of any other sovereign vis-à-vis *his* fellow rulers, since war is a contest which can be inaugurated not only by "majesties" but by any sovereign rulers. Force of arms might constrain a sovereign outside the Empire quite as much as one inside it. In fact, war constituted the only way in which even "sovereigns" could be constrained. By perceiving that the emperor's and the Empire's power to enforce their authority was in actuality reduced to war, Leibniz was in a position to demonstrate that any and all rulers of "impermeable" territory, whatever their status in regard to imperial authority, were equal in their sovereign status. He further saw that transitory capacity to exercize constraint over somebody else's territory was not sufficient to wipe out sovereignty. One acquired the latter only when one had gained "the safe and established right to enforce one's orders with the assistance of military forces capable of keeping the country subdued." [11]

Sovereignty thus conferred the power and the right to defend oneself and one's territory by force against any outside interference, including that of majesty in the pursuance of its "superior" jurisdiction. It signified that even those superior in law could no longer use the ordinary machinery of government (courts, judiciary, etc.) to pursue rights and claims against territorial rulers. This is what distinguishes the relationship between "majesties" and real "sovereigns" among their "subjects" from that between "majesties" and those "princes" and other dignitaries whom we mentioned before and who are sovereigns in name only. Leibniz, by the way of example, refers to the—nonsovereign—status of certain papal "princes," contrasting it with that of sovereign princes: "Should His Holiness desire to make obey the ones, he has merely to send out his 'sbirros' (bailiffs), but in order to constrain the others he would need an army and cannon." [12] Similarly, if the Empire wanted to constrain a sovereign member, "what would begin as court procedure in an imperial Tri-

11 *Ibid.*, pp. 352 f.: "La Souveraineté est un pouvoir légitime et ordinaire de contraindre les sujets à obéir, sans qu'on puisse être contraint soy même si ce n'est par une guerre .... celuy qui est Souverain dans ses Estats doit avoir le droit incontestable d'entretenir des forces militaires capables de les maistriser et même de se rendre considérable par dehors: et la souveraineté subsiste non obstant toutes les obligations . . . qui soumettent un Prince aux ordres de quelque autre dont il reconnoist la majesté, pourvu que ce ne soit pas une puissance présente et prompte qui le maistrise chez luy, mais la considération de son honneur et de son devoir, qui l'oblige à l'obéissance et fidélité. Il paroist aussi par là, que la souveraineté ne se perd pas par quelque contrainte passagère, et qu'un autre ne la sçauroit acquérir dans nos Etats, que lors qu'il a obtenu un droit certain et ordinaire d'appuyer les ordres d'y il y donne par un corps subsistant capable de brider le pays."

12 *Ibid.*, p. 354: "Sa Sainteté se voulant faire obéir des uns, n'avoit qu'à envoyer des sbirres; mais il falloit une armée et du canon pour réduire les autres."

bunal in execution would amount to a war." [13]   In more recent times something of the nature of the old emperor-princes relationship can be found in the relation between sovereign nation-states, as members of international organizations (like the League of Nations or the United Nations), and the organizations as such.

Thus we see that everything in this analysis reflects the internal pacification of the new territorial state and its external defensibility, conditions which had become clearly established in Europe toward the end of the seventeenth century. By giving these conditions their earliest and clearest conceptual expression, Leibniz tied the new concepts of sovereignty, independence, and so forth, to the underlying territorial pattern of statehood. His emphasis on military "constraint" as the primary prerequisite to the status of sovereignty might strike later observers as overmaterialistic and "crude." But we must not forget that the *rocher de bronze* of sovereignty was then only being established, not simply against outside interference, but also against still recalcitrant "feudal" powers within the territorial rulers' realms. Even in the latter case frequently force of arms and armed forces had to be used, which to the defeated may well have seemed to be something very much like "occupation forces." As a matter of fact, "garrisoning" is a key word in Leibniz's arguments, and having "the right to maintain garrisons" in a given territory is to him one of the criteria of independence: "So long as one has the right to be master in his own house . . . . and no superior has the right to maintain ordinary garrisons there and to deprive one of the exercise of his right of peace, war, and alliances, one has that independence which sovereignty presupposes." [14]   Indeed, on

[13] *Ibid.*, p. 358: "C'est la marque de la souveraineté de ne pouvoir estre contrainte que par le sort des armes . . . . Ainsi ce qui n'estoit au commencement qu'un procès dans les Tribunaux de l'Empire, deviendra une guerre dans l'exécution."

[14] *Ibid.*, p. 356: "Tant qu'on a le droit d'être le Maistre chez soy . . .,

this point Grotius had anticipated Leibniz, stating that partial loss of sovereignty was involved where another state had the right to introduce garrisons.[15]

The modern state had now emerged, in actuality as well as in the concepts of the most perspicacious doctrine of the age. It was a centralized area unit, whose sovereignty, independence, and power all resulted from its territoriality. Other important concepts and institutions that characterize the modern state system resulted from it as well. It was on this condition, for instance, that there could develop what we know as "modern international law." Now that power, previously diffused among various power-holders with jurisdiction over one and the same group of persons within one and the same area, had become centralized, with its "headquarters" in impermeable units, and measurable in relation to other external power, it made sense to translate power relations into legal relationships, to distinguish "rights" and "duties" of different states in their mutual relations, to speak of treaties "binding" nations, and so forth.

It is true that international law, like the system of international relations that produced it, has often been considered paradoxical, inherently contradictory, because it claims to "bind" sovereign units. Indeed, if we apply to international law the criteria of fully developed systems of internal, "municipal" law, its "weaknesses"—for instance, its reliance on uniform and generally unanimous action in law-creation and voluntary observation of rules once they have been created—are too obvious to merit further comment. But, whether or not we deny it for this reason the name and character of "genuine" law, it is important to see it in its connection with the territorial structure of the state system it served (and to some

---

et que ce Supérieur n'a pas celui de tenir des garnisons ordinaires chez nous, et de nous oster l'exercice du droit de paix, de guerre et d'alliances, on a liberté requise à la Souveraineté."

[15] *De Jure Balli ac Pacis*, in Scott (ed.), *International Law*, 1: 3, 21.

extent still serves). For only then can its functions really be understood. If we insist on considering it merely a "weak" or "primitive" variation of a law which is more nearly perfected in the internal legal systems of nations, we are liable to misunderstand its very nature as a system of rules and attitudes not contrary to, but implementing, the sovereign independence of states. Only to the extent that international law reflected their territoriality and took into account their sovereignty could it develop in modern times. It no longer made sense to conceive of it as "law of nature," a "higher law" supposed to be comprised of principles beyond, and therefore possibly in conflict with, the states' territorial nature. It has often been observed that international law, as we understand it positivistically today, outside treaty law (that is, rules which issue from mutual consent), contains primarily those rules and principles which deal with the delimitation of countries' jurisdictions.[16] Doing so, it merely gives expression to, and implements in somewhat more detail, a *de facto* condition, that of actual territorial impenetrability, by more closely defining unit, area, and conditions of impenetrability. This predominance of what is known as "*de facto* principle" in international law has often been blamed for the "underdeveloped" character of that law. But a law, under the circumstances in which modern international law has grown, must reflect, rather than regulate. As one author has rightly remarked, "International law really amounts to laying down the principle of national sovereignty, and deducing the consequences."[17] It is not for this reason "superfluous." Sovereign units must know, and know in some detail, where their jurisdictions end and those of other units begin. This is the very basis of their independent coexistence. Without such agreed-upon standards and rules

---

16 See, for instance, Morgenthau, *Politics among Nations*, p. 289.

17 François Laurent, as quoted by Schiffer, *The Legal Community of Mankind*, p. 157.

real "anarchy" would prevail and nations would be involved in constant strife over the implementation of their "independence." Thus it is important that sovereign nations adopted standards for behavior and action whenever, despite their separateness, they came into contact with each other—at frontiers, on the high seas, through nationals residing abroad, and in many similar circumstances. It has been this mutual legal accommodation which rendered their relatively "peaceful" coexistence possible in the first place.

There is one phenomenon, however, in which not the strength but the limits and limitations of "impermeability" and "peaceful coexistence" were reflected. War made its possible for a stronger power to break a weaker one's "shell" and in this way, at least in principle, to override the defeated unit's legal rights and even to destroy its existence as a sovereign unit. But if we investigate the nature and function of war in the territorial age, it will appear that it was of such a nature as to maintain at least the principle of territoriality. The close connection between "classical" war and the territorial nature of the state ameliorated its effect on the territorial system.

Not only did international law, and more so, custom and the actual conditions of the era, serve to limit the way in which war was conducted, particularly and conspicuously in the period of "limited war" which followed immediately upon the rise of territoriality. Quite apart from this, the very nature and objective of modern war was predicated upon the territoriality of the state. In Clausewitz's terms, war was "an act of force to compel our adversary to do our will"; "to achieve this object . . . . we must disarm the enemy." Therefore, one had to proceed so as first to destroy the enemy's military forces, then to conquer his territory, and, as a result of these procedures, finally to induce him to make peace on one's own terms.[18] There is no mention here of destroying the defeated unit as such. Thus an author who has often (and incorrectly) been regarded as the father of the doctrine of "total war," was still conceiving of war, not as a process of annihilation, physical or political, but rather as a "duel"-type contest of power and will, in which the interests but not the existence of the contestants were at stake.

It has certainly not been a state of complete pacification and protection in which modern man has been living since the establishment of the modern state system, either domestically or, above all, internationally. War, after all, might have and has broken walls of "impermeability" built around the units of protection and pacification. But war, even in the classical era of its greatest limitation, involved risks, even for an apparently superior power, and was therefore not undertaken lightly. With his usual perspicacity Leibniz had already realized that, while nothing, not even sovereigns, could escape "those great revolutions which the fate of arms causes here on earth," wars are always an ultimate test in which the fate of both contestants is at stake.[19] Even so, the breaking of the shell would not ordinarily presage the destruction of the unit as such or of the "way of life" of its inhabitants.[20] Now that this period is coming (or has come) to an end, and we are approaching the era of absolute exposure, with neither walls nor moats, in which penetration in its extreme form will mean not mere damage or change but utter annihilation of life and way of life, it may begin to dawn in us that what has passed with the age of "sovereignty" and "power politics" was not entirely adverse in nature and effect.

[18] Karl von Clausewitz, *On War* (Washington, 1950), pp. 3, 20.
[19] "Entretiens de Philarète," pp. 352, 353.
[20] See below, ch. 4.

4

The Territorial State

in International Relations

We have long been used to consider the international world of modern times as an insecure one where the acting unit, the territorial state, relying chiefly on its own power (plus, possibly, that of allies), struggled to survive among power-hungry, expansionist competitors. While this impression is undoubtedly an accurate indication of one aspect of the system, it neglects others which account for rather more security of unit and stability of system than one would expect from the usual image of a purely competitive condition. We shall call these the "conservative" features of the modern state system. The preceding chapter has already indicated some of the phenomena, including even war in as much as it was "limited" in conduct and objectives, which reflected a protective, stabilizing function of territoriality rather than one involving insecurity and instability. Owing to them, the modern state, embedded though it was in a basically anarchic environment, enjoyed more security than one would assume in the absence of supranational authority providing enforceable standards of international behavior.

In emphasizing the conservative aspects of the system we find ourselves in agreement with views prevalent in the earlier period of modern times. Observers then often regarded the sovereign power of the territorial state as a contribution rather than a menace to security. Thus Pufendorf made use of the then commonplace comparison between an anarchic and insecure "state of nature" and the security-providing condition of human beings under government in order to show that security was afforded not only to the people within the unit where government was established but also to the units themselves in their international relations. Hobbes had stressed the warlike posture of Leviathans in their mutual relations, where a state of nature still prevailed. Pufendorf opposed to this the picture of an international society where nations were safe in the enjoyment of security because they could trust in their own protective power. According to him, while liberty in a pure state of nature without a superior is "a thing of little joy or use" to individual human beings, because in that state "the weakness of their own resources makes their safety hang by a thread," it is different in the case of those powerful "individuals" in international relations, the states. Once they exist, "there is no similar need for universal government" because "the height of mortal achievement has been attained when security rests upon the strength of the entire state"; states "are girded with the powers which allow them the secure enjoyment of their liberty." [1]

Pufendorf and others, in this kind of argument, may have placed too much reliance on the state's territorial might as guarantor of its security. But the argument rightly emphasized one element in the territoriality of the modern state which played a greater role in the earlier classical period than it did later: under the little developed conditions of statecraft and techniques of war in the seventeenth and eighteenth

---

[1] See the references in Walter Schiffer, *The Legal Community of Mankind* (New York, 1954), p. 62. We find an echo of such earlier appraisals in theories of certain nineteenth- and twentieth-century philosophers, from Hegel, with his theory of the nation-state as ultimate judge in world conflicts, to Friedrich Wieser (*Das Gesetz der Macht* [Vienna, 1926], p. 269). They exalt the state as the highest unit in international affairs in order to discount possibilities of international integration. Here, to be sure, the argument tends to become "ideological," a rationalization to defend something beyond the actually defendable.

centuries the protective outer shell of even the smaller and less powerful states afforded them some real protection; in other words, it provided more "impermeability" than have defenses in more recent times. Nobody saw this more clearly than a realistic observer from the other side of the Atlantic who stated:

The disciplined armies always kept on foot on the continent of Europe . . . have been productive of the signal advantage of rendering sudden conquests impracticable . . . . The art of fortifications has contributed to the same ends. The nations of Europe are encircled with chains of fortified places, which mutually obstruct invasion . . . . The history of war, in that quarter of the globe, is no longer a history of nations subdued and empires overturned, but of towns taken and retaken; of battles that decide nothing; of retreats more beneficial than victories; of much effort and little acquisition.[2]

And Frederick the Great, one who certainly should have known, expressed himself in the same vein.[3]

While the changing character of war and an increasing destructiveness of weapons soon thereafter lessened the reliance which states could place on their impermeability, there were other, and more constant, elements which one must take into account to understand how the classical state system actually functioned. What has been discussed so far has concerned primarily the structure underlying international relations, the units' statehood itself. In accordance with the distinction made earlier between structure and systems of international politics, the factors which I shall now mention refer to the

[2] Hamilton, in the 8th Federalist paper.

[3] "Armaments and discipline being much the same throughout Europe, and alliances as a rule producing an equality of force between belligerent parties, all that princes can expect from the greatest advantages at present is to acquire, by accumulation of successes, either some small city on the frontier, or some territory which will not pay interest on the expenses of war, and whose population does not even approach the number of citizens who perished in the campaign" (quoted by R. R. Palmer, in Edward M. Earle [ed.], *Makers of Modern Strategy* [Princeton, 1943], p. 61). These, to be sure, were the views of a reformed—because by then satisfied —"old sinner" who had not always acted on such premises.

ways in which states in modern times have organized their relations, that is, to the international *system* rather than to the
underlying *structure* of territoriality. Some of these factors
have been given due attention elsewhere, while others are less
well known.

Among the better understood is, above all, the "balance of
power," the system of maintaining an equilibrium among the
powers. It is necessary to distinguish between balance of
power as a mere factual and possibly coincidental constellation, balance policies as conscious policies of powers having
for their objective the maintenance of an equilibrium, and a
balance system as the possible resultant from such policies.
While purely factual balance conditions have existed frequently in the past without corresponding policies and systems emerging from them (for instance, in Greco-Roman antiquity), balance of power as a conscious policy of nations is a
product of the modern rationalistic and mechanistic age, a
policy which was rendered possible chiefly by three conditions:
first, the existence, within the confines of one continent, of a
considerable but not overly large number of "big powers," not
too dissimilar in power from each other and not too distinct
in power from lesser ones; second, the existence of one insular
power which, while geographically distant from the rest, could
yet intervene as "holder of the balance" whenever the equilibrium was endangered by the expansionist policies of a
would-be hegemony power; and third, a dynastic diplomacy
which, free from considerations of "ideology," as well as from
influence of "public" or other opinion, and from any similar
"power-alien" influences, could devote itself to balancing policies as to a cool and detached game of chess.[4]

---

[4] More on problems of the balance of power will be found below, ch.
7. By the term "power-alien influence" I refer to any influence upon
the foreign policy of a given nation that is caused by considerations not
connected with power and security, for instance, sympathy with some
religious or ideological cause or issue, factional or personal preferences
and dislikes, and so forth.

That the development of the concept and policy of the balance of power was one of the primary means for checking the expansionist capacity of power and for preventing it from penetrating and destroying other power has become better recognized more recently, when emphasis shifted from a somewhat one-sided concern with the negative aspects of the balance—its uncertainty, its role as cause of unending conflicts and frequent wars, and so forth—toward its more conservative, protective effects.[5] In the eighteenth century, the period when the balance attained perfection as an art of statecraft and a technique of diplomacy, its conservative function was perhaps overemphasized, and there were even theories (not entirely lived up to in practice, of course) that nations had *legal* obligations to form barriers against a "hegemony" power in the "common interest." [6]

As the term "common interest" in this reference indicates, there was something more elusive yet also more fundamental in the structure of the old European system than balance of power, something upon which balance of power as a policy was itself somehow dependent. This may be called its community character, for, there did exist something like a community of European nations, forming a comparatively "pacified" whole, with its own standards and with rules that extended to, and mitigated, the quarrels ("wars") arising in this "family of nations." It was in part a residue from the genuine community of medieval Christian Europe; in part it reflected the "class-consciousness" and shared cultural standards of a leading aristocracy and the legitimacy-consciousness and other common interests of the ruling dynasties. As such an entity, Europe was set off sharply against a realm outside

---

5 For references see my *Political Realism and Political Idealism* (Chicago, 1951), pp. 206–21.

6 See J. von Elbe, "Die Wiederherstellung der Gleichgewichtsordnung in Europa durch den Wiener Kongress," *Zeitschrift für ausländisches öffentliches Recht und Völkerrecht*, 4: 226 ff. (1934).

Europe, the world beyond those "lines" which, by common agreement, separated a community based on territoriality and common heritage from outside "anarchy" where the law of nature reigned and no standards of civilization applied. Only recently have the existence and role of so-called "amity lines" been rediscovered, lines which were drawn in the treaties—especially the peace treaties—of the early modern period and which separated European territories, where the legal rules of war and peace were to prevail, from overseas territories and areas.[7] There was to be "no peace beyond the line"; that is, the European powers, although possibly at peace in Europe, continued to be "homo homini lupus" abroad. This practice undoubtedly served to consolidate and pacify the European "family." In particular, it made it easier for the members of the family to observe self-denying standards "at home" by providing them with an outlet for their expansionist and warlike inclinations in the vast realm discovered outside Europe. While the practice of drawing "amity lines" subsequently disappeared, one chief function of eighteenth- and nineteenth-century overseas expansion in its relation to the European community and its balance remained: a balance of power could be maintained or adjusted among the powers of Europe because it was relatively easy to divert European conflicts into overseas directions and to adjust them there. "Compensation" abroad, for instance, might pay for losses or diminished status at home (as it did in the case of France after 1871). Even in the late period of imperialism expansion and adjustment of European interests overseas still served for a while to avert "world wars" among the empires, as witness the Anglo-Russian division of spheres in Asia (Persia around

[7] See Carl Schmitt, *Der Nomos der Erde* (Cologne, 1950), pp. 60 ff.; also, W. Schoenborn, "Über Entdeckung als Rechtstitel völkerrechtlichen Gebietserwerbs," in D. S. Constantinopoulos and H. Wehberg (eds.), *Gegenwartsprobleme des internationalen Rechts und der Rechtsphilosophie* (Hamburg, 1953), pp. 239 ff.

1900, for example), the Anglo-French division of spheres in North Africa at the same time, or indeed the partition of Africa as such. Thus the "openness" of the world contributed to the maintenance and consolidation of a system built on territoriality and balance of power. The end of the "world frontier" and the resulting "closedness" of an interdependent world inevitably affected this system's effectiveness.

Another phenomenon, also less well known than it deserves to be and, perhaps, even more characteristic of the security function of the territorial system, is the almost complete absence of instances where countries, in the course of wars or other power-political events, were wiped out as such. If this statement seems astonishing, let it be added immediately that it refers only to the old territorial units "at home," that is in Europe, and not to the peoples and state units "beyond the pale," and further, that it refers only to the complete destruction of a state's independent existence, and not, of course, to mere loss of territory or similar changes which, obviously, abounded in an age of power politics. With these qualifications, however, I believe that the statement can stand. Let us consider its meaning and implications by examining more closely the concept and practice of "conquest."

"Conquest," in the sense of complete "subjugation" with ensuing annexation, partition, etc., of an enemy's entire territory, was recognized as legal title for the acquisition of sovereignty only slowly and hesitantly in the development of international law. The late Middle Ages and early modern times denied the concept recognition, chiefly because of surviving doctrines of the "just war." [8] Grotius was unclear and wavering in his treatment of the problem. Positivism, since Vattel, has been prone to accept it, but with a significant difference in point of view between Anglo-American and Con-

[8] For this and what follows see M. M. McMahon, *Conquest and Modern International Law* (Washington, 1940), *passim*.

tinental authors. The former have been more inclined to recognize it than the latter. This conflict in theory quite possibly was caused by a difference in interests on the part of the countries concerned. The Anglo-American view was primarily concerned with conditions outside of Europe, the Continental view with those in Europe itself. Outside of Europe, new units, such as the United States, as well as the colonial powers, like Britain, could not well do without conquest as a legal title to their expanding possessions, whereas the countries of the Continent, already safely established as units, were chiefly interested in legal safeguards against their own obliteration. Within Europe, some proposed that even mere changes in territorial status not amounting to complete annexation should for their validity require the consent of the "big powers" (supposedly representing, *qua* Concert of Europe, the entire European community.[9]

Did this nonrecognition of conquest on the Continent, we may ask, reflect actual attitudes, or was it primarily an ideology under which legal approval to inconvenient or immoral-appearing facts was refused? To what extent did it correspond to the practice of states? That it was far from being pure ideology can be inferred from the fact that where conquests were ordinarily the basis of acquisition of territory and title, namely, in overseas regions, early authors frankly acknowledged this by recognizing indigenous rulers as "sovereigns," so that conquest (or treaty with them) could become the legal title for the acquisition of their rights and lands. Only later, in the nineteenth century, when the procedures accompanying these acts began to seem reprehensible to many, did authors, retroactively so to say, interpret what had happened as a different kind of acquisition of territory based on a different title. Natives of overseas regions, so the theory now went, did not have the capacity to establish "sovereign," that is, "con-

[9] See Robert Langer, *Seizure of Territory* (Princeton, 1947), pp. 9 ff.

querable," states on the European pattern; their lands could be treated as mere "no man's land" (*terra nullius*); consequently, they might be acquired under the title of "discovery and occupation." [10]

All of these elements of "interest" and "ideology" notwithstanding, such doctrines of acquisition of title their had real, nonideological foundation in the actual difference between European and non-European polities so far as territoriality was concerned. European states were "impermeable," while many of those overseas were even in the nineteenth century so easily penetrable by Europeans that the earlier distinction between permissible conquest abroad and impermissibility of conquest at home was as much in agreement with the facts as the later one that distinguished units which, not being "sovereign" in the European sense, could be acquired by mere occupation on the part of the sovereign nation-states of Europe. These distinctions were a reflection of the "line" separating the community of established territorial units in Europe from the outside world not belonging to the European family. The way in which the "mighty" indigenous empires of the New World (the Aztec and the Inca) had been toppled by a handful of European *conquistadores* could not fail to impress many later generations.

Only much later, with the extension of the European territorial system beyond Europe and the emergence, chiefly in the nineteenth century, of European-style "states" on other continents, was the idea of impermissible conquest extended to them also. Eventually there was a tendency to consider their sovereignty, too, as indestructible, to be protected through a system of collective security and the outlawing—or, at least, the nonrecognition—of acquisition of title by conquest.

In Europe, in the meantime, the idea that sovereignty con-

[10] See M. F. Lindlay, *The Acquisition and Government of Backward Territory in International Law* (London, 1926), pp. 10 ff.

veyed, or should convey, protection, had already long prevailed. It was reflected, for instance, in theories of so-called
"fundamental" rights of states to "existence," "self-preservation," etc., and implied that to use one's power for the destruction of another was an abuse of sovereignty. Hand in hand
with this ideology went a practice which produced only rare
and exceptional cases of annihilation through conquest or
similar forceful means. Prior to the twentieth century there
were, indeed, the Napoleonic conquests. But this is a case in
which the exception confirms the rule, since the Napoleonic
system, as a hegemonical one, was devised to destroy the established system of territoriality and balanced power as such.
Consequently, Napoleon and his policies seemed "demonic"
to contemporaries,[11] as well as to a nineteenth century which
saw the reestablishment of the territorial balance system after
Napoleon's demise. During that century Bismarck's annexa-
tions of some individual German units into Prussia in pursuance of German unification occurred. Unification measures
in Italy, which also involved the demise of a number of hitherto sovereign states, provoked little objection on grounds of
obliteration of state units, chiefly because what happened appeared to be not so much "conquest" as voluntary merger
sanctioned by plebiscite. Bismarck's more high-handed policies, on the other hand, smacked of conquest, and therefore,
as in the case of Napoleon, they appeared abnormal to many
of his contemporaries, although the issue of national unification tended to mitigate this impression.[12]

Besides these examples of aberrance from the general practice, there was one really glaring exception, the partition of
Poland. Considering the lamentable and lasting impression
and the universal bad conscience it produced, even among the

[11] As witness the impression made on contemporaries by the destruction
of the first ancient European unit to fall victim to Napoleonic policies—
Venice (G. Ferrero, *Aventure: Bonaparte en Italie 1796–1797* [Paris, 1936]).
[12] On the relation between nationalism and conquest see below.

ruling groups in a century quite used to international skulduggery, for that event one may well claim again exceptional character.[13]

Except for these cases, we find only marginal instances of complete obliteration. The annexation of the free city of Cracow by Austria eliminated a synthetic creation of the Vienna settlement which had not had enough time to become an established member of the European family (if ever time could have made it one). The British conquest of the Boer republics at the turn of the century, if considered as an instance of annihilation of European polities in view of the European origin of the inhabitants,[14] nevertheless happened at the very rim of the world, as it were, remote from the continent where the practice of nonannihilation prevailed. Thus several centuries yield only a few scattered instances of such practice.

If, going beyond Europe, one investigates the stability of non-European states established on the European pattern in other parts of the world, one encounters even there only a few instances of conquest or similar forceful obliteration, at least prior to the age of totalitarianism. Witness, for instance, the remarkable continuity of Western Hemisphere nations *qua* units. Unstable though they may be domestically, they have proved sacrosanct in their sovereign identities. Not even at the height of American (that is, United States) imperialism were these affected. Even in our century, when the territoriality and ensuing sovereignty of nation-states have become questionable, the existence of such units has been generally safeguarded. It is surely remarkable that after the turmoil of

13 Even if one does not go so far as Carl Schmitt who asserts that Poland was exceptional because it was quasi-feudal (owing to the *liberum veto* in its diet) and therefore, even during its "lifetime," not fully recognized as being on a par with "real" centralized monarchies.

14 As does, for instance, B. H. Liddell Hart, *The Revolution in Warfare* (New Haven, 1947), pp. 47 f.

attempted world-conquest and resulting world wars, scrupulous restoration of the most minute and inconsiderable of sovereignties down to Luxembourg or Albania has been made. In contrast to the large number of new states established during the last hundred years, few old ones have disappeared. This, too, testifies to the strong roots which the practice of nonannihilation had taken in the consciousness of mankind.

In addition to "territoriality," there were other causes contributing to this remarkable stability of the statehood of nations. Two phenomena, one in each of the two main periods into which the classical age of modern international relations is divided, served this function. They are the principle of legitimacy, which dominated the prerevolutionary era of "ancient regimes;" and the phenomenon of nationalism, which characterized the era following upon the French Revolution. Territoriality of the modern state has been the ultimate foundation of that stability, for without the establishment of defensible units, internally pacified and externally fortified, neither of these phenomena would have had the proper soil in which to grow. As for "legitimacy," it is easy to see how this principle consolidated and strengthened the newly established territorial units in the Europe of the seventeenth and eighteenth centuries. These units were conceived in almost personal terms (Hapsburg, Bourbon, etc.). It was ruling heads of states, ruling dynasties, which had mutually recognized each other as legitimate potentates, that is, as rightful sovereigns of their respective lands. Depriving one sovereign of his rights by force could not help but seem to destroy the very principle upon which the rights of all of them rested. Even the mere transfer of territory through cession, for example, during that period was always based on claimed rights, such as claims arising from inheritance (to be sure, claims whose rightfulness in case of disagreement was to be proved by force of arms: "wars of succession"). It was thus mutual or common interest which generally prevented the occurrence of that extreme of power politics that the wiping out of the very existence of a country would have constituted.[15]

With the rise of nationalism interest in the personal headship of states receded; instead, the personalization of the units themselves as "nations," that is, corporate, self-determining national groups, came to the fore. Nationalism now made it appear equally as abhorrent to deprive a politically organized and "sovereign" nation of its independence as to despoil a legitimate ruler had appeared before. States, of course, had first to become "nations" in the new nationality sense of the word, and this explains why in the two regions of Europe—Germany and Italy—where large numbers of old units stood in the way of national unification their demise encountered little objection. Certainly, nationalists were not among the objectors. They did not even object, but rather cheered when in one conspicuous case, that of Austria-Hungary, the realization of the nationality principle involved the dismantling of a long-established "big power." For the most part, however (as in the Balkans, the Near East, etc.), the rise of nationalism led to the emergence of new states rather than to the submergence of existing ones, because they emerged by splitting away from multinational or, more recently, from colonial empires. But this hypertrophy of nation-states all over the world presented a new problem. Coupled as this development was with a decrease in the defensibility, or impermeability, of the territorial state,[16] it presented the need for an improved system of protection. For, despite all that has been said, the conservative, or "stability," elements in the old system should not

[15] So strong was this feeling that even in the second half of the nineteenth century, when Prussia annexed five Germanic states in 1866, whatever objections were voiced came from monarchs, such as the czar, and ultraconservative, legitimist sources; see Erich Eyck, *Bismarck*, 2 (Zurich, 1943), 305 ff.

[16] On this see below, ch. 6.

be exaggerated. Its protective function was only a relative blessing after all. Continued existence of states as such was perhaps more or less guaranteed. But apart from this, the power, influence, status, frontiers, economic interests—in short, everything that constituted the life and interests of nations beyond bare existence—were always at the mercy of historical fate, of "fortuna" in the sense that Machiavelli used the term, that is, of what international politics, power politics, wrought. Furthermore, much of the relative stability of the territorial states of Europe and the equilibrium in which they managed to maintain themselves had been due to that tremendous process which accompanied the era: the extension of Western control over the world. When the areas that could be penetrated had been subjugated, assimilated, or established as fellow "sovereign" states, the old units were thrown back upon themselves. Hence the demand for a new system which would offer more security to old and new nations alike: collective security.

5

Collective Security as an Attempt
to Maintain the Territorial Principle

In contrast to a view which considers "collective security" the polar opposite of "power politics," I propose to analyze it here as an attempt to modify—improve if you wish—certain features of a system whose basic foundations remain unchanged. That is, I view it as an attempt to maintain, and render more secure, the "territoriality" or "impermeability" of states upon which their "sovereignty" and "independence" had rested since the beginning of the modern era. To an age which took territoriality for granted, that is, approximately up to the First World War, replacing power politics with collective security would indeed seem a radical departure. We, in the mid-twentieth century, however, have become aware of the far more radical change which now in the air and nuclear age affects the very power foundations of nations. Thus, from the vantage point of the nuclear age, a plan to protect individual sovereignties by collective guarantees for continuing sovereignty appears questionable not because of its innovating, but rather because of its conservative, perhaps even outdated, nature. In any event, we are now in a position to recognize its close relation to the traditional features of the classical system.

The conservative core of any system of collective security lies in its basic objective: the protection of the territorial structure of its members. Article 10, the central article of the Covenant of the League of Nations, termed it the guarantee of the members' "territorial integrity and political independence" against external aggression. Toward the end of the classical era, besides realizing that a balance of power system had at best been a doubtful guarantor of such integrity and independence, nations had also come to fear that developments in other spheres had affected the hard-shell nature of their defensibility. The First World War showed that economic self-sufficiency, on which the old fortress-state had relied, had yielded to economic interdependence between the modern industrial states, which thus might be starved into surrender. The beginnings of air war also indicated that the old-style military barriers might be by-passed. If territorial units were to be preserved in the future—so the collective security argument ran—this would be accomplished less by reliance on individual defense potentials than by marshaling their collective power in order to preserve individual powers.

There was an additional reason for thinking in terms of collective defense guarantees immediately after the First World War. Peace treaties in the classical era had always left defeated powers their right to armaments, that is, to their shell of defensibility. Now, for the first time,[1] disarmament had been imposed upon the vanquished. This step ostensibly was to inaugurate a general reduction of armaments under the auspices of the new collective security organization set up. Disarmament and collective security were thus tied up in one package, since no disarmament could be envisaged without substituting for individual defensibility protection through joint forces.

Since, however, the idea of organizing a genuine supranational force—an international "police force"—was rejected, the states had to cling to "classical" concepts and arrange-

[1] With the relatively minor and short-lived exception of the Treaty of Paris of 1856, which imposed disarmament conditions on Russia in the Black Sea area.

ments not only in regard to the "objects" of collective security, the preservation of their individual territories, but also in so far as the procedures of protection were concerned. The guarantee to the individual states was to be the joining of forces, the formation of the "grand coalition" of all against the isolated aggressor, and this, of course, presupposed the maintenance of a certain level of armed strength by the member-states themselves. A member without that minimum of military strength would be a liability rather than an asset to the organization—in Geneva parlance, "a consumer" and not a "producer" of security.[2] Thus classical concepts (the sovereignty and independence of nation-states) as well as classical institutions (in particular, hard-shell defensibility) were to be maintained under the new system. Even where new developments in "structure" had begun to affect territoriality, an attempt was made to harness them to the purposes of the new organization. For instance, since economic blockade had emerged as a practical means to circumvent the hard shell, collective blockade of "aggressors" was adopted as one of the chief "sanctions" under Article 16 of the Covenant. But in its essence collective security was to be a mere refinement of the balance system, that is, a system which would institutionalize that "overwhelming coalition" which the old system, more haphazardly, used to provide against "hegemony" powers, and thus offer more reliable protection against "aggressors."

Institutionalizing that which so far had been based only on

[2] In the practice of the League, therefore, applications for membership of countries without this minimum of armed strength were rejected, for instance, that of Liechtenstein (see Schücking-Wehberg, *Die Satzung des Völkerbundes* [2d ed.; Berlin, 1924], pp. 252 ff.). Germany and Austria, of course, had some armed forces even under the restrictive provisions of the peace treaties. The decline of genuine collective security in our time, on the other hand, is apparent from the fact that, in contrast to this League of Nations practice, the United Nations pays hardly any attention to the question of defensibility, particularly in connection with membership applications.

unregulated practice also involved a more legalistic approach to power relations—an attempt to handle through legal commitments what previously had been achieved through reliance on considerations of interest and utility. In and of itself this attempt to legalize what so far had been relations of power might well appear novel and extreme. But in another sense, like the objective of the collective security system itself, it was in line with the conservative features of the traditional system. As we have seen, the way in which the old system functioned had in practice meant some guarantee of existence and survival to most of its member units. Collective security added to this an all-inclusive and enforceable "right to existence." Power, still measurable, and therefore calculable, in terms of military strength, economic capacities, population, etc., could be utilized for the protection and enforcement of such a right because, presumably, it could be organized to rally superior power at the side of the law. The entire system, indeed, was predicated on the assumption that even powerful aggressors could be deterred or, if need be, defeated by rallying superior power against them.

The inherent legalistic traits in a system based upon comparable and calculable power culminated in two trends which emerged in the era of collective security: the attempt to set up international law as higher law over and above municipal law, and the urge to establish legal rights and responsibilities not only for states as such but also for individual agents acting as their "organs." Under the classical system the approach to international law had been a "dualist" one. That approach assumed that international law, by its very nature, could act on and bind states only as units, so that what happened within was of concern solely to the different and separate national legal systems. This had indeed been appropriate when impermeable units coexisted, with no higher authority entitled to penetrate them, and with international law serving chiefly to delineate their spheres of jurisdiction.[3] In a working collective security system, on the other hand, international law would reflect the enforceable collective will (or policy) of the international community and thus would be effective directly upon and within the individual member states. "Legal penetrability" was of the essence in this system, and it was therefore logical to consider international law superior to municipal law (the "monist" instead of the "dualist" concept of international law). It was equally consistent with this approach to hold individuals acting for states individually responsible to the legal community in case they acted "illegally," in case, for instance, they engaged their country in "illegal aggression." The Nuremberg principles, it is true, were applied somewhat belatedly, that is, at a time when the demise of the League and the advent of the atomic age had rendered collective security legalism obsolete; but they had been elaborated at a time when the atomic age was not yet in sight—namely, at the time of the Three Power Declaration on War Crimes at Moscow in 1943—and when there was still hope of reconstituting a system of genuine collective security.

What is collective security today? On the face of it, it is still a vital concept. Collective security is still widely discussed, and not only when it is a matter of historical research into the politics of the interwar period, but also in relation to post-Second World War and present international problems. Indeed, judging from the continual references to collective security in the statements of leaders and in general public discussions, one would believe that it constitutes a major policy currently pursued by important nations. But, as frequently happens in the terminology of international affairs, actually a sloganized concept is being used so broadly as to lose its original and more specific meaning. Since honest old terms like "alliance" have come to smack too much of "power

3 See above, ch. 3.

politics" (which as a term is also discredited today), there is a preference for calling alliances and regional assistance pacts "systems of collective security," and the corresponding policy of powers so allied "collective security policy." In this manner, a policy of "collective security" has become synonymous with any policy of joining with other countries for some political or military purpose.

But genuine collective security implies the absence of specific alignments against predetermined opponents; rather, it implies the anonymity of the aggressor and the organization of an entirety of nations in a system in such a way as to counter any aggression on the part of any member of the system, whether the system be world-wide or regional.[4] Even the concept of regional collective security becomes dubious when measured against the criteria of genuine collective security. Such a system may be in conformity with a world-wide security system if its purpose is to settle intraregional conflicts through regional collective intervention before the conflict becomes a matter of more general concern. Thus, the Organization of American States (OAS) is a genuine collective security organization (disregarding cases in which the United States, a "superpower," is directly involved) in so far as it deals with conflicts arising among nations of the Western hemisphere. It is an alliance in as much as it envisages joint

[4] In this connection an incident in a *Bundestag* debate at the time when the Paris treaties on the status of Germany were discussed is revealing. Said SPD Deputy Fritz Erler: "For the rest, you, Mr. von Merkatz, as an international lawyer, should know what the difference is between a system of collective security, where the partners are mutually committed to keep the peace and collectively obligated to help each other against an aggressor, and a traditional military alliance (Applause by the SPD. Question from the CDU benches: What exactly is the difference?)" (see *Frankfurter Allgemeine Zeitung*, March 15, 1955). Erler's remark was exactly to the point, since the choice under debate was between a Germany neutralized in a European collective security system comprised of both East *and* West, and one lined up with the West against the—predetermined—potential aggressor from the East.

defense against aggression from outside the area. Similarly, NATO and related systems are alliances, or power blocs, however frequently and emphatically they are referred to as embodiments of collective security. Their members obviously are little concerned over the danger of, say, a French attack on Belgium, or even a German attack on France. What they face is an extraregional power (or power bloc). The same, of course, applies to the corresponding alliance on the Soviet side, the so-called "Warsaw Pact." The problem of "universalism" versus "regionalism," much debated at the time of the League of Nations and now under the United Nations system, resolves itself (except for the cases—now diminishing in number and importance—of genuine regional organization for collective security of the OAS pattern) into the problem of how policies pursued through traditional processes of power politics (formation of alliances, etc.) can be related to policies pursued through the instrumentality of a general international organization (such as the United Nations).[5]

The foregoing, however, does not solve the major problems of collective security. Assuming that a collective security system is consonant with certain traits of the modern state system; assuming, moreover, that criticism of recent "collective security policies" on the grounds that they do not conform to the true definition of a policy of this sort is justified; we are still confronted with the question of whether states that used to engage in traditional power politics can be expected to live up to the requirements of collective security, and if so, under what conditions. Especially in the light of the conspicuous failure of the League of Nations, could *any* organization established for such purpose play the role of a

[5] In this criticism of the abuse of the term "collective security" and the attempt to distinguish "genuine" collective security from blocs and alliances I find myself in complete agreement with the corresponding line of argument in I. L. Claude, *Swords into Plowshares: The Problems and Progress of International Organization* (New York, 1956), pp. 250 ff.

collective security organization successfully? What would be the conditions for success, what have been the reasons of failure? What, in particular, is the situation today, notably in regard to the United Nations? Can that organization be expected to implement genuine collective security?

These are difficult questions. They can, perhaps, be most profitably discussed by analyzing a number of the more recent writings on collective security, with a subsequent attempt to arrive at some over-all conclusions.

Collective security has been defined as "a system based on the universal obligation of all nations to join forces against an aggressor state as soon as the fact of aggression is determined by established procedure." [6] We may well take this definition—which corresponds to commonly accepted ones—as a starting point for our discussion, assuming that "aggression" is understood to mean violation of a country's territorial integrity (as it usually is in this connection). We then encounter in Johnson and Niemeyer's article one of the chief objections perennially leveled against the practicality of such a system: nations have (and must have) a limited range of objectives in their foreign policies; this range is determined by their own peculiar security interests. They thus can be expected to act only in regard to a carefully delineated area. If they are to join in any collective action, they must, therefore, first of all be made to recognize "a plausible and tangible relation between the aggression against which action is required and the security of the nation on the part of which action is demanded." But "aggression" determined by this power-political, or security-political, criterion no longer constitutes "an

[6] H. C. Johnson and G. Niemeyer, "Collective Security: The Validity of an Ideal," *International Organization*, 8: 20 (1954). On the earlier development of collective security concepts see Richard N. Current, "The United States and Collective Security: Notes on the History of an Idea," in Alexander De Conde (ed.), *Isolation and Security* (Durham, N.C., 1957), pp. 33 ff.

unequivocal wrong," and, it may be added, ceases therewith to be a generally valid standard for universal political action or counteraction. A genuine collective security system cannot function on the basis of potentially divergent and clashing national interests and policies.

It is to this same discrepancy between national interest and community action that another author [7] turns when he applies the term (borrowed from an earlier discussant of collective security, Francesco Coppola) "war against nature" to collective military action. "Nature" here obviously refers to the allegedly "natural" bent of nations to follow their interests to the exclusion of all other considerations. "States cannot reasonably be relied upon to 'make war against nature,' that is, for reasons they do not hold to affect their national interests." Therefore, "punitive" automatic sanctions, to be initiated on the basis of an objective aggression test, are either absurd, because nations will not subordinate their policies to them, or immoral, because, if actually applied, they imply disregard of the real merits of the case. In the latter event, they also involve the danger of extending hostilities; they are apt "to transform any particular war into a general war."

The same conflict between self-interest of nations and the commitment to act in a common interest sometimes finds a more paradoxical formulation. Collective security, so one author argues,[8] suffers from a contradiction in its basic assumption: on the one hand, it trusts in the readiness of countries to join in collective action even where their self-interest is not directly affected; on the other hand, it distrusts them because aggression is assumed to be always threatening. Collective security action is superfluous if the first assumption,

[7] Erich Hula, "Fundamentals of Collective Security," *Social Research* 24: 1 ff. (1957–58).

[8] See Walter Schiffer, *The Legal Community of Mankind* (New York, 1954), p. 199.

that of general readiness to put common before national interests, is correct. But if the second, that of the unreliability of states, is warranted, no collective action can be expected from them.

A systematic survey of the difficulties inherent in collective security is found in another publication.[9] The author of the survey, in order to cope with the question why collective security has failed in practice, distinguishes the following principal reasons: 1) The system, by protecting the political and territorial status of its members, cannot avoid defending a given status quo, which may be, or may become, unsatisfactory. This, indeed, was one of the vitiating features of the League of Nations. The post-Second World War establishment gave such a system even less of a chance because it was "created to defend a status quo which has not yet been brought into existence." 2) The proper functioning of collective security presupposes an overwhelming strength of the coalition countering the aggressor. In addition to such strength in terms of power, there must be, 3) at least "a minimum of political solidarity and moral community," among the major powers in the system. Both factors have been found wanting in past and present collective security experiments. 4) There is what this author calls "the political problem," that is, the existence of separate and conflicting national interests and policies which may run counter to the policies of the organization. The problem becomes particularly acute in connection with how the main "sanctions'" burdens are to be distributed. 5) There is the "psychological problem"—mutual national antagonisms, disdains, and distrusts. Finally, 6) there is the fact that collective security is incompatible with "peaceful change," for which it fails to provide international standards and procedures.

[9] Kenneth W. Thompson, "Collective Security Reexamined," *American Political Science Review*, 47: 753 ff. (1953).

Discussion centering on the problems of aggression and its outlawry is the hallmark of still another article.[10] Outlawry of aggression is there compared to the Roman law institution of the *possessorium,* a legal action (edict *uti possidetis*) through which possession of a thing taken away illegally could be reclaimed regardless of the merits of the underlying case (property questions, etc.). As in the case of the *possessorium,* in countering aggression there is no connection with the underlying legal or political conflict. Aggression is dealt with simply as an illegal taking-away of the peace, while the question of the merits remains unsolved at this stage. That is to be decided (as in the Roman-law *petitorium*) only after the repulsion of the aggressor. *Possessorium* and *petitorium* remained strictly separated in Roman law, and so must the question of breach of the peace and that of the underlying international conflict under collective security. The latter, conceivably, might even be decided in the "aggressor's" favor, if the merits of the case are subsequently found to warrant it, but aggression has to be dealt with first, because nobody is entitled to use force to satisfy his rights.

These procedures, however, according to the author of this article, have proved unworkable in the relations of nations. Especially under the conditions of total war it is psychologically impracticable to mobilize for an abstract, "possessorial" war. Collective security action involves "discriminating against the aggressor." Thus he is condemned as to the "merits" right away, and it becomes practically impossible to protect him in *his* rights later on. No stable peace, only armistices, can issue from such procedures, and consequently the new territorial status will be a very precarious basis for any future edict *uti possidetis.* It is better therefore, so the

10 Walter Schätzel, "Der Friede mit dem Aggressor," in D. S. Constantinopoulos and H. Wehberg (eds.), *Gegenwartsprobleme des Internationalen Rechts und der Rechtsphilosophie* (Hamburg, 1953), pp. 327 ff.

author concludes, to retrace our steps and base international politics on the balancing of power and the give and take among political and moral equals.

In questions of "what might (or might not) be" or "what might (or might not) have been" there is always a danger of either sinning through overabstractness (distinguishing possibilities and impossibilities according to some abstract schemata) or falling into the trap of overconcreteness (believing that only what is, or has been, is or was possible). I believe that there is a middle approach, and that it is as necessary as it is important to distinguish obvious impossibilities from mere difficulties. For instance, if collective security by definition implies general commitments to counter aggression by force no matter who the aggressor is in any specific instance (that which we have referred to as the "anonymity of the aggressor"), its realization will be impracticable, that is, "impossible," if at a given moment there exists one overwhelmingly powerful (hegemonical) nation, because an "overwhelmingly powerful" antiaggression coalition obviously could not be formed against it by the remainder of the states. This would be a clear case of incongruity. It is different where existing conditions *per se* are not in conflict with the basic prerequisites of a system. Congruity prevailed, for instance, between general conditions in the classical era of international relations and the balance system. It might have been, and frequently *was* difficult to maintain or restore a reasonable degree of stability to that equilibrium, but it was not impossible, and there were periods in which a relatively stable balance did prevail.

Taking these distinctions as a yardstick, I believe that for collective security the answers to the problem must differ according to the characteristics of the period under discussion. The still classical state system up to and including the period of the League of Nations must be distinguished from that of the post-Second World War era. At the time of the League there was yet in existence a plurality of territorial, impermeable states. Collective security then was aimed at the rationalization and legalization of power relations because power politics of the classical type had run into the vicious circle of increased insecurity owing to the decreased self-sufficiency of countries and the ensuing power competition and expansion.[11] The question was whether the difficulties in the path of such rationalization, which are obvious, were insurmountable. While it is always precarious procedure to indulge in "what might have been," I believe that actual trends in the interwar period were not quite as adverse to the realization of genuine collective security as current discussion, impressed by actual failure, is inclined to assert.

At a time when power was still quite widely distributed, that is, dispersed among half a dozen or more "big powers," which, moreover, were not yet too far removed in strength from a number of middle powers, the formation of the "grand coalition" against an aggressor which collective security calls for was still in the realm of the possible. In the "test cases" of the thirties, Japanese aggression against China and Italian aggression against Ethiopia, it would have been relatively easy, we now know, for the remainder of the powers, even just those who then were members of the collective security organization, to cope with the aggression by joint force. One needs only to compare the isolated condition of the aggressor nations then with the power they jointly commanded when they were nevertheless defeated in the Second World War.

With this example we also meet, at least partially, the argument concerning the "extension of local conflicts into

11 See my article "Power Politics and World Organization," *American Political Science Review*, 36: 1039 ff. (1942). I refer to this article also for a more detailed discussion of the problems dealt with in the following pages.

general wars" with which collective security is frequently charged. That possibility of course exists. Under twentieth-century conditions local conflicts are likely to extend, and collective action then implies dealing with them at a point when they are still manageable. So far as the conditions of the thirties are concerned, there was also still present that "minimum of moral and political solidarity" among the powers to which one of the authors mentioned above refers as one of the prerequisites of collective security. To be sure, this requirement cannot mean identity of internal regimes and of political beliefs; rather, it refers to an identity of views on "international morality," which, in the interwar period, meant agreement on the necessity of "indivisibility of peace" and of the desirability of a system of "paix par le droit." Despite all their internal and ideological differences, the major nonaggressive powers, precisely in their opposition to the "aggressor nations," were inclined to agree on this required minimum of common attitude. It is immaterial in this connection that this happy congruence was in some cases (e.g., Russia's) motivated by pure self-interest, in others (e.g., the United States's) by a compelling wish to be "left alone," while in still others there existed a strong "internationalist" urge to establish once and for all a precedent for the impermissibility of any "breach of the peace."

Turning now to the problem of "status quo" and "peaceful change," it must be admitted that the difficulty is a very real one. No status quo can be perpetuated. It is hardly necessary to point out how damaging the connection between the League system and the status quo of Versailles and the related peace settlements turned out to be to the reputation of the collective security organization *qua* impartial organization for the maintenance of peace. But an even more fundamental question is: how can "just" settlements ever be attained when force is eliminated as a means of obtaining change? Indeed, if it be supposed that collective security should also provide for change through "fair" or "just" settlements of disputes, a solution may prove impossible, considering that views on what constitutes a "fair" solution ordinarily differ even among the parties not directly affected. But perhaps we are aiming too high if we expect change which is both "peaceful" and "just." All we can aim at is its "peacefulness," and it would not seem utopian to believe that such solutions could be had even where states no longer rely on the threat of individual force as *ultima ratio;* that is, to expect that even after a successful outlawry of force a status quo might be modified through the time-honored means of diplomacy which comprise pressures, compromise, accommodations, etc.[12] Thompson rightly points out how difficult it is to protect a status quo which itself remains ill-defined, but this argument highlights the opposite of the "peaceful change" argument, namely, the importance of first having a stable basis from which to proceed to solve outstanding issues. It is also true, as Schätzel states, that collective security means the separation of the procedural aspects of international conflicts (maintenance of the given status by prohibition of "breach of the peace") from the substantive issues (the underlying conflict which leads to the breach of the peace). But must one assume that the anti-aggression countries, as a result of their "possessory" action, will necessarily try to "get something" from the aggressor? Collective security means the restoration of the status quo

---

12 At a time when I still believed that postwar conditions might lend themselves to the establishment of a functioning collective security system (in 1942), I wrote: "The fundamental issue would be nothing less than finding rational solutions for what rarely, so far, has been regulated in other than irrational ways. It would be more than optimistic to hope that 'inherent justice' rather than compromise would be the main device in the adjustment of still clashing interests of still more and less influential, stronger and weaker, parties, at least for a long time to come. This will, then, still be an age of relative fallibility, not of accomplished rightfulness" (*ibid.*, p. 1052).

ante, independent of the question of the merits. All one has to "get" from the aggressor is what *he* has gotten through aggression.[13]

Whether such separation of issues is possible constitutes the core of the really vital problem: the relation between "national interests" and the "common interest" in preventing aggression. One argument described above, with all its seeming logic, is not convincing. That collective security is based on trust and distrust simultaneously is true, but this is only an apparent paradox. All law is based on the possibility (and actuality) of law violation. It expects the citizen to be law-minded, knowing that there will be instances where the expectation fails. Without that failure law would be superfluous; with too much failure, however, it would be ineffective, because unenforceable. Law, as a functioning institution, is suspended between a certain minimum and a certain maximum of "effectivity."[14] The really decisive question, internationally, has been whether a "minimum" of effectivity could have been obtained under collective security law; that is, whether at a time when the power system had become world-wide, powers, and particularly the big ones, might have been made to realize that their overriding "national" or "self-interest" existed in opposing the use of force as a means of individual national policy wherever and on the part of whomever it might occur. Most discussants now tend to be skeptical on this point. But it is at least imaginable that the degree

[13] Confusion about this was apparent in connection with the Korean case (whether or not one considers the Korean action as "genuine" collective security action). Those who wanted to see North Korea thrown back behind the 38th Parallel were motivated by the idea of the "possessorium," while those who wished to solve the problem by going up to the Yalu River and thus unifying Korea had the "merits" in mind. See in this respect Hula's more pessimistic conclusions for our age on "wars for righteousness" ("Fundamentals of Collective Security," *Social Research,* 24: 1 ff. [1957–58]).

[14] As Hans Kelsen has pointed out in many of his writings.

of "rationality" in foreign policy which such realization demands is attainable once more and more states and groups within states become aware to what extent the individual nations' own security has become intermingled with the general security (in the sense of peace) in a world where conflicts usually can no longer be "localized" and aggression eventually tends to affect the most remote. I believe it is incorrect to assume that what is "natural" in the behavior and attitudes of nations must perennially follow one and the same pattern, namely, the one set by "national interests" as conceived in the classical age of their individual and individualistic pursuance. Such an assumption is implied in terms like the one that refers to collective action as "war against nature." Why should not a more rational attitude, distinguishing between short-range and long-range interest, become "second nature" to nations? [15]

If one studies the Ethiopian case in detail, the alleged "inevitability" of failure becomes a bit doubtful. One gains the impression that it was not insurmountable resistance in countries like France or Britain which defeated the "sanctions' experiment"; rather, there was a precarious balance of forces which might as easily have turned in favor of adoption of the decisive "oil and steel sanctions" which were at issue as it actually tipped against them. There are situations in international affairs in which several "might-be's" are almost equally close to becoming "are's," and where a very slight difference in actual trends and events tips the scale. In the early thirties there did exist a growing awareness in various countries all over the world, and in a growing number of groups within countries, that peace was "indivisible" and that a precedent, once set, to make this clear to all, might become a firm basis for future collective security. If everything

[15] More on the relation between "security" and "national interest," in our day and in the classical era will be found in subsequent chapters.

hinged on so (relatively) small a detail as the implementation of certain embargoes against a country so relatively unimportant in international trade as Italy in 1935–36, it is at least imaginable that the outcome might have been different, that is, successful. And if actual success was that close in the case of the League, would it be entirely chimerical to assume that a really universal organization, with all of the then "big powers" represented on its council, might have succeeded where the predominantly European League of Nations failed?

It is one of the supreme paradoxes of the postwar period that when countries belatedly realized what they should have realized in the interwar period, namely, the identity of national and common interests in an indivisible peace, they did so (and even tried to act) when the preconditions for a genuine security system had vanished. At the time of the Korean war at least three essential prerequisites were no longer extant. First, the new bipolar concentration of power had rendered the idea of marshaling preponderant force on one side nugatory. In the split world of today East and West are so finely balanced that "overwhelming coalitions" against isolated aggressors, the basic requirement of collective security in action, can no longer be formed.[16] What appears in the guise of collective action then is either bloc action or majority action by the international organization; but majorities and minorities mean little where the chief antagonists have thermonuclear weapons. If collective security is predicated upon deterrence as one of its prime instrumentalities, that

[16] Such equally balanced blocs can of course occur in a system of plural powers as well; however, in it there is at least the possibility of preponderant coalition. On the other hand, bipolarity does not preclude collective action where the big powers agree. This means collective security in regard to smaller powers and their conflicts. However, the area in which the big powers do not clash is shrinking. That the United Nations itself was not based on the idea of collective security among the big powers is clear from its structure and charter, especially the veto principle. Korean action was possible only because of the historical joke of the Soviets' temporary absence from the Security Council.

security is of course unobtainable where preponderance of collective strength is no longer available as a deterrent.

In the second place, the ideological split in today's world would render the functioning of a collective security system impossible even if there still were a plural rather than a bipolar distribution of power. "Domestic" creeds and ideologies in disagreement with those in other countries would not concern a collective security organization so long as there was general agreement on the necessity to suppress aggression. As long as the Soviet Union agreed with the Western democracies on this, or at least subordinated its own views on world relations to the practical necessity of checking fascist-totalitarian expansion, a common basis for enforcement of the peace against the aggressor nations did exist. Today, Communist and non-Communist regimes clash over what is exactly one essential collective security definition, namely, what constitutes aggression.[17] Even such a disagreement would not matter so much if the "deviator" was an isolated minority of one (or a few) as against the "overwhelming" opinion of all or most of the others (as in, for instance, the case of Italy in 1935). It matters very much where what looks like "aggression" to one half of the world appears as "defense" to the other half. In that event voting majorities of 55:5 or similar ones merely indicate that one side has managed to rally a majority of organization members to its point of view, while the other side still asserts that a majority of the actual population of the world was on its side.[18] Ideological bipolarity is as much a block to collective security as is the bipolarity of power.

---

[17] On this problem more will be said below.

[18] Something which might easily happen in the East-West conflict if India and a few other Asian countries should side with Communist China and the Soviet Union. The Western powers, of course, might then in turn maintain that populations under totalitarian rule are not free to voice their opinions. And so forth, *ad infin.*

Third, the final and, perhaps, most serious obstacle to collective security today is in the new nature and destructiveness of war itself. How the atomic bomb and related developments affect power and power relations among states will be discussed in subsequent chapters. So far as collective security is concerned, it means that the power which possession of the new weapons conveys is such that the rallying of overwhelming power against it is impossible. Nuclear power *per se* is "overwhelming." At the same time the vulnerability of a country exposed to the new weapons is such that only split-second retaliation could counter them, with no time left for discussion, voting, and similar decision making in and by a security organization.[19] Whether, under these circumstances, such an organization could still have some other sort of useful purpose is, of course, quite another question.

The foregoing consideration of trends, possibilities, and impossibilities of collective security has already touched upon the fundamental change in the structure of international relations which occurred at what may be called the end of the classical era. We now have to study more systematically the factors which have caused this change.

[19] Mr. Eban, addressing the United Nations commemorative meeting at San Francisco, rightly stated: "The grotesque potency of military force is reducing the military argument to impotence, even in the domain of collective enforcement" (New York *Times*, June 22, 1955).

6

The Decline of the Territorial State

In view of the tremendous role nation-states—or at least several of them—play in the world today, talking about the "decline" of states manifestly would be absurd. What is referred to in the title of this chapter is the decline of that specific element of statehood which characterized the units composing the modern state system in its classical period, and which I called their "territoriality" or "impermeability." The "model-type" international system built upon units of this structure was that of a plurality of countries—at first all European—bound together by certain common standards, different but not too different in power, all enjoying a certain minimum of protection in and through that system. They would quarrel, try to diminish each other, but they would hardly ever suffer one of theirs to be extinguished. In their quarrels, which they called wars, they would attack each other, but their fortress-type shells of defense could be breached only by frontal assault and thus even the smaller powers had a goodly chance to resist and survive. Self-contained, centralized, internally pacified, they could rely on themselves for a high degree of external security.

Beginning with the nineteenth century, certain trends emerged which tended to endanger the functioning of the classical system. Directly or indirectly, all of them had a bearing upon that feature of the territorial state which was the strongest guarantee of its independent coexistence with other states of like nature: its hard shell, that is, its defensibility in case of war.

Naturally, many of these new trends concerned war itself and the way in which war was conducted. But it would be a mistake to identify them with what is often referred to as the shift from limited war, the war typical of the duel-type contests of the eighteenth century, to the more or less unlimited wars that developed with conscription, "nations in arms," and the increasing destructiveness of weapons in the nineteenth century. For by themselves these developments were not inconsistent with the "classical" aim of war in the era of territorial states: the attempt by one state to enforce its will on that of the opponent by defeating the latter's armed forces and overcoming its defense installations through frontal attack. Instituting universal military service, putting the state's economy on a war-footing, and similar measures served to enhance a country's capacity to defend itself in the traditional way. Rather than endangering the territorial state they served to bolster it. This kind of "unlimited war" must be regarded simply as a more developed form of traditional warfare.[1]

Total war, as distinguished from both kinds of traditional war, limited and unlimited, is involved with developments in warfare which enable belligerents to overleap or by-pass the traditional hard-shell defense of states. As soon as this happens, the traditional relationship between war, on the one hand, and territorial sovereignty and power, on the other, is altered decisively. Arranged in order of increasing effectiveness, these new factors may be listed under the following

[1] This conclusion can also be drawn from Clausewitz's theories of "absolute" war, which were the conceptual expression of the new type of warfare and politics that had come into existence with the French Revolution and the wars of the Napoleonic era. Even "wars of movement" with their "annihilating battles" aimed not at "annihilating" the enemy politically but merely at disarming him so as to compel him to submit to the victor's will; and the means of war remained consistent with a system of hard-shell units (see Edward M. Earle [ed.], *Makers of Modern Strategy* [Princeton, 1943], pp. 96 f., 102, and quotations there).

headings: (a) possibility of economic blockade; (b) ideological-political penetration; (c) air war; and (d) atomic war. It is true that even outside and in some cases prior to the emergence of these factors, growth in offensive power and increase in range and destructiveness of conventional weapons, such as was witnessed in the second half of the nineteenth century, tended by itself to render the smaller among the traditional units of territorial power obsolete because they became too easily "breachable." [2] Countries like Holland or Belgium, once defensible through fortresses and a corresponding military setup, became simply minor obstacles, unable to resist with their own defensive strength when attacked by the concentrated offensive power of a "big" one. Thus, for example, in significant contrast to the strategy of the Franco-Prussian War of 1870–71, the famous Schlieffen Plan, developed by the German General Staff in the last decades of the nineteenth century for a future war against France, as a matter of course encompassed Belgium as merely one flank in the sweeping move into France. But, as the First World War showed, such countries might still continue as elements in contests which aimed at breaking traditional "fronts" of armed forces, if only as links in, or continuations of, fronts formed chiefly by big powers. They ceased to be even that in an age of *Blitzkrieg*, or mechanized warfare, as illustrated by the Second World War. Overrun with no possibility of offering effective resistance, their only hope lay in eventual "liberation" by their more powerful allies. In their case,

[2] The relation between size of political unit and defensibility is emphasized, in possibly too generalized a fashion, by Georg Wolff ("Das Kalkül des atomaren Krieges und die deutsche Einheit," *Aussenpolitik*, 6: 95 [1955]): "The size of political units in world affairs is essentially determined by the range of weapons, means of transportation, and means of communications." In a similar vein, Adelbert Weinstein, military expert of the *Frankfurter Allgemeine Zeitung*, states: "If space loses its military significance it also assumes a different political importance" ("Der Atomkrieg zwischen Vision und Wirklichkeit," *ibid.*, January 7, 1956).

embattled resistance had become no more than a heroic gesture
. . . . All the sacrifice of time and money their people had made
for the maintenance of their armed forces and in conscript service
was sheer waste of effort, unless they could be effectively embraced
in the defensive scheme of a greater power. Their own effective
kind of resistance only began after their armies were overthrown.[3]

On the other hand, exceptional geographic location, combined with exceptionally favorable topography, might still
enable small countries such as Switzerland to survive, if only
because of the deterrent effect of their resistance-readiness.

Turning now to the factors which, more generally, have
tended to affect old-style territoriality, let us begin with
economic warfare. It should be said from the outset that
"economic blockade" so far has never enabled a belligerent to
force another into surrender through "starvation" alone.[4] In
the First World War, Germany and her allies were seriously
endangered when the Western Allies cut them off from overseas supplies, particularly foodstuffs. Countering with the
submarine, the Germans posed a similar threat to Britain for
a while. But German postwar propaganda efforts to blame
defeat solely on *Hungerblockade* (plus alleged enemy-in-
stigated subversion), with its companion slogan "im Felde
unbesiegt" (undefeated on the battlefield), ran contrary to the
fact that a very real effort had been required to defeat the
Central Powers on the military fronts. The same thing applies to the Second World War. But blockade was an important contributing factor in both instances. Its importance
for the present analysis lies in its unconventional nature,
which premits belligerents to by-pass the hard shell of the
enemy. Its use reflects an entirely untraditional approach to

[3] B. H. Liddell Hart, *The Revolution in Warfare* (New Haven, 1947),
pp. 98 f.

[4] When referring to "starvation blockade," a term coined in the First
World War, I mean to refer not only to the cutting off of food but to
that of any supplies necessary for the continuation of the war, such as
petroleum and similar raw materials.

warmaking; its effect is due to the changed economic status of industrialized nations.

Prior to the industrial age the territorial state was largely self-contained ("self-sufficient"), economically as otherwise. Although one of the customary means of conducting limited war was to try to starve fortresses into surrender, this applied only to the individual links in the shell, and not to entire nations in order to avoid breaching the shell. When some authors [5] refer to economic blockade of entire countries as the "traditional" means of English warfare, this is hardly correct, for, prior to the twentieth century, attempts undertaken in this direction proved rather ineffective, as witness the Continental Blockade and its counterpart during the Napoleonic era. The Industrial Revolution changed all this, for it made countries like Britain and Germany increasingly dependent on imports. This meant that in war they could survive only by controlling areas beyond their own territory, which would provide them with the food and raw materials they needed. The Germans managed by overrunning food-surplus and raw-material producing areas in the initial stages of both world wars, and the British, of course, by keeping the sea lanes open through superior naval power.

In peacetime, economic dependency became one of the causes of a phenomenon which itself contributed to the transformation of the old state system: imperialism. Anticipating war, with its new danger of blockade, countries strove to become more self-sufficient through enlargement of their areas of control. I do not mean to imply that the complex phenomenon of imperialism was exclusively or even chiefly caused by economic interdependence and its impact on war. Clearly, the earlier stage of capitalist industrialism as such had already supplied various motives for expansion, especially in the form of colonialism. But an economic determinism which

[5] For instance, Liddell Hart.

sees the cause of imperialist expansion only in the profit motive and the ensuing urge for markets or cheap labor overlooks the additional, and very compelling, motivation that lies in power competition and the urge for security in case of war. To the extent that the industrialized nations lost self-sufficiency, they were driven into expansion in a—futile—effort to regain it. Today, if at all, only the control of entire continents enables major nations to survive economically in major wars. This implies that hard-shell military defense, if it is to make any sense, must be a matter of defending more than one single nation; it must extend half way around the world. This, in turn, affects the status of smaller nations, whether they are included in the larger defense perimeter or not. If they are, they tend to become dependent on the chief power in the area; if they are not, they may become "permeable" precisely because of the possibility of economic blockade.

Psychological warfare. The attempt to undermine the morale of an enemy population, or to subvert its loyalty, shares with economic warfare the effect of by-passing old-style territorial defensibility. Like economic blockade, such "ideological-political" penetration is not entirely new, but it was formerly practiced, and practicable, only under quite exceptional circumstances. Short periods when genuine "world-revolutionary" propaganda was circulated, such as in the early stages of the French Revolution,[6] scarcely affected the general practice under which dynasties, and later governments, fought other dynasties or governments with little "ideological" involvement on the part of larger masses or classes. With conscription for military service, loyalty to the cause of one's country of course became more important, but since this new approach to mobilization for war coincided

[6] On this see my *Political Realism and Political Idealism* (Chicago, 1951), pp. 78 ff.; those pages also describe the rapid transformation of this propaganda into ordinary "power politics."

with nationalism (of which it was one expression), it served to increase, rather than to detract from, national coherence and solidarity. Only in rare cases—for instance, where national groups enclosed in and hostile to multinational empires could be appealed to—was there an opening wedge for what we to-day call "fifth-column" strategies. Even then, to take advantage of such opportunities was considered "ungentlemanlike" and "not to be done" (as, for instance, in the case of Bismarck's appeal to certain nationality groups in Austria-Hungary during his war of 1866).

With the emergence of political belief systems and ideological creeds in our century, however, nations have become susceptible to undermining from within. Although, as in the case of economic blockades, wars have not yet been won solely by subversion of loyalties, the threat has affected the coherence of the territorial state ever since the rise to power of a regime that claims and proclaims to represent not the cause of one particular nation, but that of all mankind, or at least its exploited or suppressed "masses." Bolshevism from 1917 on has provided the second instance in modern history of world-revolutionary propaganda. Communist penetration tactics were subsequently imitated by Nazi-Fascist regimes, and eventually even by the democracies. To be sure, neither Nazi-Fascist propaganda directed to the democracies nor democratic counterpropaganda directed to populations under totalitarian regimes were by themselves sufficient to defeat an enemy in the Second World War; but individual instances of "softening up" countries and then gaining control with the aid of a subversive group within occurred even then. Such tactics have, of course, become all too familiar during the cold war. It is hardly necessary to point out how a new technological development and a new technique of penetration—radio broadcasting—has added to the effectiveness of political penetration through psychological warfare. The radio has rendered units accessible to propaganda and under-mining from abroad, which formerly were impenetrable not only in a political but also in a technical sense. Examples abound, from what was probably one of its first effective uses— Nazi radio broadcasting to the Saar during the plebiscite campaign of 1934–35 and to Austria in the summer of 1934 [7]— down to the present Nasserite propaganda throughout the Near East.

Thus, new lines of division, cutting horizontally through state units instead of leaving them separated vertically from each other at their frontiers, have now become possible. Un-der such political-ideological alignments, "aliens" may turn out to be friends, citizens, more treacherous than "enemy aliens"; "friendly" prisoners of war may have to be distin-guished from hostile ones, as, in the Second World War in the case of German or Italian PW's, or, more recently, in Korean prison camps; "refugees" may be revealed as spies or "agents," while "agents" may deliver themselves up as refugees; the Iron Curtain is crossed westward by those who feel that this is the way to escape "slavery," while others cross it eastward to escape "oppression" or "discrimination." How even in peace-time such a new type of loyalties (or disloyalties) can be utilized to weaken the internal coherence and therewith the "impermeability" of nations is vividly portrayed by the state-ments of French and Italian Communist leaders calling upon their compatriots to consider the Soviet Union a brother in-stead of an enemy in case of war.[8] And during actual war,

[7] For more detailed evidence see John B. Whitton and John H. Herz, "Radio in International Politics," in Harwood L. Childs and John B. Whitton (eds.), *Propaganda by Short Wave* (Princeton, 1942), pp. 12–18.

[8] See, for instance, Thorez's statement of 1949: "If the common efforts of the freedom-loving French do not succeed in bringing our country back into the camp of democracy and peace, if later our country should be dragged against its will into a war against the Soviet Union and if the Soviet Army, defending the cause of freedom and socialism, should be brought to pursue the aggressors unto our soil, could the workers and

political-ideological fissures can be utilized to counter the effects of newly developed means of attack by rendering it more difficult to "pacify" territory "conquered" in the traditional manner of breaching the outer defense wall. Guerrilla warfare then becomes another means of rendering obsolete the classical way of defeating an enemy through defeating his traditional armed forces. Using planes to establish communication with guerrilla forces behind enemy lines, or to drop them supplies or advisers, illustrates the combined effect which political-ideological strategy and air war may have upon the customary type of classical warfare.

Air war, of all the new developments and techniques prior to the atomic age, is the one that has affected the territoriality of nations most radically. With it, so to say, the roof blew off the territorial state. It is true that even this new kind of warfare, up to and including the Second World War, did not by itself account for the defeat of a belligerent, as some of the more enthusiastic prophets of the air age had predicted it would. Undoubtedly, however, it had a massive contributory effect. And this effect was due to strategic action in the hinterland, rather than to tactical use at the front. It came at least close to defeating one side "vertically," by direct action against the "soft" interior of the country, by-passing the "fronts" and other outer defenses. By striking against cities, "morale," supplies, industries, etc., it foreshadowed the "end of the frontier," that is, the demise of the traditional impermeability of even the militarily most powerful states. It "tore away the veil of illusion that had so long obscured the reality of the change in warfare—*from a fight to a process of devasta-*

people of France have any other attitude toward the Soviet Army than has been that of the peoples of Poland, Rumania, and Yugoslavia?" (New York *Times*, February 23, 1949). Post-Stalinist changes in Communist Party tactics do not affect the value of statements like this as illustrative of what is possible.

tion." [9] For "air-power has a quality of penetrativeness never approached by any army of war;" it "laughs at battlements and those who man them. It has robbed the bastion and the parapet of their ancient glory." [10]

Suspicion of what was in the offing once man gained the capacity to fly was abroad as early as the eighteenth century. Samuel Johnson remarked:

If men were all virtuous, I should with great alacrity teach them all to fly. But what would be the security of the good, if the bad could at pleasure invade them from the sky? Against an army sailing through the clouds, neither walls, nor mountains, nor seas, could afford security.[11]

And Benjamin Franklin, witnessing the first balloon ascension at Paris in 1783, foresaw invasion from the air and wrote:

Convincing Sovereigns of folly of wars may perhaps be one effect of it, since it will be impracticable for the most potent of them to guard his dominions . . . . Where is the Prince who can afford so to cover his country with troops for its defense, as that ten thousand men descending from the clouds, might not in many places do an infinite deal of mischief before a force could be brought together to repel them? [12]

That air warfare was considered something entirely unconventional is seen from the initial reaction to it in the First

[9] Liddell Hart, *The Revolution in Warfare,* p. 36 (italics added).

[10] J. M. Spaight, *Air Power and the Cities* (London, 1930), p. 120. See also the same author's *Air Power and War Rights* (2d ed.; London, 1933), where he refers to air power's "power to overleap the enemy's defenses" (p. 4); "air power can strike straight at the heart of the enemy state. It can ignore armies and fleets. Like the plot of an Ibsen drama it can plunge *in medias res*" (p. 3). After the war, admitting that he had overestimated air power's effect on morale, the author, on the evidence of the United States' Strategic Bombing Survey, emphasized the effect of bombing on oil supplies and transportation systems and thus, indirectly, on the capitulation of Germany and Japan (see his *Air Power Can Disarm* [London, 1948]).

[11] Quotation in J. U. Nef, *War and Human Progress* (Cambridge, Mass., 1952), pp. 198.

[12] From a letter to Jan Ingelhouss, reproduced in *Life* Magazine, January 9, 1956.

World War. As in the case of economic warfare, nations steeped in the tradition of classical war were at a loss to understand and appraise the new factors and what had caused them. "Revolutionary" transition from an old to a new system has usually affected moral standards. Each big change tends at first to outrage traditional standards of "fairness", etc. We have referred before to the case of the "gunpowder revolution" at the end of the Middle Ages; the same effect had been engendered when somewhat earlier the bow and arrow defeated armies of clumsy armored knights on horseback, and with them their knightly standards and rituals, or when, in mythological times of antiquity, the horse-drawn battle wagon prevailed over foot soldiers.[13] In the classical age of the modern state system the "new morality" of shooting at human beings from a distance had finally come to be accepted, but the standards of the age clearly distinguished "lawful combatants," i.e., members of the armed forces at the front or in the fortifications, from the "civilian" remainder of the population. Despite the latter's occasional involvement in direct military action or, more frequently, in such indirect effects of the fighting as requisitions or marauding by armed forces, the king of Prussia could still proclaim in 1870 that he was waging war against the emperor of France, and not against women and children. The distinction became obsolete when long-range artillery in the First World War sent shells into Paris, and bombs started dropping on cities far behind the front (on a small scale, it is true, but still "killing women and children"). At the same time "starvation blockades" had started to take their toll from civilians behind the battle lines.

All this at first shocked feelings. Germans felt that the attempt to starve them into surrender was an "unfair" way to wage war, typical of British "hucksters" (as distinguished from

[13] See the vivid account of this earliest revolution in methods of war in Alexander Rüstow's *Ortsbestimmung der Gegenwart*, Vol. 1: *Ursprung der Herrschaft* (Zurich, 1950).

German "heroes"); the heroes overlooked that they, too, had tried—unsuccessfully, it is true—to inflict the same suffering on the hucksters. In so far as war from the air was concerned, reactions differed significantly toward air fighting at the front and air war carried behind the front. In air fighting at the front a kind of "new chivalry" developed, with its peculiar "honor code" among the flyers on both sides.[14] But city bombing was felt to constitute "illegitimate" warfare, and populations were inclined to treat airmen engaging in it as "war criminals."[15] It is well known that this feeling continued into the Second World War with its large-scale "area bombing." Such sentiments of moral outrage reflected the general feeling of helplessness in the face of a war which threatened to destroy the ancient implication of protection inherent in the concept of territorial power. In fact, in the Second World War certain big powers, *qua* territorial states, were on the way to becoming obsolete.

The process has now been completed with the advent of the atomic weapon. With it, whatever remained of the impermeability of states seems to have gone for good. What has been lost thus can be deduced from statements by two thinkers separated by thousands of years and half the world. Both reflect the condition of territorial security. Mencius, in ancient China, when asked for guidance in matters of defense and foreign policy by the ruler of a small state, is said to have counseled: "Dig deeper your moats; build higher your walls; guard them along with your people."[16] This remained the

14 See Spaight, *Air Power and War Rights*, pp. 102 ff. The same phenomenon was observed in the Second World War in the case of the desert war between Rommel's Afrika corps and its British opponents, where, similar to the air war in the First World War, conditions resembling a "duel-type" war prevailed.

15 See Julius Stone, *Legal Controls of International Conflicts* (New York, 1954), pp. 611 ff.

16 See Frank M. Russell, *Theories of International Relations* (New York, 1936), p. 22.

classical posture up to our age, when a Western sage, Bertrand Russell, could still, even in the interwar period, define power as a force radiating from one center and diminishing with the distance from that center until it finds an equilibrium with that of similar geographically anchored units.[17]   Now that power can destroy power from center to center everything is different.

[17] *Power* (New York, 1938), p. 162.

II

INTERNATIONAL POLITICS

IN THE ATOMIC AGE

7

The Impact of Bipolarity

Among the revolutionary new factors which confronted the world when the Second World War ended there were, as we have seen, two above all that affected the structure and system of international relations: the bipolar concentration of power, which replaced the traditional multipower system, and the new military technology, which is summarized in the term "nuclear developments." Since both of them developed at about the same time it was easy for statesmen and students to confuse them in their effects on international politics. But a largely fortuitous simultaneity does not necessarily mean identity or even similarity of effects. On the contrary, effects may be contradictory and thus opposite in their ultimate results, which accounts for indeterminateness and even paradox in the over-all conditions thus created. What bipolarity entails—for instance, a tremendous increase in power, as measured by traditional power standards, for two powers to the detriment of all others—may be negated by what is inherent in the effects of nuclear developments upon the power position of *all* powers. This confluence of different and oftentimes differing factors renders difficult an analysis of international politics in the atomic age which would take into consideration all the new factors at once. In order to arrive at clearer distinctions, I therefore propose to study the impact of the two chief new factors separately: first that of bipolarity, then that of nuclear weapons. This, of course, involves ignoring one of these factors in each case. Only at the end, then, can an attempt be undertaken to view and assess the situation as a whole.

THE STRUCTURE OF BIPOLARITY

In the nineteenth century, we have observed,[1] a variety of factors contributed to the trends which drove the territorial states of the old state system toward expansion. There was the economic-strategic factor: while "logically," under pure economic "laws," growing economic interdependence of nations would have led to international division of labor and free trade, in a world of power politics such interdependence, which meant increasing dependence of each nation on others and decreasing self-sufficiency, enhanced the nations' apprehension about what might happen to them in case of war. It thus caused them to try to control ever larger areas beyond their own territory in an effort to diminish their dependence. At the same time the growing destructiveness of the weapons of war, which presented the possibility that large spaces could be overrun within a brief period of time, gave the big powers additional reasons for expansion and, by making the existence of the smaller powers more and more precarious, compelled them to line up with the big ones in "spheres of influence" of the latter. The result was that, on the one hand, under the impact of nationalism and its principle of national self-determination, ever more "sovereign, independent" nation-states came into existence—a process which continued into the post-Second World War world—while, in strange contrast with this process, there has been a trend toward ever more concentration of power in fewer and fewer "world powers."

The debut of terms like "world powers" itself reflected the necessity felt for expressing a new reality. Until the end of the nineteenth century the term "big powers" had been adequate to describe the actuality of a "concert" of the more

---

[1] See above, ch. 6.

powerful territorial powers. The term "world powers" came into use at the beginning of the twentieth century, and now, of course, it has evolved into "superpowers." [2] *Weltmacht*-politics became particularly fashionable in Germany just prior to the First World War; after that war it became the basic concept of the so-called "science" of geopolitics, with its emphasis on "large spaces" (*Grossräume*) and "large-space order" (*Grossraumordnung*), that is, on entire world realms organized under the leadership or control of "world powers." It is perhaps no coincidence that the initial attempts, in the conceptual as well as the practical-political sphere, to divide up the entire globe into realms controlled by only a few great powers were made by Germany and Japan, two late-comers among the big powers. They, more than the older colonial powers that had already acquired their larger "spaces" abroad, experienced the need to control large contiguous chunks of the world.[3] A perceptive German power theoretician with a particular flair for "what is in the offing"—Carl Schmitt—subsequently undertook to fashion a new theory of international law and international relations. According to him the reality underlying international law and relations in the twentieth century was leading powers or *Reiche* (realms, empires). Each should control one *Grossraum* and prohibit intervention in it by powers outside the space ("space-alien" powers).[4] State frontiers would be largely replaced by lines of demarcation separating

[2] For different attempts to define and distinguish terms in this connection see Martin Wight, *Power Politics* (London, 1946), who distinguishes "great powers," "world powers," and "dominant powers," and William T. R. Fox, *The Super-Powers* (New York, 1944).

[3] They had a kind of forerunner and model for such an attitude, however, in United States Western Hemisphere policies, especially at the heyday of American imperialism just before the First World War. There is no doubt that the Monroe Doctrine, especially with its imperialistic "corollaries," had a strong impact on the development of geopolitics and related thought in Germany, where it was much admired for its allegedly realistic and up-to-date expression of world politics in one part of the world.

[4] See his *Völkerrechtliche Grossraumordnung* (Berlin, 1939).

Grossräume. Much discussion was thereupon devoted in Nazi Germany to problems such as what would or should be the status within such *Grossraumordnung* of countries included, with respect to the "leading" power as well as in relation to countries in other spaces, and whether the control exercised by the leading power should or would be "leadership" or "domination." [5]

More important, historically, was the question as to the locus of such world power or large-space power, that is, which would be the leading powers, a problem which was, however, solved by history, and not by Carl Schmitt. The localization of superpower which would have obtained in case of a Nazi-Japanese victory is quite clear from the "greater spaces" envisaged by Germany and Japan and translated into incipient reality during the first stages of the Second World War in the form of Hitler's New Order in Europe and Japan's Asian Co-Prosperity Sphere. After the defeat of Britain and the Soviet Union the old world would have been divided up, and the only remaining question of consequence might have been the future status of the United States. There cannot be much doubt that it would have been a diminished one. As it was, the United States and the Soviet Union emerged instead, and one cannot help feeling that, if an inexorable trend tended toward the emergence of two poles of power in the world, the actual localization of superpower that prevails, apart from preferences and having regard merely for the respective geo-

[5] See, for example, G. Küchenhoff, "Grossraumgedanke und völkische Idee im Recht," *Zeitschrift für ausländisches öffentliches Recht und Völkerrecht*, 12: 34 ff. (September, 1944); Werner Best, "Grundfragen einer deutschen Grossraumverwaltung," in *Festgabe für Heinrich Himmler* (Darmstadt, 1941), pp. 33 ff. Best was a leading Nazi administrator, and there is not much doubt where he, and with him Nazi and Japanese leadership, stood on the question of "leadership" versus "domination": "In ordering international relations stronger nations enforce their will over weaker ones." The general problem of international "leadership" had been brilliantly treated previously by a non-Nazi author, Heinrich Triepel (see his *Die Hegemonie* [Stuttgart, 1938]).

graphical constellations, is somehow more "natural." For if a relatively stable division of the globe into two major spheres can be envisaged at all, widest possible separation of the two loci of power would seem best, with one in the Old World, and one in the New, one in the center of a great land mass, the other controlling the seas and thus in a position to give some protection even to remoter areas outside its own hemisphere. Compared with this, control of one half of the world by Germany and the other by Japan might "technically" even have been more complicated.[6] How would they have controlled America? By dividing the chore at a line along the Mississippi River? But one must beware of claiming too much "logic" for the present situation; after all, Europe is now divided along the Elbe.

What has been said is not to imply that geopolitical factors like location of superpowers and lines separating their realms are all that count in studying present international politics and its future possibilities. Any such analysis, of course, must in addition take up questions as to what kind of power controls what, which regimes and ideologies prevail, and, above all, what kind of policy can be attempted by the superpowers. The point which had to be made, however, is that all present actualities and all future potentialities of policy are set in a specific power system, namely, the constellation of power which emerged from the Second World War. To some extent they are determined and circumscribed by this system.

The chief characteristics of the bipolar system lie in its trend toward an extension of the hard shell, the protective wall which used to surround single territorial units, so as to include (in tendency, if not in actuality) approximately one half of

---

[6] No "preestablished harmony," of course, is claimed for the present division. The atomic factor alone renders even the relative advantages of this sort dubious. It may be, too, that the "naturalness" of the present bipolarism is a subjective impression, like that in the story of the man who observed the deadly struggle between a lion and a snake and decided to help the lion, because he seemed "the more natural beast."

the world in the case of each of the two blocs. In this way the
unit of defense and protection is being shifted from the nation to the bloc. As in Leibniz's time the consolidation of
territorial units, the states, played havoc with traditional concepts of feudal jurisdictions and led to the emergence, *contra
legem* as it were, of the new concept of "sovereignty," so today
the traditions of national sovereignties clash with the actualities of a more widely extended realm of "territoriality," and,
again, legal concepts no longer fit the facts. In the historical
case the outdated earlier concept tended to become fictitious,
while actual authority stretched as far as did the means of
effective protection and constraint afforded by military power.
The same thing is happening in today's case. Since militarily
integrated defense setups, with "bases" or friendly (that is, controlled) "people's republics" at their fringes, have assumed the
place of the "forts" and similar defenses lining the frontiers of
individual nation-states, the unit of "sovereign independence,"
legally still the nation, is now tending to shift to the bloc or
to the bloc-controlling superpower. Whether some new
Leibniz will arise to develop a corresponding conceptual
framework for the new relationships [7] matters less than having
a clear understanding of the actual trends and changes. These,
so far as bipolarity is concerned, are contained in the new system of military and political arrangements of the two opposing blocs. They constitute what, borrowing from the
new defense systems, may be called the "infrastructure" of international politics in the age of bipolarity.

In order better to understand the change, let us compare
the structure of alliances and similar arrangements in the era
of old-style territoriality with the pact system that has sup-

---

[7] The term "paramountcy," once invented by the British to fit their
own overarching authority where traditional "sovereignty" concepts had
similarly ceased to apply (namely, in their relations with Indian rulers),
comes to mind. In the following, however, we shall endeavor to make do
with the habitual terms of "sovereignty," and so forth.

planted it. In this connection, "old system" encompasses both the pre-First World War period, with its "secret treaties of alliance," and the interwar period with its "mutual assistance pacts" ostensibly concluded as integral parts of the League of Nations system. For one thing was common to both periods: all that these arrangements provided for was a mutual commitment by the parties to assist each other in case one was involved in war. But each individual nation-state remained a separate unit of power and military defense (or offense). Although occasionally such agreements were implemented through some common military planning, no further integration of the political or military setup was ever provided for. And despite the legally binding nature of the treaty commitment, it was well understood that fulfillment of an alliance obligation depended on continued recognition on the part of each treaty partner that national interest still required it. Whether or not the alliance would work only the actual outbreak of war would show.

The German-Austrian (Dual Alliance) Treaty of 1879 for instance, had as its core provision the following:

If, contrary to expectation and against the sincere desire of both the High Contracting Parties, one of the two Empires shall be attacked on the part of Russia, the High Contracting Parties are bound to assist each other with the whole of the military power of the Empire, and, consequently, only to conclude peace conjointly and by agreement.

And shortly before the emergence of the bipolar system treaties like the Franco-Soviet alliance of 1944 still repeated the old formulas. Article 4 of that treaty provided:

If one of the High Contracting Parties should find itself involved in hostilities with Germany as a result of an aggression committed by Germany, . . . the other High Contracting Party will immediately give the Contracting Party so involved all the help and assistance in its power.

This repeats almost literally the respective provision of an interwar pact, the mutual assistance pact of 1935, concluded by the same two countries. Since then, however, the "Germany" referred to in both treaties has been split by a bloc line which renders the two would-be allies, France and the Soviet Union, parts of opposing blocs. In defense of those blocs they now are lined up on opposite sides of the line. The drawing of this line all the way round the globe, making it a wall surrounding a coherent area of defense and "territoriality," has been the chief task of postwar bipolar diplomacy.

This means that, contrary to what is usually asserted, the heart of, for instance, the North Atlantic Treaty is not its Article 5. This article, with its mutual assistance commitments and related stipulations, is merely a repetition of corresponding pre-Second World War arrangements.[8] So are the corresponding provisions in other Western defense pacts. The heart of the matter, rather, is Article 3 and its implementation. This article reads:

In order more effectively to achieve the objectives of this treaty, the parties, separately and jointly, by means of continuous and effective self-help and actual aid, will maintain and develop their individual and collective capacity to resist armed attack.

This is the treaty basis on which NATO as a military organization has been integrated, with a Supreme Headquarters of Forces in Europe (SHAPE), with military areas and subareas, unified commands, combined exercises, coordinated equipment, networks of allied air bases, communications lines, supply depots, etc. In this sense NATO, as something different from an ordinary alliance of the traditional type, can be said to date from about 1952, the year when it turned from what until then had been more or less a paper pact into an integrated military establishment.

[8] With due obeisance to Article 51 of the United Nations Charter, in the case of all Western alliances, taking the place of the usual references to Articles 15 and 16 of the League Covenant in the interwar pacts.

NATO, however, is not simply what it appears to be: a defense unit consisting of fifteen countries which militarily have merged into one whole. It is both more and less than that, and this is the point at which the impact of the present bipolar structure of the world is felt. The chief purpose of the integration has been to establish a defense wall, a hard-shell outer rim of the Western world where this world touches the East in Europe, and this has been done under the leadership of the politically, militarily, and economically strongest member. That member happens to be not inside but outside of Europe. Integration thus has meant also, and most important, American troops and American bases and other installations in the border area of the bloc, that is, on the territory of the European—in particular, the Continental European—member countries. The significant feature of bipolar territoriality, therefore, is not alliances as such, and not only or even primarily the arrangements for integrated defense, but the agreements on bases, stationing of troops, and similar matters which have been concluded between the particular superpower and the individual "rim" countries.[9] Similar agreements constitute the military and political core of the security systems built by the United States to surround the Western world with hard walls at other places. The NATO system is supplemented in the general area of Europe and the Mediterranean by bases and similar strongholds not in NATO proper, such as United States bases in Spain, Morocco, and Libya, or the British on Cyprus. But the chief agreements outside of NATO are in the Pacific area and the Far East. The Japanese-American Security Treaty of

[9] For instance, the Franco-American and other intra-NATO military assistance agreements of 1950 (Department of State, *Bulletin*, 22: 205 ff. [1950]), which in their wording still cling to mutuality of making facilities, etc., available; Greek-American agreement of 1953 (Department of State, *Bulletin*, 29: 863 ff. [1953]), providing for American use of naval and air bases in Greece; and similar agreements with Denmark (concerning bases in Greenland), Iceland, Portugal (the Azores), etc.

1951 not only provides for the right to dispose American forces in and about Japan but imposes on Japan an obligation not to grant such right to anybody else.[10] Similar rights have been granted to the United States by its treaty of 1954 with the Republic of China on Formosa [11] and by many others. In Germany, American and other Western powers' rights to station troops, which until a few years ago were based on "conquest" (military occupation), now also issue from treaty arrangements.[12]

The right to maintain bases and station troops on foreign soil today has a function quite different from that of similar rights in former times. Armed forces on foreign territory in peacetime used to be a rare exception in international relations; this was in accordance with the principle of impermeability. Traditionally the right to occupy foreign territory was restricted to times of war (*occupatio bellica*) or to a temporally limited postwar occupation of enemy territory, the latter usually to guarantee the defeated enemy's observation of peace terms (thus, after the First World War, the Allied Rhineland occupation).[13] This was therefore a means of policy suited to relations among sovereign territorial units and their chief means of power politics, war. Even where powers maintained or otherwise controlled bases, strong points, or similar spots in peacetime, the function usually was "territorial" in the old sense, that is, in the sense of serving to safeguard the security and power of an individual country as a separate unit. Such strongholds might, for instance, provide

[10] Department of State, *Bulletin*, 25: 463 ff. (1951).

[11] *Ibid.*, 31: 895 ff. (1954); Article 2 of this treaty repeats Article 3 of the North Atlantic Treaty verbatim.

[12] In February, 1955, according to the United States Defense Department, almost half the American combat forces were stationed "overseas," the majority presumably not on United States overseas territory (New York *Times*, February 16, 1955).

[13] See discussion and examples in Oppenheim-Lauterpacht, *International Law*, 1 (7th ed.; New York, 1948), 758 ff.

links in the defense chain surrounding a country or an empire or, as in the case of Britain, keep open sea lanes which were necessary for the defense of the unit in case of war. And when such strategic points or areas were not incorporated into the territorial domain of the country (as were Gibraltar, Malta, and Singapore by Britain), obtaining rights to control them through garrisons, etc., fulfilled the same territorial purpose (as, for example, in the case of the Suez Canal). Thus bases and garrisons were flung here and there over the globe as parts of the several and separate hard-shell systems of individual powers. Now we find these establishments, comparable to the fortresses and garrisons formerly lining the frontiers of one territorial state in a single line or circle, arranged in what ideally (although not yet actually) constitutes one contiguous hard-shell line around each half of the world. This change of function is most clearly reflected in the continuing occupation of (or stationing of troops in) Germany and the corresponding maintenance of bases and forces in Japan, which, in contrast to the Rhineland occupation after the First World War, no longer serves to enforce the rights or interests of victor countries against the defeated enemies. On the contrary, it has rendered the latter (or in the case of Germany, its halves), because of their geographic "rim" position, outposts in and members of one of the defense blocs, and therewith allies of one or the other superpower. A different geographical location vis-à-vis the "two worlds" and the line separating them might have rendered the vanquished "uninteresting" to the superpowers long ago.

Thus, in place of some scattered outposts, bases, and other garrisoned places, all of which were parts of individual defense systems of various powers and which had their guns turned against each other, under bipolarity they are rearranged into one comprehensive hard-shell system opposing the only other one extant. The guns within each system are now lined up parallel to each other. This has meant relinquishing some of them, especially those which now have lost their *raison d'être,* while new ones have had to be established at other points. And—most significant of all changes—the United States, as leading power in the Western setup, has in many instances had to assume defense responsibilities by taking over bases, etc., from such countries as Britain or France which held them formerly.

Yet we should not forget that we are still in an age of transition. Exactly as "power" is something relative, meaningful, and measurable only in relation to other power, so hard-shell defensibility is relative too, and the new bipolar arrangements have not obliterated old-style defense units and their systems entirely.[14] What would be a "soft shell" against a polar bloc may still be a hard one regionally. To some extent (which, to be sure, it is difficult to specify more concretely), Britain, or even France, despite common NATO arrangements and United States bases, still constitute hard-shell units separate from others.[15] And in regions more distant from where the two worlds converge upon each other, hard and soft shells often still indicate old-style individual territoriality, as they did in the Central American region when the acquisition by one unit of twenty-five fighter planes threatened to make it a kind of regional superpower vis-à-vis neighboring countries possessing no air force at all;[16] or as

[14] One is reminded of the existence, at the time of the European balance of power, of regional balance systems within the over-all system, e.g., in the eighteenth century, of a "Northern balance."

[15] What this implies for relations between such countries and "their" superpower will be discussed below. Such units' sometimes desperate determination to retain a remnant of military "self-determination" is evidenced for instance in France's reluctance to have *all* of her military forces merged in the common defense system, let alone in one integrated "European army"; or in the United Kingdom's refusal to become part of such a Continental system; or, more recently, in their insistence on acquiring nuclear power of their own.

[16] The mere appearance on the scene of a few United States planes was enough to quickly restore the old balance.

they do in the Palestine region as between Israel and neighboring Arab states. In addition, of course, there still are regions in the world which have managed to remain aloof from any bloc defense system. They not only comprise large areas, such as most of South Asia and the Near East, but occasionally even small "exclaves" geographically located within or close to major defense systems, such as Switzerland or Sweden. These are leftovers from the former age, still relying on their own hard-shell territoriality.[17]

For the blocs as such, however, the shift of the hard shell from the individual member to the entire rim of the alliance region is the characteristic thing. It affects even legal relationships between the member states, with new arrangements often containing far-reaching restrictions on what traditionally has been within the most sacrosanct sphere of domestic jurisdiction, for example, criminal jurisdiction over persons within a nation's territory. Consider what is implied in "stationing-of-forces" agreements of the kind the United States has concluded with most of its allies on whose soil American troops are stationed. With ever more frequent instances of this nature, where one power "penetrates" another by having troops and military installations within the latter's boundaries, it has been found necessary to provide for complementary legal limitations of "sovereignty" by carving out, as it were, entire chunks of territorial jurisdiction in favor of the "occupying" state.

What does the new defense structure of nations, and the new legal relationship it involves, portend for the status of "sovereign independence" that these units formerly enjoyed? How has it affected the relations between superpowers and their "allies"? In order to discuss these and related problems, a few words must first be said specifically about the Eastern bloc in the bipolar system and its "infrastructure."

[17] Which they now think of bolstering up with nuclear weapons; on the problems this involves see below.

Looking at any map of American and allied bases around the world [18] one easily receives the impression that the entire business of building up a huge, world-wide hard-shell system has been a one-sided, Western, affair to which nothing corresponds on the other, Eastern, side (particularly since the Soviet withdrawal from bases in China and Finland). Are then the Communists justified in accusing the West of a vast plot to "encircle" the Soviet group of nations? At first blush, it looks like encirclement indeed.[19] In fact, there are compensations on the Soviet side. The Eastern bloc is not just "a group of nations," not even merely a group of allied countries in the traditional sense of the word. True, like the Western nations, they are bound together by what appear to be old-fashioned alliance or mutual assistance treaties—bilateral in relation to China, of the NATO type in Eastern Europe where the Warsaw Pact has replaced the previous network of bilaterial agreements. But, as in the Western case, it is not the text of agreements which counts but the implementation of the system they structure. The chief difference from this viewpoint between the East and the West lies in the fact that while the West has relied primarily on military integration, and while whatever controls the United States has gained are similarly chiefly military (bases, etc.), Eastern integration has been partly political, and some of the main Soviet controls are of a political sort too, rendering stationing of forces or establishing of bases ultimate rather than primary means. There are, of course, military controls, particularly in areas like East Germany, which themselves possess only weak or unreliable military forces, and these can be utilized whenever there is a danger that political controls will not work. Such open reliance on military means for maintain-

---

[18] See, for instance, the one in the New York *Times*, December 5, 1954.

[19] Remember, for instance, the seemingly so well justified question: "What would you say if the Russians were to establish bases in Mexico or the Caribbean?"

ing the integration of the bloc has been as much out of the question in the West as has been political control of the Eastern variety. That control in the East, of course, is exercized through satellite governments. Relations of a more Western nature seem to prevail in the Soviet bloc's arrangements with Asia, in particular in Sino-Soviet relationships. Unity there seems to be based on bilateral agreements whose conclusion and observance are facilitated by common ideology and common interests. Sino-Soviet relations, therefore, resemble that kind of relationship between Western powers that prevails, for instance, between the United States and the United Kingdom.

Despite all this fairly tight control, it might still appear to some that the Soviet bloc is at a disadvantage: while the West has managed to extend its defense system (which to the East may seem an offensive one) to widespread and remote parts of the world, the countries of the Eastern bloc have been satisfied with building up the defense of their own contiguous group. Wide geographical dispersal is characteristic of the Western build-up, compactness of the Eastern system. Such a contrast easily creates an impression that the group with far-flung possessions and bases is out to encircle the geographically contiguous opponent. Already in the age of multiple powers there was a similar contrast between the British system and that of some big land power, such as Russia or Germany. But the advantages to a power or group of powers of relying chiefly on sea power (not to mention today's air atomic power) are not even strategically unequivocal. They are in part canceled out by the advantages with which interior lines of communications provide a land power. Added to this are the advantages of manpower which the Eastern bloc enjoys. And apart from strategic considerations the East possesses one asset which, if skillfully manipulated, can easily offset any advantages which accrue to the West through ever so widely dispersed bases: they have the opportunity not only to propagate their creed or similarly to subvert the uncommitted nations and regions of the world, but even to penetrate the military barriers of the West by means of "conquest from within," particularly where, as in the case of certain outlying base-areas, there is a native population until recently or still under colonial rule for them to work on. It is true that the game of political-ideological warfare can be played by both sides, but it is easy to see that, and why, the East holds the better hand. Its own areas, which are under totalitarian opinion-management, with the means to exclude communication from without, are not readily penetrated in this way, least of all by countries which, by the very nature of their ways of life, beliefs, and value standards, are uncoordinated, often disunited, and thus ideologically usually defensive.

Whatever the differences of detail, however, both blocs have in common the essential tendency to form one vast impermeable unit of territoriality under the leadership (or control) of one predominant state within the bloc. It is the concentration of world power in these two superpowers that justifies the characterization of the system as "bipolar." What emerges as the underlying structure of the present bipolar international system is then two major power blocs, each organized so as to constitute one integrated unit of territoriality, plus some scattered old-style territorial units outside the spheres of the blocs. We shall now analyze somewhat more closely the relations and policies which are peculiar to this system. In this connection, relationships and problems which arise within the blocs, in particular those between superpower and "allies," will be studied first; subsequently, interbloc and inter-superpower relations will be investigated.

INTRABLOC RELATIONSHIPS

The sudden emergence of bipolarity, with the two superpowers preponderant over all others in today's world, has led some students of recent international politics to conclude that, in view of this concentration of power and the bloc formations resulting therefrom, all powers but these two have lost their sovereign independence, since all but the two have lost their freedom of action in the field of foreign affairs. One author writes: "Both empires have this in common, that they alone still have complete freedom of action regarding peace and war. They are still sovereign in the political sense," while "from the point of view of the world powers the other sovereign states have become security zones, atom absorbers, stationary aircraft carriers and jumping-off grounds for the reconquest of continents." [20] And another author has asserted that

henceforth the independence of small powers can not include the chief attribute of full independence, the right to an independent foreign policy . . . . A new class of powers is coming into existence, semi-powers or in the Soviet phrase 'client powers,' whose inhabitants combine patriotic loyalty to the semi-power itself with an equal loyalty to and pride in the wider world-power-system of which it forms a part.[21]

What I have said before about the "infrastructures" of both bipolar blocs would appear to justify a preliminary conclusion of this kind, at least in regard to countries included in one or the other bloc. But it is advisable to look into what actually has happened in this connection before jumping to far-reaching conclusions. In doing so, let us remember that it is necessary to distinguish between the impact of bipolarity proper, that is, the structure and trends deriving from power concentration in the superpowers, and the impact of the new developments in the technology of war. The latter will be

[20] G. Schwarzenberger, *Power Politics* (2d ed.; New York, 1951), pp. 98 f., 125; similarly, Carl Schmitt, *Der Nomos der Erde* (Cologne, 1950), p. 20: People "will transform their planet into a combination of raw materials, supply depot, and aircraft carrier."

[21] Wight, *Power Politics*, pp. 30, 32. Expectance of such harmony in "prides" and "loyalties" seems overoptimistic in view of the strains that result from the new relationships on both sides.

dealt with later. What I purport to investigate here is the impact of power concentration and bipolar bloc formation first upon relationships of superpowers to other powers within their own bloc, and subsequently upon interbloc relations. Thus I shall begin with intrabloc relations.

There is nothing radically new in the phenomenon of "in equality" and limitation, if not loss, of "independence" re sulting from an unequal relationship between stronger and weaker powers. Even under the classical system there were instances where such a relationship came close to being actual control of a client power. Occasionally—in particular in areas of imperialist expansion—the restraint was accom- panied by open assumption of control by the stronger power over the weaker one's foreign relations,[22] or by the stationing of troops on its soil ("landing the Marines," etc.). But these instances were marginal; they usually occurred at the outward rim, as it were, of the then existing state system, and not in its main area. Today, however, as we have seen, such military or political penetration is the essence of the power structure in each of the realms of superpower influence. Taking Leibniz's criterion of territorial independence as a yardstick, one might therefore conclude in a general way that "sovereignty" in the classical sense has been lost by all nonsuperpowers included in a bloc, giving rise to a kind of quasi-protectorate relationship between them and the respective superpowers. Only between the superpowers themselves, then, and possibly between them and countries outside the blocs, would traditional relations based on "sovereign equality" still obtain.

If we look into the details of actual relationships, however, we find that things are not quite so straightforward. Quali- fication is necessary. There are in-between stages, gradations

[22] When this happened in the legalized form of treaty arrangements, it was called "protectorate" relationship, and the "protected" unit was presumed to have lost its legal status of "sovereign" and "independent" unit.

of dependency, so to say, and this not only because of the still important differences in weight and influence which the various client states command even toward superpowers, but also because of a variety of "arrangements" made by them, arrangements through which they occasionally manage to achieve some degree of leeway in action or independence from controls.

Let us consider first conditions in the bloc that is commonly regarded as the more tightly knit one, where controls appear to be uniformly strict, namely, the Soviet bloc. Upon closer examination, differences, that is, gradations of dependency, become visible even there. And differences in military arrangements or conditions seem to account for some of them. For instance, having been the only satellite free from Soviet military occupation toward the end of the Second World War and afterwards, and boasting a tradition of indigenous guerrilla fighting aimed at liberation from fascism, Yugoslavia had a status different from that of the other satellites even prior to Tito's break with the bloc. Actually that enabled him to make the break. Since then, of course, the Soviets have tried to learn their lesson and to establish firmer controls. Their chief objective has been to keep military controls in the background and to rely on political control through "friendly," meaning dependent, governments. How this kind of control is achieved and maintained need hardly be detailed. Governments of satellites, outwardly in control of their countries' affairs and facilities—such as the conduct of foreign affairs and military establishments—as leaders of their respective Communist parties are under the control of the Soviet Communist Party, that is, its top leadership. Therefore, ideally, the satellite leaders can be relied upon to run their countries' affairs as much according to Moscow's direction as do subdivisions of the Soviet Union itself. But while this is the "ideal," reality, as events since 1956 have shown, confronts the Soviets with difficulties before which they have to choose between rigid enforcement of conformity on the one hand and more subtle attempts on the other to deal with "nationalist deviations" and similar problems. While Stalin preferred rigidity, his successors have in general been more subtle, permitting degrees of autonomy which seem bold by comparison with the older practice. Hence, the gradations of dependency between, for instance, Rumania and Poland. Whenever·concessions permit avoidance of enforcement, present Soviet policy seems to prefer them to the military alternative. However, there are limits, and, as the case of Hungary shows in its contrast with that of Poland, they are being drawn where the unit's status as member of the bloc is, or seems to be, endangered. When the action of the Hungarian revolutionaries threatened to take the country out of the military alignment (i.e., when they denounced the Warsaw Pact), the Soviets intervened. Thus, bloc coherence rather than ideological conformity seems to be the overriding interest.

Things are vastly different in the West. Here, the major distinction between what happened in Leibniz's time to feudal powers that were absorbed into the new territorial states and the way in which nations of the Western bloc are affected by their inclusion in the bloc rests in the formers' complete loss of independence versus the latters' continuing possession of domestic and foreign political autonomy in both a legal and, to a large degree, a practical sense. This appears most clearly in these countries' relations with the world outside the bloc. In relations within the bloc, however, it has meant a conflicting interplay of "sovereignty" and dependence which has lent the countries' present status ambiguity and lack of definition, the character of an indeterminate condition which may now mean one thing and now another. Much, therefore, depends on day-to-day developments, much also on arrangements made between them and the superpower. For, an apparent uniformity of arrangements, status, and ensuing dependency conceals considerable differences in practice and detail. As an example, let us compare the status of Norway with that of Greece in the Western alignment, particularly as members of the NATO arrangement. On the surface, both units' relationships to that organization and to the United States as its leading power seem identical. Both countries have assumed the same membership commitments in the community established by the North Atlantic Treaty, they participate in similar fashion in the coordinated defense arrangements, and so forth. But there is one important difference: while Greece, by agreement with the United States, has opened its territory to American armed forces, which, with their equipment, "may enter, exit, circulate within and overfly Greece and its territorial waters," [23] Norway has refused to do so. Indeed, such refusal was a kind of entrance reservation which the Norwegian government made prior to giving its consent to Norway's becoming a member of NATO. At that time, on Soviet protests, it declared that it would "never join in any agreement with other states that contains obligations for Norway to open bases for the military forces of foreign powers as long as Norway is not attacked or subjected to threats of attack." [24] This policy has been maintained even since NATO's integration into a common defense organization after 1952.[25] Thus, in a way, the difference between Greece and Norway, despite all the similarities in commitments and arrangements, is one between a state garrisoned and a state not garrisoned by another state, a criterion which, as we have

[23] Article 1, para. 2, of the Greek-American Bases Agreement of 1953 (Department of State, *Bulletin*, 29: 863 ff. [1953]).

[24] Text of Norwegian note to the Soviet Union in New York *Times*, January 2, 1949.

[25] See New York *Times*, October 14, 1952. Denmark so far has likewise refused to grant other powers the right to maintain bases or station troops. Similar attitudes emerged in the fall of 1957, when the question of missile bases was ventilated at the NATO "summit" conference.

noted, was the decisive one in the eyes of certain classical theorists of sovereignty. To be sure, the garrisoning is designed to afford protection from foreign attack, and is not occupation to control the country itself. Nevertheless, it can hardly fail to have some influence on the freedom of action of the "protected" unit.

Such implementing or "detail" arrangements, not the pacts or general treaty stipulations, have often been "the heart of the matter" in foreign affairs. Thus, in the interwar period, what was decisive for Switzerland's international status was not its membership in the League of Nations as such but rather those specific agreements with the League which exempted Switzerland from sanctions' obligations that would have made Swiss territory available for the transit of foreign troops. In this way Switzerland could continue its traditional status of "permanent neutrality" into an age when neutrality was seemingly becoming obsolete. Similarly, Norway's freedom from foreign bases may not only imply greater freedom of action in relation to the United States and other NATO countries, but, since bases today are potentially launching points for nuclear weapons, it may also mean a relationship toward the other superpower vastly different from that of a garrisoned country. Seen from Moscow, a country like Norway, I surmise, appears "more neutral" than others in the Western bloc. To Moscow, Norway must seem like one link in a chain of decreasingly neutral units located in northern Europe between the cores of the two blocs. Moving from east to west, there is Finland, which, though not a Soviet satellite, is closest to the Soviet orbit and to some extent, economically, though not politically, dependent on the Soviet Union. Then comes Sweden, which in 1949 refused to enter NATO and has since become one of the neutral countries in the classical sense. Norway, forming the bridge from neutrality toward

Western integration, follows. Finally, west of Norway, the area of full integration begins.

Again, however, it is necessary to beware of overemphasis on the importance of one factor alone. Norway, for instance, despite its freedom from bases, has voluntarily been following a policy of close alignment with "Atlantic" policy. It also is enmeshed in the general defense organization of NATO. And outside the military and the political realm there is the economic one. The impact of economic factors on allied relationships since the advent of bipolarity can hardly be exaggerated. Both superpowers, and in particular the United States, emerged from the Second World War as the only powers economically still strong and, to a degree, self-sufficient, thus being the only ones able to rebuild and assist others economically. Whether this has been done by gift or loan, by favoring vested interests or reform (in the case of America, it has been both in different instances), whether it has been done for the purpose of establishing control (as in the case of the Soviet Union) or not (as generally in the case of the United States), such economic aid, plans, or measures could not help being important instrumentalities of actual influence, causing *de facto* dependencies of various degrees. While in Athens, for instance, or in Paris, the American embassy continued to be the symbol of traditional relations between "equal" and "sovereign" powers, the American Marshall Plan representative, or Mutual Security Administrator (or whatever his rapidly changing title) could hardly avoid cutting a more important figure than his diplomatic colleague. And even in "neutral" areas, and regarding ostensibly neutral, "nonpolitical" programs of technical aid and so forth (Point Four), the emphasis has invariably shifted from "disinterested" assistance toward aims of "mutual security." The United States wants to get something for its money after all, and even where no specific *quid pro quo* is expected, it wants at least an assurance that the receiving unit will remain or become a stable and reliable unit of resistance to possible Communist penetration. Therefore, it is understandable that this country might insist on certain guarantees, for instance, safeguards against an internal assumption of control by the Communists or even against their participation in government. To implement such a guarantee, it may further be necessary to suggest certain domestic measures or policies, e.g., the adoption of some election system better able to keep down leftist parliamentary strength and so forth. Thus a country is almost imperceptibly led from "guidance" in another's foreign relations to "guidance" in its domestic policies. This brings us to the question of the impact of bipolarity on the foreign and internal affairs of "allies." [26]

In talking about domestic or internal policies, I refer to a nation's fundamental decisions about its social and economic structure, political constitution and freedoms, and similar basic issues, and not to the details of day-to-day policy making. It was one of the characteristics of the classical era that these issues were settled freely and without outside interference within the territorial units themselves. There were, of course, exceptions in which through wartime interference, or defeat in war, or through strong peacetime pressure, decisions of this sort were imposed from the outside; but they remained resented exceptions. Generally, states were autonomous in their domestic affairs. Political institutions grew out of each state's native soil, and changes, even revolutionary ones, were due to indigenous forces and indigenous movements. Foreign influences were not without effect, but they were commonly transformed and shaped to fit the needs of the nation respond-

[26] An excellent survey of this impact is contained in Karl Loewenstein's article "Sovereignty and International Cooperation," *American Journal of International Law*, 48: 222 ff. (1954).

ing to them. Thus, "reaction" as well as "reform," revolutions and even "international movements" proceeded within
the framework of the territorial states; they had to be implemented through national parties or similar indigenous institutions. All this went hand in hand with the nations' freedom to arrive at their own decisions in foreign policy, that is,
in issues of war or peace or neutrality, in decisions on isolation
or alliances, on expansion or *status quo*. Together, autonomy
in the domestic sphere and freedom in the conduct of foreign
affairs amounted to that independence which, with the sense
of relatively high security it created, enabled countries to develop their own "ways of life."

In today's bipolar world, which is split ideologically as well
as geographically, such independence outside the superpowers
themselves is greatly imperiled. Especially within the blocs it
becomes more and more difficult even to separate domestic
affairs from affairs "international," that is, bloc affairs. With
each of the superpowers and each of the corresponding blocs
representing a specific economic, social, and political system of
its own, and with the other bloc opposing the opponent not
only as a power but also as a system, the type of policy, movement, parties, institutions, and doctrines of one, which formerly would have been within the range of free domestic choice,
tends to become suspect within the bloc of the other, even
where it is not officially banned as treasonable. The East
need hardly be mentioned in this connection, since it is clear
that anything non-Communist or not officially aligned with
Communism is impermissible, minor leeways which we have
noticed notwithstanding. But even in the "free" world, freedom in this respect is qualified exactly because it no longer
applies to Communism. True, Communist parties are still
legal and strong in countries like France and Italy. But as a
result of the cold war and of American pressure, they have
been excluded from official positions of power wherever they

held them, in particular in government coalitions. This is because such internal alignments in our days are liable to have foreign political connotations. So long as Italy, for instance, is in NATO, it would be difficult to envision Communist participation in a government where Communist ministers might share the secrets of the military alliance. The Communist Party, as a French statesman has put it, is "neither Left nor Right but East." This statement reflects the change that has affected domestic affairs under bipolarism. Superpowers first of all want to make sure that the fortress is safe within. And there is sometimes little difference in the way in which East and West have acted. For instance, if we reflect on how the respective bipolar fortresses were originally established, we see that the two superpowers (or those acting at their side) both proceeded little mindful of what the people in question or their majorities might have wanted. They did not bother to find out. What happened in Athens at the time of the liberation (as reported by Churchill) differed little even in detail from what happened at the same time in Bucharest. "Democracy," whether as "people's democracy" or the Western type, was allowed to prevail only after the basic decision, namely that on (Eastern or Western) "orientation," had been imposed.

Such preclusions or exclusions are not limited (in the West) to Communism. Other trends tend to restrict a seemingly still wide range of choices. Thus, one or another alternative, in the eyes of the superpower and those representing its policy in the allied country, may seem so closely connected with the latter's "stability," "political health," or "reliability" as an ally, that it should no longer be left to the exclusive domain of the country concerned. Thereupon, one particular policy, decision, or solution, by intimation or pressure, is "suggested" or imposed. These procedures run counter to the still officially accepted standards and policies of noninterference and respect

for sovereign equalities; they tend to offend national sensibili-
ties and strain allied relationships, and are not usually
splashed over the headlines; [27] but the public does occasionally
get a glimpse of them.   An American ambassadrice, on the
eve of an election, voiced threats of measures that would be
taken should the election go the "wrong" way (Italy, 1953).
The United States twice intervened in Greece in order to influence a change in its electoral system, not because it feared
that the existing system might result in the victory of what
was, in any case, an outlawed Communist Party, but in order
to enhance the chances of one group of parties believed to be
more favorably inclined to the West over those of another.[28]
As in Italy, outright American backing of one man and his
party (Adenauer and the Christian Democrats) in West Germany in 1953 was not without effect on their victory over the
also Western-oriented but less trusted Social Democrats.   The
possibility of an "agonizing reappraisal" of American policy
was made known to a France hesitant to integrate itself with
Europe, and particularly with Germany.   In a manner which
reminds one of the typically Communist appeal from the allegedly "unrepresentative ruling circles" to "the masses," a
foremost and usually objective American newspaper denounced
the French parliament's rejection of the European Defense
Community, as not constituting "a free expression of the
French will." [29]   A French journalist at that time was said to
have declared that he would now take out American citizen-
ship papers so as to be able to exercize some influence on
French affairs!

[27] In the words of James Reston, "It is still part of the mythology of
world politics that one sovereign government never does anything for the
purpose of influencing the outcome of an election in another country"
(New York *Times*, May 11, 1955).

[28] See New York *Times*, August 23 and November 16, 1952.

[29] New York *Times*, September 3, 1954.   Similarly, when a democratic
election in Iceland "went wrong," the same newspaper complained of
"the fantastic distortions of the democratic process revealed by the election results" (New York *Times*, June 28, 1956).

It is easy to see why such pressures and suspicions affect the more leftist, notably socialist, trends and groups, however democratic and Western-oriented they may be: they do not agree with the "free enterprise" philosophy of the leading power, and were they in government, they would be liable to disturb that philosophy. But it cannot be said that American intervention has always been in favor of "reactionism." There is some reason to assume, for instance, that the transformation of Turkey from a one-party dictatorship into something resembling a two-party democracy was not unrelated to that country's reception into the Western system at the time of President Truman's Greek and Turkish aid policy.

Another and perhaps even more important trend is that domestic issues, including those which used to be considered the most vital ones (e.g., "socialism" versus "capitalism," etc.) tend to recede before foreign affairs, that is, they tend to be overshadowed by the great foreign policy issues involved in bloc formation and bipolarity. Whereas in former times foreign affairs remained rather "foreign" to the public at large and foreign policy issues were seldom those over which movements, political parties, and so forth were primarily divided, these issues now concern everybody so immediately that such questions as neutralism versus alignment with a superpower, or whether to grant bases to a foreign power, often preoccupy minds and policies to the exclusion, or at least to the detriment, of internal issues. This cannot fail to affect traditional party systems and policies. Once a country chooses "Western orientation," for instance, and then opens its territory to foreign troops and installations—thus becoming part of the bipolar hard-shell—the vital foreign policy issue has been settled. After that, what usually happens is either that such an orientation becomes the only "permissible" one and opposition to it, regardless of the grounds, will be regarded as "disloyalty;" or that the country divides into those favoring and those opposing the decision, with the former indicted by the latter as "slaves of American imperialism," and the latter maligned by the former as "agents of Communism." [30] In any event, this sort of thing interferes with traditional party alignments, either by compelling all important groups to back the official orientation in a kind of "bipartisanism," or "me-too-ism," or by causing the issue of orientation to cut right through parties and alignments and thus render them increasingly ineffective.[31] In the Soviet sphere pro-Western or even mere neutralist orientation can obviously exist only underground. But even in the West there are sometimes tendencies toward a general rally to a pro-American party or group of parties. Party trends in West Germany, at least until recently, offer an example: The pro-Soviet group (Communists, plus possibly some small groups outside it) has been driven into illegality; radical Rightist forces seem to have no chance so long as they tend toward neutralism or "fence-sitting"; spokesmen of democratic neutralists—who are politically quite insignificant—are maligned as "fellow travelers"; Social Democrats, the major opposition group, cannot afford to oppose Western orientation in principle because of their opposition to Communism and Communist control over East Germany, and thus, for a long time, they opposed mere details in the problems of such an orientation. Only recently have some seemed to veer toward the other alternative, neutralism. In France, on the other hand, the internal political system has at times been imperiled by intraparty divisions over foreign

30 As in another instance of "bipolarity" in history, that of Athens and Sparta in the Greek city-state system, where factions in the lesser units tended to be pro either one or the other orientation.

31 As O. Kirchheimer ("The Waning of Opposition in Parliamentary Regimes," *Social Research*, 24: 127 ff. [1957]) has noticed, party leaders and politicians cannot usually relate "the broad canvas of international politics to their domestic objectives"; this must then result either in an aimless and vacillating conduct of foreign affairs or in an assumption of foreign policy decision-making by elites outside the traditional party setup.

policy. With the exception of the Communists, and to a lesser extent the Mouvement Républicain Populaire, there was not a single French party which was not split nearly equally over the issue of the European Defense Community. In Britain, where the two great parties have customarily been bipartisan on foreign issues, opposition to current foreign policy, as, for example, in the form of neutralism, has occasionally cut through one or the other party and weakened it from within.

Thus, in the West, the issue of Western orientation may tend either to make any but the alliance orientation appear subversive and thus compel all major groups and parties to agree basically on one and the same foreign policy; [32] or it may tend to split all or most of the existing groups and parties over this issue. In the latter event, a Western orientation may raise more political and general antagonism than it is worth militarily. It may even lead, as in Iceland, to threatened denunciation of arrangements for bases or the stationing of troops, which will leave the "occupant" confronted with the choice of trying to hold on by force or letting the unwilling ally go his way.

In any event, international issues influence the relations, alignments, and strength of those political forces within nations which used to be guided primarily by domestic issues. One other factor, also connected with the international situation, seems to have a bearing on the recession of domestic in favor of foreign policy issues: Increasingly larger portions of national budgets must now be allocated to expenditures for defense and security. This means that less and less of that *nervus rerum*, money, remains available for such domestic

[32] In the West German election of 1957, Adenauer's charges that the Social Democrats' lukewarm attitude toward NATO was helpful to the Soviets undoubtedly damaged the latters' cause; exactly the same kind of charge was used by the Democratic party against the opposition People's Republicans in the Turkish election of that year.

policies and purposes as internal improvements and reform programs, over which parties and political movements used to struggle.

Unequal relationship between superpower and "ally" is occasionally reflected in the stipulations of treaties themselves. The Japanese-American Security Treaty of 1951,[33] for instance, provides for an opportunity for future intervention if any should be desired, by enabling the United States to render assistance "to put down large-scale internal riots and disturbances in Japan, caused through instigation or intervention by an outside power or powers." Even in the absence of written agreements to this effect, such a power may be inferred from such texts as that of the NATO treaty, in which, according to a statement by (then) Secretary of State Acheson, "armed attack" might also be "indirect" attack "from within" by Communist groups under the control of Soviet Communism. This reflects the territoriality-undermining potentialities of present-day bipolarity. On the other hand, attempts to influence or control the affairs of less powerful countries too closely or too rudely may backfire. The "nationalist" reaction to too much pressure could result in driving a unit out of its ally relationship through the—now typical—alignment of nationalism with neutralism, or it might give Communist propaganda an entering wedge and thus strengthen the internal opposition to Western orientation until the validity of that orientation becomes doubtful.

What has just been said highlights the possibilities of maneuvering which remain available to allies even in their relations with a superpower. In other words, "inequalities" and the trend away from old-style sovereignty are not the only characteristics of intrabloc relations in the bipolar age. We should therefore beware of overestimating them and thus overlooking the difficulties with which superpowers have to con-

[33] See Article 1 (Department of State, *Bulletin*, 25: 463 ff. [1951]).

tend so long as sovereignty continues legally to remain a condition of other bloc nations. Conflicting interests are likely to exist among units of the same bloc or defense system and may cause differences in policy and approach. Difficulties arising within alliances in the classical age are well known, of course, and we still encounter such difficulties, whether they are due to strains arising from superiority and inferiority in power (this is particularly marked in the age of superpowers), or whether they arise from conflict of interests among the lesser and more equal allies. In the latter case, the superpower will try to assume the role of arbiter; but it often proves difficult to avoid antagonizing one country when establishing close relations with another. This difficulty is illustrated not only by the perennial Franco-German problem (or, on the Eastern side, the corresponding Polish-German problem), but also by the problems encountered when new alignments are sought in regions which are considered vital for bipolar defense but at the same time are areas of clashing regional interests. The superpower then runs the additional risks of having the newly aligned country "desert" after receiving aid, or of having such aid "diverted" to that country's own national and nonbloc power politics. Western efforts to build Asian and Near Eastern links of the bipolar hard shell offer examples of all of these pitfalls: aid to Pakistan antagonizes India, and may be used to fight India over Kashmir; military assistance rendered to Arab nations could be used against Israel; and so long as no actual Western bases or similar controls are established, there is no guarantee against a change in the political orientation of the respective country toward neutralism or even toward a pro-Soviet attitude.

Thus, unless ironclad totalitarian controls are maintained—something from which relations between Western superpower and allies are still far away and which could hardly materialize so long as the underlying ideology remains one of freedom and independence—the superpower is going to be confronted with counterforces and counterinfluences on the part of its allies, particularly the stronger ones among them. They may try to push the leading power into a more peaceful or a more belli-cose attitude toward the other bloc, as the case may be. Oc-casionally, a small but vigorous (or desperate) ally will try to pull the entire bloc into major war, and may have to be thwarted by the superpower; in other cases, stronger allies may have to exert their influence to tame the "big brother." [34] This proves that even under the accentuated conditions of bipolar inequalities, Hegel's dialectic of "master" and "ser-vant" persists, with the master needing the servant's services, and being as dependent on the servant as the latter is on him. Whether, considering all the new trends in intrabloc relation-ships, one should substitute novel concepts for the traditional concepts of "sovereignty," "independence," etc., seems at this point a matter of terminology. What is certain is that the old concepts no longer retain the full meaning peculiar to them under the classical system of territoriality.

INTERBLOC RELATIONSHIPS

"The greatness of an estate, in bulk and territory, does fall under measure; and the greatness of finances and revenue does fall under computation. The population may appear by musters, and the number and greatness of cities by cards and maps; but yet there is not anything, amongst civil affairs, more subject to error than the right valuation and true judg-ment concerning the power and forces of an estate." [35] This statement, made when the modern state system was in its

[34] Twice in recent history Britain seems to have averted a major threat of general war by pulling America from the "brink," namely, during the Korean conflict, and in Indo-China, and possibly a third time, when the first crisis over the off-shore islands of Quemoy and Matsu occurred.

[35] Bacon, *Essays Civil and Moral*, in *Works*, ed. B. Montague, 1 (Phila-delphia, 1842), 36.

earliest phase, calls attention to a difficulty that has plagued not only statesmen but students of international politics as well: How, even on the basis of known "power factors" or "power elements," can the over-all "power" be assessed so as to have some measure or criterion with which to appraise the international situation at a given point in time? Today, for instance, how can we know whether, as the prevailing thought on the structure of present international politics holds, the two superpowers leading the two major power blocs are about "equal" in power? While it always—and especially during the classical era of modern international politics—has been difficult to measure power in any more precise way, there are a couple of reasons why this task is even more complicated today. Quite apart from the fact that nuclear developments have rendered the concept of measurable power doubtful as such, changes in other fields (e.g., in nonnuclear technology affecting industrial strength, or in nuclear power for non-military purposes) have frequently been so rapid that the dust has hardly settled after the last change before another requires reappraisal. And, compared with the simpler nature of the fewer factors that had to be taken into consideration in former times, especially in regard to preindustrial countries, the very complexity and number of factors affecting the relative power of powers (including superpowers) today are staggering.

This uncertainty is illustrated by the fact that at the end of the Second World War, which through its impact on victors and vanquished itself produced bipolarity, major doubts concerning the new power structure prevailed even among leading statesmen in charge of a postwar settlement. It is common knowledge that America expected Britain rather than itself to emerge as the chief antagonist of Russia (and to be of approximately equal "weight"); and as late as 1946, when the United States and the Soviet Union had quite clearly emerged as the leading powers, Churchill and de Gaulle were still dreaming of a Britain and a France that conjointly would be in a position to play the role of "third force," capable of constituting a decisive weight in the world balance. Stalin, at Yalta, still seems to have conceived of the postwar world as one in which a concert of several major powers would play the predominating role in the world, "realistically" referring to certain military standards as the criteria of "bigness" (his famous "entrance ticket of having five million men on the battlefield"). Subsequently, Stalinist terminology, in distinguishing what was officially referred to as "great" peoples from peoples without such honorific title, continued to apply similarly simplistic criteria, for instance, population, for assessing power in world affairs. Having approximately 100 million inhabitants or more was to be the standard of "bigness." [36] But was it so simplistic? Perhaps not if we try to assess future developments and the potentialities they seem to offer for countries like China and India, Japan and Germany.

A further difficulty in the accurate appraisal of power and power relations lies in a subjective factor. Countries, like individuals, may add to their status, or diminish it, according to how they feel about it. Even more importantly, power status may be increased or decreased according to the ideas others have about one (in other words, what one's "prestige" is). For instance, when after the Second World War the United States emerged as the only power in the world with an atomic weapon, many outside America felt that the United States was now a dominating or hegemonical power, since it was now in a position to dictate to the world.[37] But can one

[36] At least this is the most plausible conclusion from the fact that, regardless of "friendship" or "enmity," the Russian, American, Chinese, Indian, Japanese, and German peoples, and only these, were referred to as "great." Another crude standard of appraisal is revealed in Stalin's alleged query: "The Pope—how many divisions does he have?"

[37] As Arnold Wolfers put it: All nations were "at the mercy of our peaceful intentions" (in B. Brodie, *The Absolute Weapon* [New York, 1946], p. 113).

say that the United States actually had that status? It is a strange but undeniable fact that the United States itself—that is, its leaders in foreign policy as well as most of its people—considered itself inferior rather than superior to others at that juncture, particularly in relation to the Soviets who then not only had not demobilized but were making all kinds of expansionist moves. All America, in its own mind, was able to do was to check the Soviet Union through the atomic menace, and thus balance the latter's power. "Actual" or "real" superiority—if these terms make sense at all—is transformed into mere "equality" where consciousness of superior might, and therewith ability to conduct policies on that basis, is absent.

However this may be, or was in 1945, we have in the meantime become used to what was novel and unexpected twelve years ago; we now appraise the existing power structure as one of two superpowers by and large balancing each other in the world. And this appraisal may be roughly correct, considering that the two superpowers, regardless of their ultimate objectives, have maintained themselves in equipoise for over a decade, despite frantic competition for superiority and despite the occurrence of frequent and often major changes in the technological and the political sphere which have benefited now one and now the other power or bloc. This is what, for the most part, justifies the application of the name and concept "bipolarity" to the present power situation in the world. It does not by itself indicate what *system* of international relations has emerged, or can emerge, from such a power structure. This is the question to which we must now turn.

One possibility has already been dealt with and excluded: that of establishing a system of genuine "collective security" on a structure characterized by a split of the world into two power blocs of preeminent and fairly equal power.[38] So far

38 See above, ch. 5.

as these two blocs are concerned, I have suggested, genuine collective security cannot be practiced because no "overpowering" coalition can be marshaled against the "aggressor" or "aggressors." The use of terms like "sanctions," "police action," or "enforcement measures" against a "lawbreaker," by a majority of countries in the world (or of members of such an organization as the United Nations), then merely indicates that certain legitimizing verbiage is at the disposal of one superpower rather than the other; it does not alter the fact that there are two basically equal opponents.

But what about that system, and that policy, which seem to be the most natural, indeed the almost obvious, result of an equilibrium structure: a balance of power system, and balance of power policies? Here it is necessary to scrutinize conditions somewhat more closely in order to understand the similarities as well as the dissimilarities between the present situation and that of the times when balance systems and balance policies received their most significant, their "classical" expression.

The balance of power, as we have seen, became accepted as the chief regulatory principle of international politics with the rise of the modern state and the modern state system. In those centuries balance policies were developed into an art, which became almost synonymous with diplomacy, especially by Britain, the classical "holder of the balance," and by those countries which, from time to time, with Britain opposed whichever one was the "aggressor" of the age, the would-be hegemony country. There was then nothing pejorative in the term or the art itself. But disillusionment with them set in when during the nineteenth century standards of morality were applied to foreign affairs by middle classes more actively participating or at least more seriously interested in their conduct. And the prestige of the balance, together with that of power politics generally, reached its nadir during the interwar period. With the emergence of bipolarity, however, it has come to the fore again, at least among the more serious students of world affairs. Having turned full circle, it is now considered the only or chief principle which does or should underlie present international politics by the "realist school" of international relations.

Yet the situation is not so simple. If we do not want to identify balance system with the mere factual existence of equilibrium, it is necessary to ask questions like these: Can a balance system function with only two major "players"? Does it require a "holder of the balance" as an equilibrating third force, and, if so, is there such a balancer in the present situation? Can it exist where major powers pursue policies of supremacy rather than of balance? Can balance policies be pursued where the major actors are split ideologically? Certain recent publications have delved into some of the objections that can be leveled against the applicability of the concept and policy of balance under present conditions, and as I did in the case of "collective security," I shall discuss some of the problems concerning the balance of power through analyzing these writings.

One author, Ernst B. Haas,[39] has listed a number of factors which, so he contends, render both the concept and practice of balance outdated. According to him, the balance of power was based on the "institutional and cultural consensus" of the eighteenth century, which disappeared in 1789, although the

[39] "The Balance of Power as a Guide to Policy-Making," *Journal of Politics*, 15: 370 ff. (1953). A more recent article by the same author ("Types of Collective Security: An Examination of Operational Concepts," *American Political Science Review*, 49: 40 ff. [1955]) deals with its topic with much less conceptual neatness. The term "collective security," there is used to embrace policies and processes as varied as "the concert principle," "permissive enforcement," regional bloc action, and, finally, "balancing"! All that remains of "collectivism" here seems to be the existence of an international organization, the United Nations, in whose formal framework these processes occur and which, in the end, itself emerges as a "balancer."

assumption continued that it could function so long as there
was a system of sovereign states competing for power. It had
functioned on the basis of a number of "operational" or "procedural" assumptions: the possibility of at least roughly
measuring power (something more difficult in industrial than
in preindustrial ages); great flexibility, or adjustability, of
policy, necessitating secret and rapid, often instantaneous, decisions (something difficult to obtain in an age of democracy,
which entails accountability of governments to parliaments,
public opinion, etc.); continuity of foreign policy in the face
of internal changes; indifference to the "merits" of issues, to
"ideologies," etc.; and a willingness to go to war in the interest
of the maintenance or restoration of the balance. At the same
time, "national interests" had to be stable and well defined.
Even under the *ancien régime* divisions among the ruling
elite over such interests endangered the homogeneity of foreign policy. Pluralistic-democratic societies of our time rule
out consensus on national interests exactly because they are
pluralistic. They are even less able to fulfill the various pro-
cedural-operational requirements of balance policies. Such
policies, in democracies, would require the establishment of a
"permanent foreign affairs elite" to make up for the "deficien-
cies of democracy in the operational-conceptual areas of balance of power conduct."

This is an able presentation of the difficulties encountered
in and by democracies in regard to balance of power policies,
and in as much as half the world today utilizes democratic
procedures for its conduct of foreign policy, they must be
taken very seriously. The factors mentioned by Haas do account for the frequent "power-alien" and "balance-alien"
motivations and influences which have beset a conscious and
consistent pursuit of balance policies on frequent occasions
both past and present. But can we say that they have rendered such pursuit impossible under or for democratic re-

gimes? In the long run, and despite intermittent deviations, have not considerations of power and balance prevailed in Britain even since cabinets have become responsible to parliament and to the public? Does not increasing bipartisanism with respect to fundamental foreign policy issues there and in the United States and elsewhere bespeak the same fact today? The weakness in this author's argument lies in his overlooking that, while the national interest may be variable in many respects in pluralistic societies, it may yet be constant in as much as it can be defined as interest in the maintenance of the balance itself wherever countries pursue balance policies. Disagreements in those circumstances refer to how best to achieve the balance, that is, to details which may legitimately constitute objects of disagreement despite a consensus on the balance principle as such. Thus, whether to implement its balance policy by lining up with Germany against Russia, or with Russia and France against Germany, or whether to continue temporarily its "splendid isolation" from any alignments, were legitimate questions discussed by and in Britain at the turn of the century. The very fact that such disagreements can exist, refutes one of Haas's chief arguments, because it allows leeway to foreign policy makers, for different ways to attain the end are open. This enables different groups—political parties, for instance—to disagree "pluralistically" without rendering balance policies impossible. To be sure, the conduct of balance policies, like that of any long-range, consistent, "principled" foreign policy, has become more difficult in an age of "open diplomacy," democratic control of foreign policies, etc.; it can hardly be said to have become impossible. Today, however, under bipolar conditions, there exist additional complications, which this author does not mention, but before discussing them, another suggestion, equally skeptical of traditional balance concepts, will be analyzed briefly.

The author of this suggestion, J. Liska,[40] proposes to replace the traditional concept of an exclusively military-political balance of "powers", now said to be obsolete, with that of a multiple balance which places checks and restraints on individual powers—a kind of "constitutionalization of power" in the international realm; to the military-political balance is added an "institutional" and a "social" one. "Institutionally," international organization serves to equilibrize power through legal voting equalities and similar devices favoring smaller units. In the "social" sphere, balances have to be established between colonialism and independence movements, industrialization and economic specialization, different cultures and religions. This may lead to cooperation in supranational processes, e.g., in prevention of world-wide depressions. Only broader conceptions of national interest, which take these equilibria into consideration, can be lastingly successful: "The achievement of a right measure, a 'just equilibrium,' between a too narrow and a too diffuse conception of the national interest is the criterion of statesmanship in our time." Thus, the United States can be the "equilibrator" in the free world, between Germany and France, Israel and the Arabs, colonialism and anticolonialism, Franco and Tito, capitalism and democratic socialism. But it needs institutional equilibria, international organization, to achieve its purpose. While power analysis reveals only relations of super- and subordination, control and subjection, "equilibrium analysis" partly reverses power analysis and partly refines it, without rejecting it. Under equilibrium analysis "the multiple equilibrium replaces the balance of power as the 'constitutional principle' of international society."

This theory has the merit of showing up certain limitations

[40] "The Multiple Equilibrium and the American National Interest," *Harvard Studies in International Affairs*, 4: 35 ff. (1954).

of a "realistic" power analysis which, if it takes power in the narrower sense as the sole factor in the analysis of international politics, overlooks the role played by "power-alien" factors, as well as the power role of units and organizations which may restrain the major powers. It is also legitimate to stress the role of international cooperation and the potentialities of an internationalist approach, because there is an inclination to overlook them under the impact of superpower and superpower conflicts.[41] But the author's analysis becomes unrealistic when he places "institutional" and "social" balances on an equal footing with the balance of power. It is one thing to emphasize the real but limited role international organizations and agencies can and do play in international relations today; it is quite another to claim for them, actually or potentially, an importance in and influence on world affairs commensurate with that of, say, United States or Soviet bloc policies. Multiple influences (to use a more suitable term than "equilibria") do exist in international politics but the limited role of those stressed by Liska becomes painfully clear through his own major exemplification. Where the United States plays the role of balancer, it does so exclusively within its own sphere, that is, within its half of the world, the free world, and not in relation to the world as a whole. There, bipolarity prevents America as any other body from "equilibrizing," and this fact itself shows that "balancing" plays only a moderate role today, while the balance per se looms ever larger in its military-political sense.

At this point must be mentioned that feature of the present balance which, curiously, is not referred to by either of the two authors quoted above since it constitutes the most obvious and the most far-reaching of all departures from the classical pattern. A direct result of the bipolar structure, it

41 Chances of international or supranational attitudes and policies will be discussed in another context below (see below, ch. 12).

consists in the fact that there are no longer a large number of bigger and smaller "weights" but basically only two in the balance. Two can of course balance each other, but the resulting sort of equilibrium is very different from the one among multiple "weights." Above all, there is no longer an effective "balancer," that is, a country whose vital role it is to maintain or redress the balance by shifting its weight to the momentarily weaker side. Today, the two sides are predetermined, and their equilibrium is precarious, without there being much of a chance for others to intervene decisively in order either to safeguard or, if necessary, to restore it. Everything in balance policy now, therefore, is more rigid. There is little opportunity to shift from one of the two rigid blocs to the other, and the still existing uncommitted powers, although in a position to exert some influence, are not equipped to intervene in the decisive fashion of the "holders of the balance" of yore. This difference between traditional balance policies and what is possible today has been well summed up by Hans Morgenthau, in whose words the superpowers can either only

advance and meet in what is likely to be combat, or they can retreat and allow the other side to advance into what to them is precious ground. Those manifold and variegated maneuvers through which the masters of the balance of power tried to either stave off armed conflicts altogether or at least make them brief and decisive, yet limited in scope—the alliances and counter-alliances, the shifting of alliances according to whence the greater threat or better opportunity might come, the sidestepping and postponement of issues, the deflection of rivalries from the exposed frontyard into the colonial backyard—these are things of the past.[42]

Under what circumstances, then, can the present system be supposed to achieve that primary purpose of the traditional balance system which consisted in preventing any one power

[42] *In Defense of the National Interest* (New York, 1952), p. 50. See also H. Butterfield, *Christianity, Diplomacy and War* (London, 1953), p. 91.

or group of powers from attaining hegemony? Under present conditions, this question is synonymous with asking: How can the superpowers be prevented from making a war upon each other which could only result in world control by the victor? [43] Two views oppose each other in this respect. One maintains that only an exact balance can deter the two blocs from attacking each other; the other one asserts that only utter imbalance can. It is probably correct to assume that in either of these circumstances the threat of war is less than in the case of a *slight* imbalance. In the latter event, the disfavored side might fear that the trend was toward even less favorable conditions and thus might be driven to go to war at what appears to be a (relatively) still favorable time. The favored side, on the other hand, might feel that "this is the moment" and that missing it might mean "missing the boat" forever. But the other "solutions" to the question are dubious also. Great imbalance would indeed be an assurance against conflict so far as initiation by the disfavored side is concerned, unless (and this possibility can by no means be excluded) it acted in an "irrational" manner. But so far as the more powerful side is concerned, the assurance would exist only if and so long as it was "nonaggressive," that is, so long as it was satisfied with having more but not all of the power. In any event, unless one starts with a situation of great imbalance, one can get there only from balance. That means passing through the most dangerous stage of all, namely, a slight imbalance. All this leaves as a (relatively) "ideal" condition that of exact balance. Here, again, however, one cannot demand too much from "objective circumstances," nor form purposeful policies. Even if it were possible to have a situation which, "objectively," could be called an "exact" or "perfect" equilibrium (and this,

---

[43] At this point I have not yet taken into account the impact of the atomic factor, which may well render terms like "victors" and "vanquished" meaningless.

of course, has never been the case, considering the impossibility of assessing all power factors exactly), the respective powers, "subjectively," would still view with alarm any situation that would not give them at least some margin of superiority. Thus balance and balance policies today can at best be only minor evils.

If the decade following upon the Second World War brought about a comparatively equal balance between the two major blocs, inflexibility in their equilibrium has also been growing apace and constitutes a constant danger in regard to its maintenance. The two leading powers' chief concern has been with gaining or retaining a margin of superiority rather than with maintaining equality. And even where they have striven to maintain a balance, there has been intermingled in their concern for continuing equality a strong motive for trying to line up on their respective sides the still uncommitted countries, whose number therefore has dwindled and is still dwindling. And the more rigid the alignments, the greater the sensitivity regarding any changes or threats of changes in the existing line-up. Such sensitivity endangers world peace over the most minute of issues or incidents. If the passing of China into the Eastern camp or that of most of a rearmed Germany into the Western camp are, perhaps, legitimately considered major imbalancing events, it is more difficult to understand why the possession or loss of some tiny, strategically unimportant islands along the China coast—or the possession or loss of Hungary, for that matter—should make a tremendous difference. Or why small and possibly unintentional [44] border violations should pro-

---

[44] It is different in the case of intentional ones. Indeed, "defense technological" developments today offer temptations which hardly existed previously, for instance, penetration of the opponent's air space for purposes of photographic reconnaissance or detection of radioactivity or of radar stations, etc. See Hanson W. Baldwin, in New York *Times*, September 14, 1954.

duce war crises. An apparent paradox lies in a situation, and in a system, in which the slightest technological or general change, as well as the slightest political shift or realignment, is felt to be an imbalancing and threatening factor, while at the same time even major groupings of nations can no longer function as "balancers;" indeed, whatever shift or realignment they might perform, it would not affect the balance essentially. The answer is as follows: Countries outside the superpowers cannot serve as balancers in the classical sense because it was the function of the latter to tip the scales against a would-be hegemony power by intervening in a "war for the restoration of the balance" or by threatening such intervention. Under conditions of bipolarity, such a war would naturally include the superpowers and would result either in the hegemony of the victorious superpower or (if fought with nuclear weapons) in their mutual destruction. But if "balancing" in this sense has become meaningless, this does not imply that shifts and other changes may not affect the balance at all; on the contrary, the more rigid the balance is, the greater the danger that, in the absence of countershifts and realignments, such events may sooner or later lead to that imbalance in which the more powerful can either destroy the opponent or blackmail him into submission. Sensitivity, if sometimes exaggerated, is therefore understandable in an age where so little room for maneuvering is left, where the hard shells of the two world-wide blocs touch each other almost everywhere, and where distances which formerly sufficed for buffer protection no longer amount to anything in view of space-annihilating supersonic speeds.

All of this is evidence that calling the present system a balance of power system is a doubtful use of the term. If the essence of the classical balance system lay in the possibility of restoring a disturbed or lost balance by force of arms—through the grand coalition war—the impossibility of attaining such an objective indicates that there is no such "system" today, only what in contrast one might call a "stalemate," a "balance" in the mere factual sense of the word. And the situation is rendered even more complex because of "ideological bipolarity."

It has been asserted that even if the two superpowers were not divided by conflicting ideologies and "ways of life"—for instance, if there were a Russia with a socioeconomic structure and a political constitution not too dissimilar from those of the Western democracies—the bipolar rift would still exist. In view of the "security dilemma" in which sovereign units coexisting in a single international system find themselves, and which reaches its acme precisely where bipolar superpowers face each other,[45] there is reason to fear that this is true. But the rift, though it might exist anyway, is immeasurably widened on account of the fact that ideological cleavage is superimposed upon bipolar power concentration.[46] This, besides the rigidity of a two-power system, constitutes the great impediment to balance policies today.

The ideological cleavage leaves the possibility of the pursuance of balance *policies* open to question. The aim of maintaining a balance may still constitute the minimum each superpower wants and will strive to achieve; the maximum, or preferred, objective is different. It is the victory of the superpowers' respective "worlds," that is, world control by the Communists in the one instance, and defeat of Communism, with its corrollary, destruction of Soviet power, in the other. Is it possible today to "bury" the opponent with-

[45] On the meaning and effects of the "security dilemma" see below, ch. 10.

[46] In what follows the term "ideology" is used as a shorthand notation for the entire congeries of "world views" and creeds, socioeconomic-political "systems" connected with such belief systems, ways of life, etc., which confront each other from, respectively, Communist totalitarianism and Western liberal democracy.

out destroying the balance? Here is where the impact of bipolarity is decisive. Under the classical, multipower system a country or countries could indeed defeat their opponent and, if the opponent were an ideological one intent on spreading his ideology over the world, could "bury" him without destroying the balance of power. On the contrary, this was the way to restore the balance of power after defeating the hegemony strivings of such a power, as witness what happened in the case of revolutionary and Napoleonic France.[47] But under bipolarity the defeat of one would-be hegemony power would mean, not restoration of balance, but hegemony of the victor.

Pending such an ultimate clash, the ideological split is deepening the gulf between the power blocs. It tends to consolidate the units and blocs on each side even more than does power competition; it tends eventually to create a crusading fanaticism which leaves opinion and policies on either side with nothing but an exclusive concern for a mutual *écrasez l'infâme!* To say that ideologies possess such group-consoli-

[47] The hegemonical system which any such ideological power (whether it be revolutionary France, or Bolshevist Russia, or Nazi Germany) strives to create, found its classical description in Burke: "The balance of power had been ever assumed as the common law of Europe . . . by all powers . . . . But the revolutionaries changed all this: As for the balance of power, it was so far from being admitted by France . . . that they constantly rejected the very idea . . . . They avow their design to erect themselves into a new description of empire, which is not grounded on any balance, but forms a sort of impious hierarchy, of which France is to be the head and the guardian . . . . They permit the temporary existence of some of the old communities . . . and invest them on every side by a body of Republics, formed on the model of the mother Republic, to which they owe their origin. It is in this manner that France, on her new system, means to form an universal empire, by producing an universal revolution. By this means, forming a new code of communities according to what she calls the natural rights of man and of States, she pretends to secure eternal peace to the world, guaranteed by her generosity and justice, which are to grow with the extent of her power" (Third Letter on the Proposals for Peace with the Regicide Directory of France).

dating and therefore bloc-dividing effects may seem to con-tradict my previous analysis of the *dis*-integrating effect which ideologies and political-psychological warfare can exert on the territorial coherence of states. Doctrines and belief systems may indeed divide populations, and even under bipolarity they may and do cut through orbit lines and set group against group within countries and blocs. I have pointed out that this gives the Soviet side an advantage over the West. But I have also pointed out that bloc formation and bloc controls tend to render it ever more difficult even in countries with freedom of opinion to organize and adhere to the respective "hostile" type of movement. Totalitarianism, of course, forces any ideological enemy underground, where it generally is ineffective or at least unable to affect the coherence of the unit which utilizes opinion control and indoctrination to consolidate itself. By way of reaction, nontotalitarian coun-tries are driven toward adopting increasingly numerous and far-reaching measures against "subversion" in order to counteract the disintegrating effect of ideological bipolarity. In ideological competition, too, "the bad money tends to drive out the good." With the ideological gap widening between the camps it becomes ever more difficult to conduct policies of adjustment and compromise, even where adjust-ment and compromise would clearly serve the maintenance of the balance between the blocs and therewith the national or bloc interest in the balance of power.

Ideological bipolarity, however, has another, even more divisive effect. Even where there is still a readiness to ac-commodate (be it ever so provisional or qualified), it may be frustrated by what threatens to become the loss of a common language, a common conceptual framework, without which no understanding as to the aims of policies is possible. Policies, and also events as such, then lose their unequivocal meaning; the world is no longer comprehended in the same or similar terms.[48] A few "diplomatic" problems may serve as examples.

First, "recognition." In times without ideological conflict recognition of states or governments indicates the consensus among the existing members of international society on which units are fellow nations and which persons are entitled to represent them as their rulers. That is, in more technical language, units of international relations, and regimes representing them internationally, are recognized uniformly either because they exercise *de facto* control in a given area or because they comply with common standards of legitimacy. The situation becomes different when such consensus or ideological homogeneity yields to heterogeneous and mutually hostile creeds. Today, as in previous ages of creeds and countercreeds (for instance, the time of the French Revolution, with its "world-revolutionary" doctrine of democratic and national self-determination opposed to the legitimacy concepts of the *ancien régime*), there is no longer agreement between the two worlds on what constitutes "legitimate" rule. That is, there is no longer a basis for common or mutual recognition. This disagreement tends to blur the very criteria by which the units of international relations are defined and distinguished. Recognition tends to be granted, not on the basis of actual control but to "like" regimes only, and to be withheld from the ideological opponent regardless of actual rule. Actually, therefore, powerless groups may enjoy recognition because of ideological-political affiliation, and may be perpetuated far

---

[48] Burke, as quoted before, goes on to say: "To talk of balance of power to the governors of such a country, was a jargon which they could not understand even through an interpreter. Before men can transact any affair, they must have a common language to speak, and some common recognized principles on which they can argue, otherwise all is crosspurpose and confusion."

beyond the time their control over territory and people has ceased, if it ever had begun.

This kind of policy started with the emergence of exile groups or exile governments, claiming to be the only legitimate representation of their respective nations or peoples, after the Bolshevik Revolution and then with the rise of the Italian, German, and Spanish fascist regimes. Sometimes, a territorial "remnant-headquarters" like Formosa serves to corroborate the claim. On each side of the "curtain" largely fictitious groups are thus maintained diplomatically, sometimes not only because they are felt to be related to the cause but also because they are considered politically serviceable: at the very least, they can serve to maintain claims to future repossession. If it is a Western purpose sometime in the future to regain the Chinese mainland, Chiang on Formosa will do as the visible symbol of such an intention; a similar purpose may be symbolized through the continuation of Latvian, Estonian, and Lithuanian diplomatic representation in Washington, which represents a policy of "nonrecognition" of the *de facto* situation in regard to the Baltic republics.[49] Such recognition or nonrecognition policies have been paralleled on the Soviet side when certain "liberation" groups or "liberation" governments were recognized during a civil war or occasionally even when still outside the territory to be "liberated." Needless to say, in such instances ideas and words of the two sides, divided as they are by their "world views," no longer have reference to the same "things."

Another illustration of the same confusion can be drawn from the ancient problem concerning the "identity" or "continuity" of states in case of revolutions or changes in

[49] Lack of consistency in these policies, which is characteristic of the whole history of nonrecognition since the enunciation of the Stimson Doctrine in 1931, is illustrated by the contrary policy followed in regard to the Eastern European satellites.

territory. In former times nations were usually agreed that even far-reaching changes in boundaries or internal structure of a country were internationally irrelevant so long as the country in question remained recognizably the same territorial unit. Again in more technical language: To well-defined territorial units as units of international relations there applied recognized rules of customary international law which stated, for instance, that even far-reaching and revolutionary changes in· their internal government and structure were not to affect their continued existence as the same "legal person" in relation to the others. Today, owing to bipolar ideological splits, there are many twilight situations where agreement about which unit is identical with what area is difficult to attain. Where, for instance, is pre-Second World War Germany today? Is it continued in the (Western) Federal Republic or the (Eastern) Democratic Republic, or in a Germany comprising both but represented, in Western eyes, through the Bonn regime, in Eastern eyes through that of East Berlin? Or has it ceased to exist? In that event, what has taken its place? Similar problems exist in respect to other *de facto* partitioned, although legally still somehow "united," units, like Korea or Vietnam. Traditional criteria are seldom applied in these instances, and new ones differ because of the different ideologies and interests. As in the famous case of the term "democratic" used in the Yalta "agreements," common language conceals divergent concepts. What to some appears as legitimate rule by consent on the part of formerly "exploited masses" is sheer tyranny to others. What to one side appears to be self-determination of a nation through free elections may constitute fraudulent corruption of the people's will to the other side. An ever so minute but "class-conscious" group of "toilers," in sympathy with the "camp of peace and democracy," in Moscow's eyes represents a nation more genuinely than its numerical majorities, while, conversely, in Western eyes, slave workers, underground opposition, or other suppressed portions of a Communist-controlled population constitute a more legitimate representation of the respective nation than do those controlling it through terror and indoctrination. As the preceding sentences indicate, language in international relations now tends to consist primarily of "fighting words," no longer suitable to discussion and peaceful agreement, but fit only for clubbing the opponent.

What then is "Germany," or "China," or "Indo-China" to the parties concerned? There is hardly hope of diplomatic agreement if there is not even agreement on the meaning or identity of the objects of agreement. Whether, despite bipolar ideological confusion of language and concepts, a minimum agreement on terms and notions might yet be attained will be discussed at a later point. What is to be stressed here is the trend toward a divergence in concepts and attitudes which not only renders a policy of balance of power more difficult to operate but endangers even the continuation of mere "peaceful coexistence" of the two opposing worlds.[50]

Ideological bipolarity may eventually lead to the domination of all bloc relationships by assumptions of "conspiracies," that is, beliefs on either side that the other side is conspiring aggressively against it. Because the two sides are divided ideologically, it is easily assumed that policies, at least "on the other side," are exclusively controlled by ideological considerations. "Conquering the world for Communism," then, is considered the only and the overriding motivation of Soviet

---

[50] The term "peaceful coexistence" illustrates the present Babylonian confusion in language too. Meaning "objectively" nothing more nor less than the continued side-by-side existence of the two blocs without all-out war, it has been used by Soviet propagandists to indicate a situation in which the West ceases to put obstacles in the way of "peaceful" Communist penetrations, while in the West, for this very reason or because it denotes the opposite of preventive war, it has tended to become synonymous with "appeasement."

foreign policy by the West. "Imperialist aggression," to the East appears the sole policy means of the West in its effort to destroy Communism. "Objectively," of course, both assumptions may be ill-founded. Supposing that it is the ultimate objective of Communist regimes to spread Communism all over the world, or, correspondingly, that Western countries aim at making Communism disappear eventually from the face of the world, it would still be rash to conclude that the more distant objective must control the more immediate policies in uniform fashion. Soviet policy, while naturally not omitting opportunities for the extension of Communist influence in the world, may at times be chiefly concerned with maintaining and defending what the Communists hold; and even where it turns expansionist, it would be naive to expect expansion in the form of military aggression only. Soviet leadership may well believe that time is on its side, and may therefore expect countries to fall to Communism by internal disintegration, or through economic penetration, or through foreign policy alignment with them. By the same token, while in the West, and particularly in the United States, there have been advocates of "crusade," "liberation," and "preventive war," they have so far been unable to control actual foreign policies. "Conspiracy" theories correspond to a boy's "cops and robbers" fantasy rather than to the more complex realm of facts and motivations in international politics. Even in the instance in which the term perhaps corresponded most closely to the actuality—namely in that of "Nazi conspiracy and aggression"—the phenomena were not quite so clear-cut as the Nuremberg indictments would have them appear.

Still, there is great danger in conspiracy doctrines. It lies in the very fact of their existence, in that they may come to be believed by the public and the policy makers in regard to the other power. Such a belief, then, by rebound as it were, motivates and justifies the first power's own conspiracy *policy*, and thus mutual suspicion affects decision making. To the extent that the West becomes convinced that the East is scheming to attack it, will it be inclined to counter this "conspiracy" by its own more active policy; this, in turn, may strengthen the Soviets' convictions that the West is out to attack, and cause them to take countermeasures, and so forth. Or, beginning with the East: To the extent that the Soviets believe they are being "encircled" in preparation for all-out war, will they be inclined to take counteraction, which, in turn, will strengthen Western suspicion that their immediate aim is "world conquest." Whether "Communist world conspiracy" here, or conspiracy of "imperialist aggressors" there, either assumption is damaging of any kind of foreign policy save one: a policy of preparation for war.

This vicious circle of suspicion and countersuspicion, then, leads to the insistence, perennially and drearily repeated in each side's propaganda war, that the other side must "give up its aim of world conquest" or its "aggressive imperialistic designs" before any concrete problem, such as disarmament, or German unification, or Chinese recognition, can be approached. With this type of mutual recrimination, not even day-to-day diplomacy is possible, since neither side can admit publicly of conspirational intentions.[51] Continued repetition of such charges is a one-way street which precludes discussion —except for propagandistic reasons—of any more concrete issue; rather, logically, it must result in crusading war. There is, indeed, a legitimate question whether, in view of the nature and threat of "the other" system and doctrine, bringing matters to a head and "having it over with" is not preferable to prolonged accommodation and "coexistence." This

[51] If, as happens, not only verbal confession but "tangible" evidence of peaceful intentions or change of heart is demanded, the situation is even worse, since practically nothing short of complete surrender or voluntary abdication by one side or one regime is likely to satisfy the other.

question shall be discussed at another point. Here the purpose was merely to trace the relationship between ideological conflict and bipolarity, and to demonstrate their general impact on international politics. The conclusion is that they allow, at best, a rigid and perpetually endangered equipoise which —this being a matter of terminology—may be called a balance of power, but, if so, one which is far from constituting a system that would guarantee powers against hegemony of the strongest. Ideological bipolarity in particular adds to the perils with which a bipolar "balance" is confronted, and, by the same token, shows up another—it may be *the* other— potentiality inherent in bipolarity, namely, that things will move toward a situation of "irrepressible conflict." Such a conflict, in turn, would result in the replacement of bipolarity with something which would leave no "system of international relations" at all any longer. Rather, the final result would be either hegemonical control of and by one of the contesting powers or—more likely—mutual annihilation.[52]

[52] Supposing that global war leaves anything; it would be ironical, indeed, to find in the end that the crusade had not destroyed the vanquished cause after all but merely driven it underground. It is not likely that a world controlled by Communism would be in a position to extirpate "freedom movements" altogether; nor is it likely that American world control could root out all Communist ideas and movements. Soviet control could hardly hope to stifle everything, nor could the West, unless it solved all problems of economic and social injustice or racial and other inequalities, so as to prevent something like Communism from exploiting dissatisfaction. Under world control by one superpower such suppressed ideologies and movements might even regain that "idealism" and appeal which they lose when they are in control themselves.

8

The Impact of the New Weapons

The impact of bipolarity on international politics which we have investigated can be deemed comparatively clear-cut. Despite the difficulties that are always involved in applying traditional concepts and ways of thought to a new situation, it is possible to talk meaningfully about what happens to national power and interest, to sovereignty and independence of larger and smaller nations, to alliances and balances, when power becomes concentrated at two poles. To be sure, under such conditions, it may well be that accustomed concepts must be adapted to the new situation, as for instance, when the sovereignty and independence of certain countries are affected by the extension of the hard shell of defense from the old-style territorial unit to the bloc; or that traditional relationships or systems of relations must be reinterpreted, as for instance, when alliances turn to some extent into dependency relationships, or a balance of power changes from a multiple into a bilateral and rigid one. But there remains at least meaning in the basic terms themselves, in "power" and "power unit," "increase" or "decrease" of power or influence, and even in "territoriality" as the underlying structural factor in modern international relations. And so long as we regard the power of nuclear weapons as merely another addition to an existing arsenal which increases the military strength of nations (or of some nations) without affecting the essence of power and power relations, we can still conceive of a bipolar world system as one built on the traditional impermeability and relative security of separate and distinct units—in this case not the now too small nation-states but, except for the uncommitted units, rather the blocs and defense systems which now constitute the hard-shell-rimmed entities of territoriality and security.

But this cannot be done. To conceive in this manner of the new weapons and their impact would constitute a radical misconception of their nature and effects. I have pointed out earlier that part of our consciousness and even part of nations' policies still proceed on the preatomic level of assumptions. This is only natural in view of the newness and unprecedentedness of developments in this field. Indeed, so radical is the new departure, so bewildering the continuing rate of change that one is inclined to question whether any meaningful framework of concepts relating to any coherent power system and to any consistent foreign policy can be built up at this point. As the Austrian critic of culture and language, Karl Kraus, remarked when faced with a phenomenon that stunned even him, "On Hitler I have nothing to say," so nuclear developments seem so unfathomable in their effects as to make them appear no longer "à la mesure d'homme." But we have to advance into this unknown even though the result of our probing may be uncertainty or, worse, contradiction.

AMBIGUITIES IN THE EFFECT OF THE NEW WEAPONS

One of the tenets of the new physics is that "the traditional doctrine of the distinct independence of each bit of matter should be replaced by an emphasis on the pervasive presence of everything everywhere."[1] If we apply this tenet to the realm of nations and their status in the atomic age, it means that the decisive change is from "distinctness" and "separateness" to "pervasion," to the absolute permeability of each unit by each of the others, so that the power of everyone is present

---

[1] A. H. Johnson, in "Introduction" to A. H. Johnson (ed.), *The Wit and Wisdom of Alfred North Whitehead* (Boston, 1947), p. 10.

everywhere simultaneously. There is, or will be, unlimited might, the capability to inflict absolute destruction, which will go hand in hand with absolute impotence, that is, the impossibility of defense against the same infliction on the part of the others; complete lack of "security" within the most accomplished, the most powerful "security" systems ever devised; disappearance of the protective function of the state, or the bloc, despite all its might and power.

It is true that we have not gone quite that far yet. I was projecting present tendencies into the future. What distinguishes the present from the future are the still existing—partly technical, partly political—limitations of nuclear power. Thus, not all, or even many, units possess the new weapons or the faculty to make them; but where there was only one at first, and then two, there are three right now, and there will in all probability be more. And, the less powerful fission weapon left some chance for effective defense; it may be that some measure of defense is still possible against effective delivery of the H-bomb today. But it seems safe to say that with further improvement of the weapon and the means of delivery these chances for defense will become ever more slim. We are in the transition stage, conceptually as well as factually. We are in a twilight zone for another reason as well. We do not yet know what kind of system and what kind of policies will actually be adopted for and within the new structure which the new weapons will determine. It is conceivable, for instance, that certain powers will bank on means other than all-out war as the primary means of policy, or that even all major powers, and particularly the superpowers, will somehow agree to forego the use of the new weapons. All this proves that, in studying the impact of the nuclear weapon, it will not do to start from the assumption of its most extreme effect, as it were. Even when assuming that a situation will materialize in which the weapon will have its ultimate effect, we must still remember that we are in an interim period. We need to know how much it counts now. The trouble is that as we try to do so we are overwhelmed by the rapidity of change: what I write today may no longer be valid at the time this book is published. Therefore I shall not venture to ask at the outset the fundamental questions, such as, what is going to happen to sovereignty, to power, etc.? but rather, shall pose those more specific questions which are more immediately connected with the concrete situations as we find them in the world to-day, such questions as, what will happen to certain specific kinds of power, or to certain kinds of powers, under given circumstances? Answers to such questions are, I believe, more readily and more safely deducible from the atomic factor than those concerning the broader problems.

We may begin with what used to be known as "power factors," or "power elements," those factors which entered into an assessment of "national power" and which one "added up" in order to arrive at comparable over-all appraisals. Size, location, configuration of territory, quantitative and qualitative aspects of population, economic and above all industrial development, and, of course, military strength, actual as well as potential, were among the chief traditional power factors comprising the total power of different nations in their mutual relations. What happens to some of them under atomic conditions can be perceived. Like atomic power itself in its effect, they tend to become ambiguous, contradictory in themselves, "positive" and "negative" power factors in respect to over-all power at one and the same time. "Industrialization," for instance, which is still—and especially now—a necessary condition for military and, in particular, atomic strength, simultaneously renders a country more vulnerable because industrial and urban concentrations must be among the chief targets of atomic warfare. Lack of industrial development, while "negative" in its impact on a country's power status in the traditional sense, on the other hand becomes an asset in nuclear times because it makes the country in question a less likely victim of atomic attack. Compare, in this respect, China and the United States. There is no doubt that the very basis of American superpower status, its economic-industrial strength, renders its great urban-industrial areas primary targets for atomic attack. China, inferior to the United States so far as traditional power assessments go, is much less vulnerable in this respect, and "atomic superiority" in a United States—China conflict could not so easily be brought to bear upon that country, a fact which may have played a deterrent part in American policies toward Peiping China.

"Location" becomes similarly ambiguous. On the one hand, that protection through distance, "ocean walls," and so forth, that used to give countries like the United States security from attack upon their own territory vanishes when everything is in reach from everywhere, as it is, or will be, when countries' intercontinental missiles have become operative. In addition, there also vanishes the difference between "front line" and "rear," when countries near the formerly protective outer shell were more endangered, and the central unit protected. "Frontier area" may even be safer, "rear" in greater danger. Contrariwise, remoteness and "out of the way" location vis-à-vis major contestants in the atomic race may become a "positive" power factor, when, for instance, a country is underdeveloped and thus offers little temptation to either side. This does not imply, of course, that such a nation thus becomes more "powerful" in the traditional sense of the term but simply that it may be better protected than the traditionally "powerful" ones are in our day. But even in the case of the latter, a power factor such as "location" may occasionally gain or regain its "positive" nature, while simultaneously having the "negative" effect just outlined; this again attests to the ambiguous impact of the new developments. If we take Britain for an example, we see that no major country is in more mortal danger of instant annihilation (the surrounding "silver sea" no longer, of course, being protective "in the office of a wall"); but one element which used to be adverse in preatomic times, namely, her distance from overseas regions from which she had to import food and resources in war, no longer constitutes a "negative" power factor in all-out war. A war of that type will be decided one way or the other within so short a period of time that overseas communications will no longer be material; whatever Britain needs in order to resist or counterattack will have to be available within the country at the time the war breaks out. But, we may ask, would a country like Britain, in view of its exposure and vulnerability, be in any position even to envisage resisting nuclear attack or counterattacking? This leads us to a brief consideration of how intrabloc relations are affected by the nuclear factor.

We have seen before how bipolar bloc integration affects the relations between superpower and "allies" by reducing the latters' independence to a greater or lesser extent. The first impression of the effect that nuclear power as possessed by the superpowers has on these relations is that it increases the dependence of all the others within the blocs. For a small and exposed country, becoming part of the defense structure of a superpower or a bloc may be its chief, indeed its only, avenue of protection against major attack, its only guarantee of survival as an independent unit in case of a major war. Simultaneously, however, this makes it a major target for atomic attack by the other superpower, which otherwise would, or might, by-pass it. Sovereignty or independence of such a country is thus in double jeopardy, namely, in regard to its own superpower, to which it is "allied," and in regard to atomic penetration on the part of the other superpower.

Any "remnant sovereignty" in this connection seems to depend on whether and to what extent a base-country (thus may we refer to the unit where bases or similar installations have been established) is still in a position to arrive at vital decisions alone, for instance, as to whether to stay neutral in war, whether or not to allow other powers (including its super-power) to use its installations in the event of war, whether or not to permit them to inaugurate military action on its territory, such as launching "the Bomb" or the missile from there. Discussion within the Atlantic alliance so far (with regard to who has the right to decide about use of the atomic weapon, the United States alone, or the United States in agreement with its allies, or with some of its allies) [2] seems to indicate that questions of this sort are, as usual, left "in the air." Whether a paper answer is written into the text of some pact or not, it would appear that the real answer is likely to be given only when it comes to what the Germans call the *Ernstfall,* i.e., during an actual crisis or at the outbreak of large-scale hostilities. There is then a whole welter of possibilities, and it will probably depend on actual power, controls, interests, possibly personalities involved, whether or not such permission will be requested and obtained, whether, in case it is refused, the stronger power or powers will do what is deemed necessary anyway, whether or not this will lead even to conflict between "allies," and what not. Similarly, the degree of independence or dependence of nations of the Eastern satellite type may well be revealed only in and through such an *Ernstfall.* If I were to venture any prediction at all, it would be to the effect that what is most likely to be revealed in these contingencies is the loss of actual freedom of decision which the status of being part of the

[2] On this see, for instance, the discussion in *NATO: A Critical Appraisal,* report prepared by Gardner Patterson and Edgar S. Furniss, Jr., on Princeton University Conference on NATO, Princeton, N.J., June 19–June 29, 1957, p. 38.

hard-shell defense of a bloc conveys upon the units concerned under the conditions of the nuclear age.

The impression of increased dependency is heightened when one looks into the impact of the nuclear factor upon bloc nations' relations with countries and areas outside the blocs. One might have assumed that they are still somehow independent in this connection. But since there are very few regions, and problems, left in which the superpowers are not interested, their nuclear power is usually felt there as well. The Suez crisis of 1956 showed, as in a flash, some implications of the nuclear age on power and its use in the conduct of foreign relations. It proved that powers like France or even Britain ("minor nuclear power" though she is) have little discretion in the conduct of their affairs even toward a minor country if the latter is backed up by the nuclear threat of its "protector." It is true that in this instance France and Britain lacked the backing of their superpower. To what extent nuclear threats may be neutralized by deterrent counterthreat will be discussed below. As the simultaneous Hungarian events showed, such deterrence may be effective. In the absence of this sort of counterprotection, however, Suez was a "demonstration of their [Britain and France's] impotence" [3] in the face of a nuclear superpower.

Realizing their increased dependency on their superpower in the face of nuclear threats issued by the other, "allies" have tended to see in the development of nuclear power of their own a way toward a "new freedom." But pending such a development, we can already see—as we saw it in connection with the impact of bipolarity—that there is a dialectic element in these relationships: dependencies are never one-directional, and the reverse side of the picture of allied dependency is the influence they may be able to bring to bear on the leading

[3] Henry A. Kissinger, *Nuclear Weapons and Foreign Policy* (New York, 1957), p. 251.

power itself. The very fact that base-countries incur grave risks in case of all out war provides them with grounds to intervene should the superpower or stronger ally engage in too active or bellicose a policy or venture. Thus Britain and other European powers had a chance to influence American policy not only in Europe but even elsewhere when they could argue that an American Far Eastern policy involving a threat of war there might eventually involve them too; they then have demanded at least consultation. As the British have said, "No annihilation without representation."

Especially within NATO this dialectic of dependence and counterdependence has complicated alliance relationships ever since their inception through mutual suspicion regarding *who* needs whom most, and *who* will defend whom? At a time when the United States was still protected through distance from immediate nuclear attack on her territory, the suspicion involved mostly the readiness of her allies to participate in common defense. Would the European nations—more directly vulnerable to nuclear attack—fulfill their commitments if war involved the two superpowers first? What would happen if the Soviets should couple an attack on United States troops in Germany with an ultimatum threatening the other NATO partners with nuclear holocaust unless they immediately declared their neutrality? But already at that time there also existed the opposite fear, namely, that the United States might abandon Europe in the event of a Soviet attack on some NATO power or area not deemed "vital" to American interests or defense. With the United States in reach of Soviet nuclear weapons the question of whether this country will help if it means sacrificing her own cities has come to the fore; but of course there is still the suspicion of an—enforced or voluntary—European neutralism or neutrality in the event the United States needs help. Both sides are in danger of developing a kind of "split personality."

The United States wants to be sure that her allies will side with her in any event, but also resents the idea of being "pulled in" by them. Her allies, on the other hand, want United States bases as guarantees of American involvement and United States troops in Europe as "hostages," but at the same time they do not want them in as much as their presence might "pull *them* in" and render *them* vulnerable as targets of nuclear attack.[4]

Would building up a nation's own nuclear power be a way out of these dilemmas and dependencies? The importance of possessing such weapons, and therewith some power over strategically vital questions like choice of targets in case of atomic war, was stressed by Churchill when he undertook to justify Britain's decision to produce her own H-bombs. He said:

Unless we make a contribution of our own . . . we cannot be sure that in an emergency the resources of other powers would be planned exactly as we would wish or that the targets which would threaten us most would be given the necessary priority . . . . I cannot feel that we should have much influence over their policy or actions while we are largely dependent, as we are today, upon their protection.[5]

Since then Britain, more even than the United States, has chosen to emphasize nuclear armaments for nuclear deterrence at the expense of almost everything else. This involves tremendous risks, as the defenders of the British White Paper of 1957 themselves realized: "Deliberately to make ourselves a greater target is a grim undertaking, but, given the need for economy in defense, it is probably the best way out."[6] Rationally, it would appear, a division of labor taking into consideration the capabilities of the different partners—such as

[4] As a West German publication once put it: "The only thing worse than the presence of American forces in Germany would be their absence."
[5] Speech in Commons, March 1, 1955 (New York *Times*, March 2, 1955).
[6] *Manchester Guardian Weekly*, February 2, 1957.

leaving the task to provide for nuclear force to the United States while letting the others provide for conventional armaments and, so far as is still necessary, bases and similar facilities—would be a better "way out," even economically. For the building up of both nuclear and conventional machinery for war is so expensive a task that only the collaboration of a huge bloc of countries would seem capable of coping with it. Adding France and, possibly, West Germany and others to the roster of allied nuclear powers would bring about the opposite of the desired result. By making each power more independent it would also render each of them less able to retaliate effectively (or to threaten such retaliation), while it would make it more difficult to bring the combined weight of the alliance to bear upon the opponent. Simultaneously, coping with conflicts in which the nuclear weapon is not usable becomes more difficult with the weakening or absence of conventional arms. The present trend is largely irrational or emotional; it reflects nostalgia "for a time when security was absolute and control over a great power's survival rested entirely in its own hands." [7] Thus, strangely, an extreme urge to be up-to-date technologically and strategically combines with a lack of insight into what the nuclear factor really implies in this connection: the demise of the defensibility of independent units, whose hope for survival can lie only in the deterrent function of superpower nuclear capacity, coupled with availability of nonnuclear force, to deal with the outbreak of actual "conventional" hostilities. As nuclear powers, nations such as the European NATO countries can hardly become equals of the superpowers at this stage of development, if solely for economic reasons. But they are still vital for balancing the Eastern bloc in a coordinated system of "division of labor."

In one sense, it is true, one might perhaps say that "allies"

---

[7] Kissinger, *Nuclear Weapons and Foreign Policy*, p. 276.

in the atomic age are those powers which themselves have developed atomic weapons and that which goes with them (planes, missiles, etc.), as well as those to whom they entrust atomic weapons and/or the secrets connected with manufacturing and using them. Other countries in blocs and defense systems would be "satellites," without the standing and influence the atom powers would enjoy and used primarily as bases for atomic warfare, or as areas for communications, supply lines, or, lastly, as manpower reservoirs. Under these criteria, Britain today would be a genuine ally of the United States, and so, probably, would Canada, while France would still be a "satellite." This would correspond to, and partly cut through, the distinction made previously between "allies" and "satellites" on the basis of degrees of discretion in regard to bases, freedom from stationing of troops, etc. But under conditions of total nuclear power both distinctions become ambiguous. When nuclear power is not sufficient to deter, or to destroy the opponent completely, to have "some" of it may be worse than nothing at all in regard to a unit's security, while being a member of a more integrated bloc may lend some protection even to the nonnuclear units within it. The result is that what under nonnuclear considerations detracts from nations' sovereignty and independence, namely, integration into a bipolar bloc, has the effect of bolstering them up when the impact of nuclear power is taken into consideration.

How does nuclear power affect relations between nuclear countries (or others included in a bloc) and the "neutrals," that is, the units in what is usually referred to as the "uncommited" third of the world? I have already mentioned the fact—strange at first glance—that a country not tied to a superpower and its bloc and at the same time "out of the way" geographically and "underdeveloped" economically is in a way favored today, because absence of commitment lessens the risks of becoming involved in conflict, and remoteness as well as backwardness render it less worth a big power attack. In addition, it retains more room for maneuvering, that is, more actual independence in the conduct of its affairs. Thus units, under former standards inferior in power in every respect, actually may now have more of a chance to provide their inhabitants with protection than superior and even nuclear powers possess for theirs.

This is not to deny that there is a tremendous gap between the "power" (as measured in conventional terms: economic, military, etc.) of a superpower or other "major" power, and a "backward" nation. But even in this respect the nuclear factor reveals its ambiguity. It has been rightly observed that "although the margin of superiority of the industrialized over the underdeveloped nations has never been greater, it has also never been less effective," and this primarily because of an "incommensurability between the power of nuclear weapons and the objectives for which they might be employed." [8] It is not only for technical reasons that the nuclear weapon may be a useless weapon in relation to underdeveloped areas; it is not only that these areas do not contain "worth-while" targets for H-bombs. There are also moral and political considerations which might make it inadvisable to bring such awful power to bear on what appears to be a helpless victim. Above all, there is the impact of nuclear deterrence which can be observed not only in the mutual relations of the superpowers,[9] but also as an interdicting factor in the attitude of one superpower (or one of its allies) toward an uncommitted country. And this not only in regard to the application of nuclear power but to that of any superior force to the "neutral" unit. In this connection the Suez crisis again furnishes an example: It showed up, not only the impotence

8 Kissinger, *Nuclear Weapons and Foreign Policy*, pp. 127 f.
9 On this aspect of deterrence see below.

of Britain and France in the face of a Soviet nuclear threat but also Egypt's (relative and, as it were, borrowed) power as a unit shielded by its nuclear protector. Had the United States been the "aggressor" in this case, the result might well have been the same; or, inversely, it might be the same should the Soviet Union openly attack an uncommitted unit and the United States threaten nuclear retaliation. Thus deterrence, supposed to prevent attack in bloc relations, may have similar effects in relations between bloc powers and "third" countries whenever the other side is sufficiently interested in the latters' fate.

If, because of nuclear deterrence, resort to nuclear or even conventional force is no longer possible, what then can replace it, or its use as a threat, in the relations between nations? Have the nuclear powers in particular become so impotent that they can no longer apply even that kind of pressure which was behind ordinary diplomacy in classical times as the ultimate regulator of international relations? This would constitute another, and an ultimate, paradox in the effects of the so-called "absolute weapon." [10] Moreover, it raises a more general problem of power, one we touched upon in another connection, namely, when asking what could ensure "peaceful change" if resort to force was successfully outlawed in a collective security system. Similar to that eventuality is the situation in which unavailability of force renders it equally doubtful how a country can protect its status quo interests or its rights when harmed by action of another. Supposing the British and the French had vital interests or rights at stake in Suez, how were they to defend them without use or threat of force? Can anything replace

[10] See, in this connection, George F. Kennan's statements to the effect that "the suicidal nature of this weapon renders it unsuitable both as a sanction of diplomacy and as a basis of an alliance . . . . There can be no coherent relations between such a weapon and the normal objects of national policy" (*Russia, the Atom and the West* [New York, 1958], p. 55.

military power pending world government? Can diplomacy
retain efficacy without being bolstered by the *ultima ratio
regum?* On the other hand, it may be asked whether it is
realistic, under all circumstances, to base the concept of power
on the asumption of "ultimate violence." Is this what is done
in trade negotiations or similar day-to-day diplomatic relationships? We may concede that some kind and amount of
pressure and counterpressure must always be present in the
conduct of relations between independent units which "want
something from each other." But these pressures may be
nonmilitary, and economic especially, in nature; and at a time
when public opinion bears increasingly on the conduct of
foreign affairs, "moral" pressure may likewise assume increasing importance. But even where such pressure, for instance,
the economic one, would seem to give more "advanced"
countries an advantage over "backward" ones, the latter, if
uncommitted, may actually still hold the advantage: under
conditions of bipolarity they may, and do, play off one superpower against another. Threats to cut off economic aid or
similar pressures lose their effect if their object can turn to
the other side which may be waiting on the sidelines for just
this opportunity to enter the field. Such things go far in
explaining the considerable influence of noncommitted
countries in a world where power—in the traditional sense—
is concentrated so largely in the superpowers. Relative
strength of the uncommitted is nothing entirely novel, of
course; it could be seen in classical times whenever blocs
fought for the "soul" of neutrals. What is new is the enhanced difficulty for the traditionally most powerful to fight
such a fight when use of their military power is precluded or,
if not that, involves the danger of world destruction.

This dilemma would be heightened, and the stature of in-
dependents might be immeasurably increased, if they, or
many of them, should acquire nuclear power themselves.

Again, a problem is involved which not only affects relations to "backward" nations but constitutes an over-all problem in world politics. It has already been referred to in this book under the heading of "multipolarity," a system into which bipolarity changes when more than two opposing powers or power groups acquire nuclear capacity. What relations among nations would be like in such a system is hard to foresee. It might no longer be anything that could be called "system" at all, since this term implies at least a minimum of generality and calculability of attitudes and relationships. In principle, such countries acquire equal power status. True, as I have indicated before, possession of nuclear weapons as such does not necessarily mean equal power to destroy or retaliate, especially when nuclear units included in defense blocs with some amount of coordinated policy are involved. But when any number of uncommitted and uncoordinated units have this power, the situation may be different. There would be among them some who, whatever the consequences for the world at large, might be inclined to utilize their capabilities for the attainment of the most narrow and minute but to them the most "vital" objectives. The emotionalism and, in terms of world-wide policies, irresponsibility of some of these units or their leaders might add to this danger. The world would not only be at the mercy of each power as such but would also be dependent upon whoever—that is, which person, group, regime within each unit—was controlling the military establishment and had the final word about its utilization. So long as fairly stable and reasonably responsible regimes, such as the American, the British, and even the Soviet (which so far has proved cautious rather than rash) are the arbiters of the world's fate in this respect, there still is hope. What will happen if and when our fate depends on a new Hitler, or even merely a new Mossadegh, a Nasser, any new junta or *caudillo* of the Latin American type? The present superpowers might yet want to cooperate in order to forestall adventurism of this sort.

Even where such a situation was at first only a regional threat, it might suck in major powers. Thus, each power, and each power holder in such power, could for all practical purposes hold up the world. But since it, and he, would also be totally exposed to annihilating retaliation, there would be no saying who would bluff, or blackmail, or terrorize whom. There would also exist the possibility of instigating nuclear war between others without being personally involved. Suppose a "small" power does not want to attain anything for itself through threat of nuclear war but rather desires to involve two "big" ones in mutual destruction; who could find out whence the nuclear surprise attack had actually come and prevent the victim from suspecting its major opponent and from retaliating immediately and "massively" against *him?* Who, in such a world, could know anyway what came from where and what it was meant to imply? On the other hand, multilateral deterrence might at first be effective in such a system, which would mean that everything and everybody would for a while be frozen in terrified inaction until, most likely through failure of nerve, somebody would start the process of annihilation. Among all the various possibilities of future developments, this is the most unpleasant to envisage, and at this point it seems to be the most likely to materialize.

THE IMPACT OF DETERRENCE

So far as the relations between the superpowers are concerned, "deterrence" has been the major effect nuclear developments have added to or superimposed upon bipolarity. It is true that sometimes a policy to achieve the highest possible degree of atomic preparedness has been advocated not so much as a way to avoid the catastrophe of atomic war through deterrence but rather in order to be able to launch "preventive war" successfully at some point.[11] But most of those who believe in a policy of atomic preparedness, a majority of leaders as well as citizens, in America as well apparently as in the Soviet Union, profess to see in it a safeguard against the occurrence of atomic war. As a matter of fact, the belief that nuclear armament sufficient to strike an overwhelming blow against the adversary will, *qua* threat of instantaneous retaliation, deter· him from undertaking atomic attack or even from resorting to any kind of "aggression," has now become almost a dogma. And like all dogma it involves a tendency to take certain conclusions unthinkingly for granted: for instance, the optimistic one that fear of annihilation will lead to exactly the opposite of what is feared, a kind of *pax atomica;* the utmost threat of the greatest of all imaginable destructions will bring about peace on earth. In Churchill's prose, "it may well be that we shall, by a process of sublime irony, have reached a stage in this story where safety will be the sturdy child of terror, and survival the twin brother of annihilation." [12] This thought was voiced several years ago, and while it certainly cannot be said that a man like Churchill took this outlook unthinkingly for granted, too many have since repeated his words without giving much thought to the doubts and difficulties inherent in such a theory of deterrence.

A first problem concerns the relative atomic strength of the two superpowers: Is deterrence effective only as unilateral deterrence, that is, only in case the deterrent power enjoys

11 Thus "Ferreus," in his article "Courage or Perdition? The Fourteen Fundamental Facts of the Nuclear Age" (*Review of Politics,* 16: 395 ff. [1954]), leaves little doubt that this is what he wants to advocate. The New York *Times's* Arthur Krock is more devious in what seems to amount to advocacy of preventive war. In his view, a "military policy of striking an enemy before an assault he obviously is about to make" "cannot be burdened with the unpopular name of 'preventive war'" (New York *Times,* December 20, 1957). It is of course exactly that!

12 Speech in Commons, March 1, 1955 (New York *Times,* March 2, 1955).

nuclear "superiority"? Or will it have its optimum effect as mutual deterrence, that is, where two nuclear powers are in a state of nuclear equality, or "parity"? Those who believe that only a large margin of superiority can function as reliable and sufficient deterrence, point out that it was exactly such a superiority, an absolute one as it were, that deterred the Soviets from further expansion and aggression when the United States held its atomic "monopoly." We have seen previously that in those early postwar years America did use the atomic monopoly as a deterrent, that is, in order to maintain a balance against the Soviets, and not in order to establish hegemony. When the monopoly was lost, continuing superiority (or what appeared as such) was relied upon by many in the United States as the primary guarantee of safety. Only the maintenance of vast nuclear superiority, it was believed, could impress the opponent sufficiently to deter him from major aggression.[13] There existed, one is inclined to say, a Maginot complex in reverse, an uncritical, almost naive belief in the offensive power of the nuclear weapon and its capacity to work an atomic super-Blitz which might annihilate the enemy in no time, should it ever be necessary to "give him the works," while we remained safe from counteraction. But unless this approach is tied to an advocacy of preventive war (and comparatively few have been ready to so tie it), it suffers from at least one large fallacy: the identification of superior numbers of bombs, planes, missiles, etc. with superiority in the over-all effect of their use. Due to the "absolute" character of the nuclear weapon, there comes a point at which inferiority in numbers becomes meaningless because the "inferior" power is capable of reaching and destroying all enemy targets of any consequence. In other words, the "superiority" doctrine over-

---

[13] See, for instance, Thomas K. Finletter, *Power and Policy: US Foreign Policy and Military Power in the Hydrogen Age* (New York, 1954), *passim*.

looks the fact that in an atomic Blitzkrieg two Blitze are possible, and likely. Churchill, realist that he is, also tried to put minds aright in this connection when he saw a couple of years ago that

in three or four years time—it may be even less—the scene will be changed. The Soviets will probably stand possessed of hydrogen bombs and the means of delivering them not only on the United Kingdom but also on North American targets. They may then have reached a stage not indeed of parity with the United States and Britain but of what is called "saturation" . . . . "Saturation" means the point where although one power is stronger than the other— perhaps much stronger—both are capable of inflicting crippling or quasi-mortal injury on the other with what they have got.[14]

It has since become abundantly clear that "superiority" in this or another matter of detail can no longer prevent actual stalemate in the total picture. Whether one or the other power overtakes the competitor in this or that particular field, regarding this or that specific weapon or means of delivery, does not seem to be decisive any more, at least so long as effective retaliation remains possible to that side which at a given moment seems disadvantaged. Thus, whether one or the other side possesses ICBM's first does not matter too much so long as IRBM's enable the "slower" side to retaliate from territory closer to the opponent. Not realizing this, American overenthusiasts of "superiority" tended to become equally overdespondent when the Soviets suddenly appeared "supe-

[14] Speech of March, 1955. The following day President Eisenhower made a statement which stressed the same element in "the awful arithmetic of the atom" (New York Times, March 3, 1955). See also J. Robert Oppenheimer's recent statement according to which "it is a long time since we have had atomic plenty: weapons adequate in number for the targets of the strategic air offensive . . . . Those who have occasion to know our stockpile are terrified by them; everybody is terrified by estimates and assessments of Soviet capabilities. Total nuclear war has begun to take on that desperate, perhaps genocidal, perhaps suicidal, quality which was anticipated from the beginning" ("The Environs of Atomic Power," in Atoms for Power: United States Policy in Atomic Energy Development, The American Assembly, Columbia University, New York, December, 1957, p. 31).

rior" in the fall of 1957. Previously they had been almost ludicrous in their naive confidence in America's alleged superiority, never noticing (or, at least, publicly acknowledging) the inconsistency in their claims. Thus, there were boasts about the protective possibilities of Nikes or similar "anti-missile missiles," overlooking the fact that their possession by the other side, supposing the missiles actually were able to protect, would blunt our retaliatory threat, since our counter-blow would in that event no longer be effective. In reality, as most experts admit, no means have been discovered, or are likely to be discovered, that will provide adequate protection against an all-out blow. But this works to the disadvantage of both powers also. Or, SAC spokesmen and others would never cease bragging about the devastating blow, or "Sunday punch," the Strategic Air Command was able to inflict, not mentioning the other fellow's capacity to inflict the same on us; or, they would boast of being able to pinpoint all enemy targets, though, were this true, the enemy could probably do so too.[15]

Thus, excepting the unlikely case of a really decisive technological "break-through" by one or the other side, what realistically has to be assumed in a discussion of deterrence is not superiority (or any specific superiorities in detail) but that stalemate under conditions of "atomic plenty" or "saturation" which derives from the mutual capacity to retaliate with "absolute" power; that is, mutual, not unilateral deterrence. What does this mean? In discussing the deterrent effects of a nuclear equilibrium, Churchill, in the speech quoted before, went on to say: "It does not follow that the risk of war will then be greater. Indeed, it is arguable that it will be less, for both sides will then realize that global war would result in mutual annihilation." Can we bank on this? If we cannot trust in atomic superiority, can we at least rely on nuclear

[15] Unbelievably, John Foster Dulles was still talking in terms of nuclear "superiority" at the NATO Conference of December, 1957 (see his speech of December 16, 1957, New York *Times*, December 17, 1957).

parity, an atomic "balance of power," as a guarantor of peace? It is inviting to believe in such wholesome results of an atomic stalemate. There then opens up the vista of a pacified world where, in the course of time, the use of atomic weapons will *de facto* have been outlawed by common if tacit consensus; where atomic weapons, although still in existence, would be "used" merely for purposes of assertion of power, to "encourage" the continued peaceful behavior of the others; where periodic weapons demonstrations might be held, with, for instance, the atomically balancing powers, like so many whales, alternately blowing off their steam, but strictly within the limits of innocuous radiation and permissible fall-out. Everybody would know that nobody would "blow his top" in anger.

Unfortunately, again, it is not quite so simple as it looks.[16] We must be sure in our minds and policies of the specific circumstances in which deterrence is to deter; and since it is to deter mutually, we must, moreover, have clarity about the meaning of mutuality.

Considering the confusion of opinion and policy which we encounter at this point, it is necessary to reconsider the situation in its simplest logic. Under conditions of nuclear satura-

[16] How strong a temptation to engage in wishful or optimistic thinking can be even in the case of realists is shown by certain statements of Reinhold Niebuhr, who has spoken of the "fortunate recognition by both sides that large scale war would be suicidal for both victors and vanquished" and of the "recognition of the existence of a stalemate and of the impossibility of conducting a war with hydrogen bombs"; "the summit conference at Geneva was the symbol for this mutual recognition" (Reinhold Niebuhr, "Yesterday's Anticipations and Today's Realities," *Christianity and Crisis,* June 25, 1956, p. 81). Of the many similar utterances we refer to only one other, one by the military expert of the *Frankfurter Allgemeine Zeitung,* because it so candidly argues that that which must not be therefore cannot be: "No statesman or general is today still of the opinion that nuclear world war can be conducted as the continuation of politics with other means. The recognition of the theory of mutual deterrence is a first result of reason . . . . Nuclear armament proceeds with the proviso that one is accumulating an explosive which *one knows will never explode because it must never explode*" (Adelbert Weinstein, July 25, 1956; italics added).

tion—as we assume them here—each side is in a position to inflict nuclear devastation of approximately equal, namely, absolute, scope on the other; each of the two opponents, therefore, can be assumed to be deterred from doing so because each must expect that his opponent will react (retaliate) with nuclear force against him once he has used the nuclear weapon first. After you have suffered initial devastation you have nothing worse to fear and can, therefore, afford to inflict the same on your opponent.[17] From this it follows, on the other hand, that only if retaliation is threatened against *nuclear* attack can it have a deterrent effect. If it is meant to deter the opponent from less than this (for instance, from attacking by conventional means), its effectiveness becomes doubtful, for then it must either be bluffing or betray unreadiness to be deterred by nuclear threats made by the opponent. For, in that event, the opponent can be assumed to be relying on *his* power of nuclear retaliation to deter you from making good your threat. In a word, the threat of counterretaliation renders the threat of retaliation nugatory in such conditions. Supposing A wants to deter B from engaging in "ordinary" (that is, nonnuclear) aggression against A or against anybody

[17] Rationally, of course, there is no "reason" for the attacked, once his threat of retaliation has proved futile, actually to make good on his threat and retaliate; he will do so only to satisfy his "irrational" urge for revenge. However, prior to an attack (that is, during the period of "mutual deterrence") his determination so to retaliate must be assumed to exist, because otherwise the would-be attacker would feel free to attack, that is, would not be deterred. The dialectic implicit in the situation has been well formulated by Carl Friedrich von Weizsaecker: "If we try to get at the ultimate logic of the idea of protection through weapons which must not be used in actual practice, we seem to arrive at a mere bluff. These bombs can protect peace and freedom only on condition that they never fall, for if they should ever fall there would remain nothing worth protecting. But, on the other hand, they cannot protect us either if everybody assumes that they will never be dropped, for then the opponent can act as if they did not exist. Ergo, we must be determined to drop them if necessary, and this means that they may very well be dropped one day" ("Ethische und politische Probleme des Atomzeitalters," *Aussenpolitik*, 9:306 [1958]).

else. In that event, threatening all-out (that is, nuclear) war is illogical and probably ineffective as the means of deterrence, for, since B can be expected to react with nuclear force against nuclear action by A, A either does not really mean it (that is, he is using his threat as a bluff) or, if he is actually ready to inflict nuclear devastation even at the risk of being so devastated himself, he denies, at least for his part, the deterring force of the nuclear threat. Why, then, should A assume that B will be so deterred? To be even more concrete: Supposing the West wants to deter the Soviets from committing "aggression," can it rely on the effectiveness of its threat of nuclear retaliation under conditions of "nuclear plenty"? Doing so, the West would risk its own destruction as the result of Soviet nuclear counterretaliation. If the West threatens nuclear retaliation nevertheless, it can do so only because it expects the Soviets to be deterred by something (threat of nuclear war) which, in this instance, does not deter the West; in other words, deterrence would not be "mutual"; or it is not really ready to follow through and "take" Soviet re-retaliation, in which case its bluff may work, or it may not. But in the latter event—that in which the Soviets commit aggression and the West fails to live up to its threat of "massive retaliation"—it would mean a massive victory for the East and an equally massive defeat for the West. All of this naturally applies in reverse in the event the other side engages in such a policy.

Has not something like this been actual Western policy? It has indeed, and this is what makes Western, and particularly American, policy so doubtful under conditions of nuclear stalemate. So long as the West was genuinely superior to the East—that is, so long as the United States enjoyed an atomic monopoly, and even into the period when Western nuclear armaments were still vastly superior to those of the Soviets—there was at least some logic in the argument and in the corresponding policy of deterrence: Threat of nuclear action against "ordinary" Soviet advance could be effective so long as the Soviets were unable to inflict anything like equal atomic destruction on the West. At that same time, in view of the West's inferiority in terms of conventional arms and forces almost everywhere in the world and especially in Europe, this unilateral atomic deterrence was an effective—and perhaps the only available—means of policy for it. But even at that time the way in which it was implemented was open to grave objections.

In order to utilize nuclear retaliation as a means of deterrence, there must be some mutual understanding as to the conditions under which it will be used, for, if the opponent is left in the dark as to what he is supposed to be deterred from, he may through sheer misunderstanding involve himself and the world in nuclear war. The "deterrer," therefore, must threaten the "deterree" with something at least minimally qualified, that is, must couple it with certain clarifying conditions, for instance, that retaliation will come forth subsequent to specified actions on the part of the opponent. A simple, that is, unqualified, retaliation policy would involve the world in constant danger of atomic war. Policies perhaps meant to eliminate this danger have indeed been elaborated, but the qualifications usually attached to the threat were of such a nature as to enhance rather than decrease the difficulties inherent in the situation. The stipulation most common in Western statements concerning nuclear retaliation has been to the effect that retaliation will occur "only" in the event of an "aggression." Instead of clarifying the situation so as to leave the other side in no doubt about the circumstances under which it could expect retaliation and thereby deter it from resorting to steps which would provoke "instant massive retaliation," reference to "aggression" blurs the picture so completely as to make everything more doubtful than it would be without such qualification. This is because of the vagueness of the term "aggression," which—like the term "peace" or "democracy" in Eastern verbiage—has become one of the worst catchall phrases in the present dictionary of international affairs.

The problem of how to define aggression will occupy us at another point. Suffice it here to refer to a few statements in which the vagueness, indeed, frequently the meaninglessness, of the term is revealed. Secretary of State Dulles declared in connection with the United States defense commitment to Taiwan (Formosa):

The United States continues to evaluate the words and deeds of the Chinese Communist regime to ascertain whether their military actions, preparations and concentrations in the Formosa area constitute in fact the first phase of an attack directed against Taiwan and whether the United States must proceed on this assumption.[18]

This seems to imply that even prior to an "overt act," preparatory measures (or measures so interpreted by us), for example, troop concentrations, might be considered aggressive, and, if need be, would encounter atomic counteraction; but these measures were not further defined. Or, Senator Knowland is quoted as having said: "Any Communist gain anywhere by any means, including subversion," constitutes aggression.[19] In a similar vein, a former chairman of the United States Atomic Energy Commission, Gordon Dean, declared:

Let's tell them we will tolerate no debate as to the meaning of aggression. Such debate might take years. We'll know aggression when we see it. But if there be any doubt on this score let's make it plain that it is an aggression when a mortar or weapons carrier from the Skoda Works of Czechoslovakia is found next to a dead man from the Western world. That's enough. It is enough when a MIG, employed to assist an aggression,[20] can be traced to a Russian factory.[21]

18 See New York *Times*, March 4, 1955.
19 New York *Times*, November 16, 1954.
20 Note the circular definition of aggression by aggression!
21 New York *Times*, October 24, 1953.

Obviously, such definitions, or clarifications, tend to eliminate all limits. They include anything one does not like, anything which in someone's view may appear as a threat to one's "vital" or "national" interests. For instance, when "subversion" is included in such "definition," not only coups à la Czechoslovakia but Communist victories at some polls, or even the mere danger of such election victories, or an alleged "general influence" of some Communist organization over a non-Communist government, may all be included. They also leave everything undetermined and undeterminable in cases of contested boundaries or ill-defined territorial status. The lack of agreement on "what's what" in the relations between the two blocs and ideologies, which has been mentioned in connection with "recognition" and similar questions, here acts as an aggravating factor.

Now, under conditions of actual or approaching nuclear parity, there is, as has been shown, no consistency at all in threatening nuclear action as a deterrent against anything less than the opponent's first use of the nuclear weapon, for example, against committing undefined "aggression." But apart from this it is clear that the very vagueness of this kind of retaliation threat may turn more and more to the disadvantage of the Western powers. Suppose that the Soviets, getting stronger and bolder, should apply a similarly broad aggression test. They might then define as "aggressive" such United States "imperialist" policies as the signing of a defense pact with another country, or the establishing of military bases somewhere outside of United States territory, or the launching of balloons carrying propaganda material from the American Zone in Germany. Obviously, both sides would then have ample opportunity to start preventive war in the guise of "war in self-defense" (individual or collective) against "aggression." On the other hand, if the intention is not to have a justification, or pretext, for launching such a war but, on the contrary, to use this test merely in order to deter, it is a poor and dangerous way to attain the desired end. Assuming that the Soviets should, rationally, abstain from any action which might provoke atomic retaliation on our part, can we rely on their doing so if they know that almost anything they do might be considered "aggression" by us, that is, as ground for retaliation? Might they not, in the face of this uncertainty, be tempted to re-retaliate first? And, aware of this possibility, might *we* not prefer to "re-re-retaliate"? And so forth, *ad infin.* There is here a clear danger that, instead of preventing nuclear war, this policy might provoke it.[22] The Soviets, rather than forego everything which might conceivably be considered aggression by the West and thus rather than limit their freedom of action in what they might consider an unbearable fashion,[23] might be induced to start all-out atomic war "to get it over with." The same would apply to the West if the Soviets adopted a broad aggression test.

Supposing, on the other hand, that the Western qualification of its retaliation threat should actually deter the Eastern bloc from its more conspicuous policies of expansion, it might the more forcefully drive it into a policy of subversion, of "boring from within," economic penetration, and so forth, which, while potentially also falling within the broad aggression test, would lend itself less conveniently to atomic retaliation in practice. Korea, Malaya, and Indo-China have shown

[22] "We must realize that the threat of instant retaliation will not prevent war, and may invite it." Thus spoke Admiral Radford in 1949, when defending Navy views and interests against those of the Air Force. Then he also condemned the slaughter involved in nuclear war as "morally reprehensible." Wearing a different hat, as chairman of the Joint Chiefs of Staff, Radford subsequently emerged as chief protagonist of a "one-weapon" nuclear strategy (whose "morally reprehensible" nature apparently had been forgotten in the shuffle).

[23] As the examples mentioned above show, the situation might even include events over which they actually would have little control, e.g., the starting of hostilities by an overenthusiastic satellite, or "war preparation" on the part of China.

that whenever it is a problem of combating "populations" or "movements," of countering guerrilla action, or of fighting a war in a "backward" area or an underdeveloped country, the atomic bomb may be a less than ideal weapon, unless one is ready to start an all-out global war over the issue involved. If this is so, the indeterminateness of present standards of deterrence seems either to enhance the danger of atomic war or to force the East into increasing emphasis on "world-revolutionary" practices. Especially when coupled with a defense policy which discounts "conventional" war and "conventional" armaments, reliance on nuclear deterrence conjures up the gravest danger of an involuntary rush into the very conflict we want to avoid. It would be tragic indeed if for lack of preatomic means of force conflicts which might still be fought over in the traditional way would either involve the world in atomic annihilation or compel the West to retreat abjectly before Communist expansion.[24]

But is not this type of retaliation policy the only way in which the West can hope to "contain" Communism? Or at least, has it not been the only way so far? This is the major argument which the proponents of such a policy have presented in its defense. Without the threat of instant atomic retaliation, it has been contended, the East, with its vast superiority in manpower and conventional arms, would be free

[24] A suggestion to restrict "massive retaliation" to three grave contingencies has been submitted by William W. Kaufman (in *Military Policy and National Security* [Princeton, 1956], p. 27). These contingencies are: "an attack on areas which have to be regarded as of vital interest to us; the use by the Communists of nuclear weapons; and that range of actions by the enemy which demonstrates that there is a clear and present danger to our society." Of these, the middle one corresponds to the one I favor (see below); the others, I am afraid, offer no clearer standards for ourselves, our allies, and our opponents than the use of the term "aggression" itself. Even if the term "attack," in the first instance, is meant to denote military action only, the "action," in the third contingency, which is to be subjected to a "clear and present danger" test, might easily be defined as broadly and vaguely as it has been domestically by the United States Supreme Court in the Dennis case.

to commit aggression wherever it wanted to, and to overrun areas and countries vital to the West, such as Western Europe. Indeed, it is asserted that solely due to the atomic deterrent was all of Europe not so overrun in the years following 1945.

This argument, as has been pointed out before, bears some conviction so far as its historical reference goes. For, so long as the United States possessed an atomic monopoly, and the West was vastly inferior to Soviet armed force, it may be assumed that the Soviets, to put it mildly, would have been more active in their European policies than they were under the threat of atomic retaliation. But the threat has now become a wasting asset: It is the less effective the larger the counterthreat of Soviet atomic retaliation (or re-retaliation) waxes, and it may by today or tomorrow be altogether ineffective. And even assuming that there is still some effectiveness in the threat, is it, together with its concomitant, the danger of an actual nuclear war of mutual annihilation, worth maintaining? To put it differently, shall risking global hydrogen war be dependent upon the varying strategic situations and calculations regarding conventional war and conventional forces? Let those who assert that the Western position would be hopeless without the atomic weapon ask themselves this question: Supposing the atomic bomb had never been invented, would responsible leaders in the West have advocated giving in to the East without a fight because of "hopeless" inferiority? The answer can only be "no." We would then have tried to make the best of available possibilities; and even though the East might have overrun a considerable part of the world, there would have remained the chance of "liberating" it and of achieving final victory, as happened in the Second World War under similar circumstances.

Foregoing the nuclear threat for the case of "aggression" does not, of course, imply renunciation of the weapon as such; neither does it mean renouncing it as a deterrent. On the contrary, it can—and, so long as effective nuclear disarmament is not achieved—it must remain the foremost means of deterrence that can be relied upon to prevent a nuclear holocaust. The way in which it can, perhaps, best be used to such purpose is simple and was repeatedly suggested even prior to the advent of nuclear "saturation," in particular at the time when the decision to manufacture the hydrogen bomb was debated in the United States.[25] Now (or in the near future), under conditions of equal nuclear power of both sides to retaliate, it appears to be the only way which, outside of bluff or irrational behavior, makes nuclear sense. Each nuclear power (separately or by agreement) would declare that under no circumstances whatsoever would it use the nuclear weapon first. In other words, the weapon would be used exclusively as retaliation against the use of the nuclear weapon on the part of the other side; it would not be used in (alleged or genuine) defense against attack with nonatomic, conventional weapons, nor in defense against other types of vaguely or nondefined "aggression." The situation would then be clear and devoid of the ambiguities surrounding the term "aggression" as well as the other possible qualifications. Each side might, of course, still be tempted to break the pledge and use the weapon first. But it would thus automatically define itself as the "aggressor" and provoke the then genuine retaliation of the opponent. Since it appears to be difficult, if not impossible, to disguise a first use of the weapon (at least so long as there are only two chief atomic power blocs), the aggressor would be clearly revealed to the world, without the excuse of self-defense. No side, once committed by its own declaration, could use the threat for "blackmail" any more. The West

[25] I made such a suggestion at that time in a letter to the editor of the New York *Times* (February 12, 1950). Since then, and probably under the impact of the relentless propaganda for the official "antiaggression" line, less has been heard about this. It is likely to come up for discussion again when the implications of nuclear parity have finally been grasped.

would not be tempted to employ the weapon to "stop aggression," or for similar general policy ends; the East would not be tempted to use it in its belief that the West *might* do so for preventive purposes. Each power would know exactly when, and when only, to expect retaliation in kind; in all likelihood both would for this very reason abstain. When counteraction is likely to be as destructive as action itself, being "the first" no longer offers advantages. Thus would the innate deterring force of the retaliation threat have a better chance to come into operation. Nuclear power would become self-policing.

A familiar argument is sure to occur at this point. To announce to the world, including the Soviets, that under no circumstances except the East's own first use of the weapon would the West make use of its nuclear might, would seem to mean a standing invitation to the former to go ahead and get what it wants through nonnuclear aggression. Would this not, then, involve a gratuitous throwing-away of Western advantages? This argument was not even completely convincing at a time when the West possessed atomic superiority, for, as we have seen, the opposite of a certain and unambiguous threat, vagueness and ambiguity, might also invite aggression, or it might be inducive to indirectly aggressive policies and tactics of "peaceful penetration." However this may be, once the condition of parity prevails and the East can threaten the West as effectively as the West could and can threaten the East, any advantage in leaving the situation uncertain may accrue to the East as well as to the West. As a matter of fact, the recent development in Soviet attitudes, following the revelations about the East's nuclear achievements and potentialities, has been anything but reassuring. Far from even defining as "aggression" the case in which, as Mr. Khrushchev put it, "the rockets will fly," it has been left entirely to the concrete situation as it develops whether the threat will be intimated or made. This involves an "atomic blackmail" which can be tried at any international crisis. It can be tried not only to deter or stop actual use of force (as at the time of Suez) but also, when no such use of force is contemplated, merely to inflict diplomatic defeat on the West or to gain some other advantage (as during the largely synthetic Turkish-Syrian crisis in the fall of 1957). Thus it might now be positively to the advantage of the West to induce the East to adhere to a policy of self-limitation such as is here suggested.

There is one point in the "disadvantage argument," however, which holds some validity. So long as a nuclear power follows a strategy of "putting all its eggs into the nuclear basket," it deprives itself of practical ways to counter an opponent's nonnuclear strategies effectively. Then this power is indeed faced with a horrible alternative: on the one hand, unconditional surrender to any conventional attack, or even in the face of the threat of such an attack; on the other hand, the risk of launching the holocaust in any and all cases of serious menace to its interests. But this dilemma can be avoided. It cannot, to be sure, if the West goes on cutting down its conventional armaments and potentials and insists on exclusive or preponderant preparation for the "big blow." This, however, is a matter of policy, and not of "given" and unchangeable factors, such as "inadequate manpower," for instance. It has been correctly pointed out that "the combined manpower of the United States and its European allies has always exceeded that of the Soviet bloc in Europe. The disparity has not been the availability of manpower but the willingness to mobilize it"; [26] and, it may be added, the readiness to make the necessary economic and financial sacrifices which a two-way military establishment involves. Here again, it is necessary to emphasize the overriding importance of avoiding a "monoemphatic" approach to strategy in the nu-

[26] Kissinger, *Nuclear Weapons and Foreign Policy*, p. 308.

clear age, and of leaving various possibilities open so as to be prepared for both nuclear *and* conventional war. "Strategic doctrine" turns out to be a determinant of what is possible and what is likely to happen in the nuclear age, and thus even of the fate of the world. Surely, if ever war and its preparation was "too serious a business to be left to the generals" (as Clémenceau is reputed to have remarked), it is so today.

Supposing then that mutual deterrence "makes sense" if limited to the case of retaliation against the "first user," can we now confirm the conclusion, suggested previously, that it will be an effective guarantee of peace—at least in the sense of avoidance of all-out war? Two more questions have to be answered before that inference is warranted. These concern (1) what is meant by "nuclear" war and use of "nuclear" (or "atomic") weapons, and (2) what are the area and units to be protected by the threat of retaliation, or, upon whom is nuclear attack to be considered an attack on the retaliator? The first question concerns the question of "limited nuclear war" and related problems. They will be taken up in another context. Suffice it to state here the conclusion: None of the various suggested distinctions as to "graduated deterrence," targets, "tactical" as opposed to "strategic" atomic weapons, and so forth, seems to offer a sufficient guarantee against eventual (or even immediate) outbreak of all-out nuclear war; only avoidance of the first use of any and all "atomic" and "nuclear" weapons (in the sense of the fission and fusion weapons) might guarantee this.

The question relating to the areas and units to be protected through the retaliatory threat is a decisive one for the effectiveness of deterrence. If deterrence refers only to the political units which themselves possess nuclear weapons, nuclear force could still be inflicted upon all others with impunity. Supposing that the United States and the Soviet Union, having both declared that they would retaliate against the other side's first use of the atomic weapon, interpret this as referring only to a first attack upon their own specific territory or bases, there would be no assurance of retaliation in case the attack was launched against another nation, whether allied to the retaliator or not. This would still leave deterrence ambiguous. To render it completely unambiguous it would be necessary to extend the retaliatory threat to nuclear attack wherever it occurred. The United States, for instance, would have to make good on its threat not only in the event of attack against herself but also should Egypt, Israel, or Indonesia become victims. It would hardly be realistic to expect deterrence to become so comprehensive. As I have pointed out, its effectiveness lies in the consideration that, after one country has itself been assaulted with nuclear weapons, it has nothing worse to fear any more if it now inflicts the same on its opponent. What a country considers as being included in "itself," in other words, with what or with whom it identifies itself in this connection, depends on strategic, political, and general attitudes of the nation and its population. While it might not be entirely visionary to assume that sometime in the future we will be ready to identify ourselves with humans everywhere in the world, it would be too much to expect Americans (or Russians, for that matter) to risk their "national substance," their cities and all, for the sake of any indeterminate nation, or for the sake of establishing the principle of nuclear deterrence. But it may not be expecting too much to think that a nation might risk its existence if that of a close ally is at stake. We have discussed the doubts applying even here in dealing with the various problems facing NATO. Everything might be clarified on this point if nuclear powers, when declaring not to use the nuclear weapon first, would indicate (that is, list) those nations whose attack by nuclear weapons would result in immediate atomic retaliation. This in all likelihood would prove to comprise the units of the respective defense blocs and would thus reassure a super-power's allies at the same time its opponent was effectively deterred.[27] But might not the listing of protégés be misused by including all (or most) of the world? This is not likely. While politically there might be a temptation to pose in this way as the protector of all, the superpowers would be deterred from doing so because listing too many would involve too broad a commitment. The bluff might be called if, say, the Soviets, having listed Egypt, shrank from risking devastation of their own territory in the face of an actual threat to that country. Thus the device is in a way self-policing.

What about the countries thus left unprotected? They would in all likelihood include chiefly the uncommitted third of the world. It is true that deterrence would not work there, at least so long as those countries were not themselves nuclear powers. But there are compensations. First of all, the re-taliatory threat, although not certain in these instances, might be effective after all, and because of its very uncertainty. The Soviet Union, to take an example, might be deterred from attacking a "neutral" with nuclear weapons because the United States (or Britain), although not committed to do so, might yet choose to retaliate in such an event. And apart from this, the uncommitted are politically in not too unfav-orable a position. Under bipolarity, as we have seen, the po-sition of the more remote and backward among them can be relatively safe. Not only are they poor nuclear targets, it would also make a very poor impression on world opinion to

[27] It might also be necessary to list those groups of nations which the powers threatening retaliation would hold jointly responsible for the first use of a nuclear weapon by any one in the group. Otherwise, subterfuge might occur. A major power could make the weapon available to a minor ally or satellite through which it might want to commit nuclear attack. Joint responsibility, it is true, involves the risk that retaliation might be applied against a country not actually responsible for the at-tack; by the same token, it would encourage the major powers to super-vise closely their allies as to the nonuse of the weapon.

make them the victims of such cruel attack. Moreover, the status of all the neutrals is likely to be one of relative political strength. Both sides desire to be their friends or, at least, not to drive them into the opponent's camp. The system of deterrence here advocated would thus have its strongest effect where the tension is greatest, that is, among the bipolar blocs themselves; it would be doubtful in its effect where the danger of nuclear war is least. Such a system would clearly accentuate bloc formation. But it would also lend itself to the drawing of bipolar "demarcation lines" which, as I shall elaborate later, should be considered one of the primary means of arriving at a diplomatic adjustment of bloc problems. The blocs would in this way surround themselves with "nuclear hard shells" which, if the system works, would make the respective areas "impenetrable" again, with mutual prohibition of intervention.[28] Only beyond these lines, as outside the "amity lines" of yore, would the realm of a new-style "anarchy" prevail.

We may finally consider an interesting suggestion one student of the nuclear problem has made in terms of a full-fledged "collective security system" concerning the use, or rather nonuse, of the weapon.[29] According to this suggestion, all powers would conclude a pact outlawing the first use of the weapon, even if the first use was "defensive and against an aggressor who was delivering a heavy attack" with conven-

[28] This exclusion of interference would have one strange but logical result: no deterrence would apply to the use of atomic machinery within blocs; such machinery might, if technically feasible, be applied against "allies" or satellites such as Hungary, or even in civil war against one's own population. This would correspond to the unlimited "right of war" (even of unlimited and unregulated war) that governments had against "insurgents" within their own territorial jurisdiction in the age of classical territoriality.

[29] E. L. Woodward, "By Man Came Death," *Bulletin of the Atomic Scientists*, 11: 19 ff. (1955). See also the same author's earlier essay *Some Political Consequences of the Atomic Bomb* (New York and London, 1946).

tional forces. To this would be added a commitment, on the part of *all* powers, to apply atomic sanctions against the first user "without any reference to the political situation" and "however close the relationship of one or other of the powers concerned to the signatory who had launched the first bomb." The United States, for instance, would have to retaliate against Britain in a war with the Soviet Union if Britain was the first user, or Britain against the United States if the United States was the first user. For use of the weapon must be regarded as "an overriding act of treason to humanity." "The sanction is not against war; it is against atomic war."

Part of this plan is plausible, indeed necessary: the outlawry of the atomic weapon even where the other side was clearly the "aggressor" with conventional armaments. In other words, nuclear retaliation in conventional war would be impermissible even in self-defense. This much is implied in my own suggestion. But, while the unconditional character of the outlawry should be accepted, this plan's other features seem utopian. As has been pointed out earlier, genuine collective security cannot be had in a bipolar situation. It would be too much to expect powers lined up on one side of the "great divide" to turn around and actively assist—possibly even during the war—the enemy side. Something less along these lines, however, might well be within the realm of the possible: a commitment on the part of all concerned "not to make war on or participate in a war against a country against which an atomic weapon has first been used." [30] Although it may be doubtful to what extent satellites or even allies would be in a position to stay neutral or drop out of a war in such an event, there would at least be an inducement to inde-

[30] See my letter to the New York *Times,* referred to above. This suggestion is patterned on the undertaking of League of Nations members under Article 15, para. 6, of the Covenant.

pendent action and, conversely, a counterinducement for the would-be user of the weapon not to use it.

Have we now delineated a nuclear utopia? We must beware of overoptimism. Even if the system of mutual deterrence just outlined could be put into practice it would still be fraught with the many technical and political uncertainties which we have indicated. And beyond this, we must be aware of the fact that everything here depends on the rational behavior and the rational calculations of the powers concerned. Churchill himself, when putting forth his theory of deterrence, mentioned "a blank": "The deterrent does not cover the case of lunatics or dictators in the mood of Hitler when he found himself in his final dugout." The case of Hitler, of course, refers to a situation in which general although not atomic war has started and one side is about to be defeated. But this raises a second doubt. Not only in the case of a Hitler but in that of any leader of any power about to be defeated in a conventional war, it is more than doubtful that threat of retaliation can be relied upon to deter that power from using one more, the ultimate device "in desperation." Does one assume that in an all-out although nonnuclear war between, say, the United States and the Soviet Union, an America about to be defeated would shrink from hurling "the bomb" even though sure of instant retaliation? Or vice versa? Once war has started, the deterrent force of retaliation can be said to decrease in the ratio of one side's weakening to the other side's growing stronger in the war.

Even so far as initial deterrence is concerned, however, the problem is not merely one of "lunatics." It is the problem of the power of rational considerations quite generally. The history of pacifism and peace movements attests to the relatively low impact of rational thought in this respect. Norman Angell and others might prove ever so convincingly that war "did not pay" economically, but the argument failed to make the necessary impression. It has often been said, and history so far seems to prove, that frightfulness and destructiveness of new weapons are no guarantee against their use. It is the theory and expectance of the believers in nuclear deterrence that this will be different in the case of the "absolute weapon." And indeed, the new weapon is so extreme and "universal" in its effect that there may be some basis for a belief that its impact on attitudes and policies may also prove unprecedented. The ultimate difficulty lies in the uncertainty, on the part of all concerned, as to what "the other side" will actually do, that is, whether it actually will behave "rationally." This is the point at which what we shall later discuss as the "security dilemma" reaches its culmination. Each side, we may assume, wants to act rationally, but, not knowing for sure that the other side can be trusted to do so, each feels that the possibility of irrational behavior by the opponent must be included in its own calculations. For instance, assuming that rationally—that is, remembering the suicidal nature of nuclear war —the United States would not permit itself to be provoked into nuclear action, can this country rely on Soviet abstention from nuclear attack for similar rational reasons? Or can the Soviets, who may actually believe that the "imperialist" powers are ready to inflict the worst on them, rely on Western rationality? And if, knowing that the other side may be swayed by considerations like these, one side takes these amended calculations as yardsticks for its own behavior, what rational considerations remain? Policies then become so dependent on ever-reflected reconsiderations of what one believes the other side believes, etc. *ad infinitum*, that no sane calculations are any longer feasible. One is caught here in the vicious circle inherent in the problem of the effects of assumptions, of what has been called the possibility of an "infinite regress of effects." [31]   In the face of this prospect, as Herbert Butterfield says, "the mind winces and turns to look elsewhere." [32]

And beyond irrationality there looms an even greater danger. It lies in something apparently purely technical and as such even puny but in reality of ever greater importance: the possibility of nuclear war breaking out through misinterpretations of situations, misunderstandings of orders, or arbitrary action by subordinates. First, there is the possibility of misunderstanding a situation somewhere down the line by those who are in charge of "instant retaliation"; a speck on a radar screen caused by a meteorite or a swarm of birds or "electronic ghosts" may be mistaken for a plane or missile, or an unidentified plane or similar object might actually penetrate a radar line and be mistaken for an attacker, and this may cause atomic retaliation as an almost "automatic reflex action." [33]

Second, there may be misunderstanding or misinterpretation of orders on the part of bomber crews, crews of missile-launching submarines, or similar subordinate groups to whom a secret order or signal would be transmitted and who alone, without further action or participation by anybody else,

[31] "Like the limitless vista of images on two opposed mirrors, knowledge of each revised generalization produces a new condition which must be taken into account and results in a new set of circumstances to be considered—and so forth to infinity" (David Easton, *The Political System* [New York, 1953], p. 27). In behaviorist parlance this problem is known as that of "anticipated reactions." It may be doubted that even the theory of games as applied to international relations can cope with this one.

[32] *History and Human Relations* (New York, 1952), p. 23. See also his shorter essay on "The Tragic Element in Modern International Conflict," *Review of Politics*, 12: 147 ff. (1950).

[33] As Hanson Baldwin has termed it (New York *Times*, December 21, 1954); see also the same analyst's article in New York *Times*, February 4, 1958, and E. W. S. Hull, "A Steel Ring for the Iron Curtain," *The Annals*, May, 1955, p. 57: "The gun is loaded. It is as automatic as pushing a button. It could take even less to set it off; an accident, for example. An unavoidable risk."

would be in charge of readying and launching the death-carrying weapon; and this risk increases in proportion to the number and dispersal of crews which are up in the air or similarly held in readiness for immediate retaliatory action. Finally, there is a possibility of action on the part of such a group or its commander on their own, through "trigger-happiness" or overexcitement or similar psychological conditions. Some situation, order, or signal then may be "misinterpreted" on purpose, and the world thus plunged into nuclear war.

Especially when one imagines the state of nervous excitement prevailing at times of great international tension and war crises, such possibilities must be taken into account. It is difficult to see what sort of precautionary measures against such occurrences could be ironclad. And while in former times, in such conditions, similar misfortunes could also happen and did, their effect was comparatively limited, and the damage could usually be repaired with relative ease. Today, or tomorrow, an exchange of intercontinental missiles caused by inadvertence could—and in all likelihood would—destroy the countries concerned and much of the world. World destruction by mistake! This danger, in what Charles Lindbergh as early as 1945 called "an age of split seconds and of splitting atoms," [34] grows as authority to make decisions must be sub-delegated and decentralized, something that becomes more and more necessary as long-range weapons leave only minutes of warning time. "Instant retaliation" may ultimately become a matter for any missile battery commander, and the possibility of "war breaking out by mistake or inadvertence, perhaps even as a result of equipment malfunction," [35] cannot be

[34] New York *Times*, December 18, 1945.

[35] See New York *Times*, August 2, 1956 (statement by a "former Air Force research specialist"); see also H. Baldwin (New York *Times*, February 4, 1958): "Our reaction time will be still further reduced and the defense be confronted with a terrible question. Are those blips on the radar

excluded. We are at the mercy of almost incalculable things, and, in the face of this prospect, too, "the mind winces and turns to look elsewhere."

The foregoing was written prior to the spring of 1958, when the revelations concerning the Strategic Air Command's practice flights in the arctic area provoked a controversy which, perhaps fortunately, has drawn public attention throughout the world to the problems and dangers which have been pointed out above. For it must now be clear to every thinking person that even the allegedly and so called "fail-safe" system used by SAC is anything but fail-proof. Who guarantees that the bomber commander who is supposed to turn back at a given point unless he receives orders to proceed will actually do so? There can be no absolute protection from human aberration or failure, be it insanity or fanaticism. Moreover, what of the case where the object discovered on the radarscope, which caused SAC to dispatch its jet fleet toward enemy targets, remains unidentified during the few minutes available for identification? And finally, how are the Soviets, discovering approaching aircraft on their radar screens, to know whether this is a case of return or one of no return? The extreme danger pointed up by this situation should cause more general awareness of the desperate urgency of finding ways of easing tension, and of the pressing necessity for avoiding complacent reliance on a system of deterrence which by its very nature cannot be foolproof.

THE OUTLOOK FOR DETERRENCE

We have seen how much effective deterrence depends on at least a minimum of rationality, self-restraint, and ability to

---

screen moving toward our shores the real thing . . . or merely false alarms? There will be little time to decide and the consequences of mistake are disaster . . . . In the age of the missile, recall is impossible." See also B. H. Liddell Hart, "Die Gefahr der Bereitschaft," *Frankfurter Allgemeine Zeitung,* January 17, 1958.

subordinate immediate "national" interests to over-all world interests in avoidance of destruction on the part of the powers. It is at this juncture that attitudes and behavior patterns of those who make up "powers"—that is, people—and those who act in their name—that is, leaders—become decisive. What has the impact of nuclear developments been on them? If this question leads us to some extent into internal developments and the domestic affairs of nations, we must remember that there is a two-way relationship between nuclear developments and such affairs. Nuclear facts affect domestic affairs; in turn, domestic affairs, so affected, react on the nuclear world situation. For example, if nuclear factors render concentration of power in a few leaders within nations necessary, the way in which these few view nuclear developments and react to them in their decisions may be vital for nuclear strategies, foreign policies, and international relations in general.

It is hardly surprising that the paradoxical character of the unaccustomed new phenomena and the intermixture of the new with the still persistent old have had a bewildering impact on countries and publics all over the world. A good deal in recent foreign policies—with their often violent swings from one extreme to another, from "appeasement" and apathy to truculence and threats of war—and also much in internal policies— with their suspicions and hysterias, their secrecies and purges— can be explained by the fact that publics and often policy makers, while now aware of the new facts, are still at sea with respect to their implications. In the face of the new facts can old systems, institutions, and policies still be relied upon to safeguard traditional aims, interests, and ideals? If and to the extent they cannot, which new approaches, processes, and policies are to replace them?

In this respect statements of leaders and policy makers have for a long time betrayed much confusion. It is true that most of them have gradually become conscious of one foremost implication: the suicidal nature of all-out atomic war. Britain, one of the most exposed among the powers (in the old *and* in the new sense), was also one of the first to become aware of it. This is why Winston Churchill, early anti-Communist crusader and archprotagonist of a collective stand against aggression when collective security action was for the last time possible (in the thirties), gave up this "dynamic" policy after the Second World War. In doing so, the likelihood of race-suicide through war in the hydrogen age seems to have been his decisive motivation, since nothing permits one to believe that the old realist suddenly took flight into idealism. "Mankind has never been in this position before. Without having improved appreciably in virtue or enjoying wiser guidance, it has got into its hands for the first time the tools by which it can unfailingly accomplish its own extermination." [36] But also such disparate leaders, or ex-leaders, as President Eisenhower,[37] General MacArthur,[38] and at one point even Soviet leadership through the then Premier Malenkov [39] have seen that much.

Conclusions drawn from this premise, however, have been less clear-cut. MacArthur arrived at the—for him--strangely Jacobin or anarchistic inference that "the ordinary people of the world" will see to it that their "laggard" and power-befuddled leaders outlaw war.[40] Eisenhower, after his earlier pessimism, for a while emphasized a mere palliative, international agreement on peaceful uses of atomic energy. With him, many have

[36] *The Second World War,* 1 (Boston, 1948), 40.

[37] See, for example, the somber forecast in his speech of April 16, 1953 (New York *Times,* April 17, 1953): "The worst to be feared and the best to be expected can be simply stated. The worst is atomic war. The best would be this: A life of perpetual fear and tension; a burden of arms draining the wealth and the labor of all peoples."

[38] Address at Los Angeles (New York *Times,* January 27, 1955): "No longer is war the weapon of adventure whereby . . . a place in the sun can be gained. If you lose you are annihilated. If you win, you stand only to lose . . . . It contains the germs of double suicide."

[39] See his admission that atomic war would mean the destruction, not merely of "capitalism," but of "civilization" as such.

[40] Address at Los Angeles (New York *Times,* January 27, 1955).

come to believe that "atoms for peace" somehow would make "atoms for war" "go away." In the case of the Soviets, post-Malenkov leadership seems to have returned to Marxist-Leninist orthodoxy, that is, to the belief—by some means entertained even in the face of the latest nuclear advances—that, though nuclear war would spell the demise of imperialism, it would enable socialism to emerge victorious, in spite of the great suffering involved. It is of course impossible to know whether this kind of bravado reflects Khrushchev's *et al.*'s actual convictions or whether it has to be taken at its mere propaganda value. Churchill, as we have seen, has at times embraced the cheerful prospect that "the annihilating character of these agencies may bring an utterly unforeseeable security to mankind":

When I was a schoolboy I was not good at arithmetic but I have since heard it said that certain mathematical quantities when they pass through infinity change their signs from plus to minus—or the other way round. It may be that this rule may have a novel application and that when the advance of destructive weapons enables everyone to kill everbody else nobody will want to kill anyone at all.[41]

Subsequently, as has been shown, belief in permanent peace through mutual deterrence became so widespread that at one point (about 1955), a "Geneva spirit"—fostered by the (in personal terms) harmonious but otherwise resultless Summit Conference of 1955—seemed to presage a general *détente*. Since then, however, the combined impact of new and ever more harrowing weapons developments and new political intransigence has caused this optimism to wane and yield to new fears and deepening pessimism.

Thus the general picture is one in which confusion, despair, or easy optimism have been rampant. Since to arrive at consistent, rational solutions often seems hopeless, the inclination has been toward adopting emotional and largely ir-

[41] Speech in Commons, November 3, 1953 (New York *Times*, November 4, 1953).

rational attitudes, and policies which promise some kind of an easy, "wishful-thinking" way out of the difficulties. Desire to "give in," "keep out," or "get it over with" underlies advocacy of appeasement, neutralism, or preventive war. In the case of countries as well as group attitudes within countries such mutually exclusive attitudes are often found following each other in rapid succession. Frequently, there is also a quick succession of public alarm and worry, euphoric confidence, and general apathy. Long stretches of the latter have been particularly striking in the case of the United States. Earlier opinion studies [42] revealed an amazing degree of public and private indifference, leading to the conclusion that the atomic problem "has strikingly little place in the conscious life of the American people." [43]

It is likely that this indifference was at first due to the usual lag in popular awareness in cases of sudden new developments, similar to what happened when the advent of the air age destroyed the foundations of the traditional attitudes and policies of "isolation." After that stage there followed the period when a flight into the comforting expectation that atomic stalemate between the superpowers would have a permanent deterrent effect led to the new belief in "permanent peace." At that point it could be said that, "By and large American opinion has lost its fear of war as conviction of the deadly nature of war won acceptance." [44]

Whatever remains of apathy today, however, may be not so much due to lack of realization of the new or to overconfi-

[42] See, for instance, E. Douvan and S. B. Withey, "Some Attitudinal Consequences of Atomic Energy," in *Annals of the American Academy of Political and Social Science*, 290 (November, 1953), 108 ff. Another study, which, to be sure, was not directly concerned with the atomic problem, similarly revealed very little conscious concern with the dangers threatening from that quarter (see Samuel A. Stouffer, *Communism, Conformity, and Civil Liberties* [New York, 1955], pp. 66 ff.).

[43] Douvan and Withey, "Some Attitudinal Consequences of Atomic Energy," p. 108.

[44] Raymond J. Sontag, "History and Diplomacy as Viewed by a Historian," *Review of Politics*, 18: 182 (1956).

dence in deterrence but rather to conscious or unconscious suppression of latent fear. There often prevails a sense of impotence amounting to something like fatalism. This may lead to the usual inclination to leave the whole problem to others to worry about, for example, to "the people in Washington." Even nuclear scientists may thus "try to keep the tormenting picture of a future atomic war out of their consciousness, believing that there is nothing they can do about it." [45] J. Robert Oppenheimer, in his article quoted earlier, talks of the over-all sense of "oppression which any group always finds when it touches seriously any part of the problem of the atom." [46] There is thus a tendency to evade responsibility for grappling with the "mess" by always shoving it off onto the other fellow. People at large leave it to "Washington," or to "the scientists," the latter, claiming that these problems are not nuclear but social and political, defer to politicians or military experts, until, eventually, responsibility may come to rest on the frail shoulders of "social scientists," in particular, the poor specialists in international relations.[47]

Similar escapism reveals itself in public attitudes toward civil defense and related matters. It is quite understandable that the public has so far paid little attention to the obviously incommensurate and insufficient advice given it in connection with so-called "civil defense preparations." "Fraud" is perhaps not too strong a word for signifying what, in this con-

[45] R. L. Meier and E. Rabinowitch, "Scientists Before and After the Bomb," *The Annals,* May, 1955, p. 125.

[46] "Atomic Weapons and American Policy," *Foreign Affairs,* 31: 534 (1952–53).

[47] Albert Einstein, himself certainly no escapist but modest enough to recognize the intricacies of other sciences, is reported to have been asked once: "Why is it that when the mind of man has stretched so far as to discover the structure of the atom we have been unable to devise the political means to keep the atom from destroying us?" He is said to have answered: "That is simple, my friend. It is because politics is more difficult than physics." He must have felt that physics, as pure science, and politics, as combined thought and action, and enmeshed in the contingent nature of the world, are indeed incomparable.

nection, has been and still is being perpetrated against an un-wary public, particularly when, like the American public, in contrast to the European and other populations, it is entirely innocent of the effects of even prenuclear large-scale bombing attacks. It has been expected to believe that "Distant Early Warning Systems," air-raid sirens, or similar installations can protect in the complete absence of effective shelter, dissipation, or similar measures. It is like having a perfect fire alarm system without fire trucks and fire-fighting equipment. But most experts doubt that there can be any effective civilian protection in case of thermonuclear attack. What might be done by leaders is to take the people into their confidence and make them aware of the situation. Apathy, then, might indeed yield to alarm, but the latter can be beneficial if it leads to a realization of what atomic war implies and which policies might render it less likely to occur. One of the ways to render it less likely is by making mutual deterrence more effective, that is, by doing all that which communicates to the opponent one's readiness to retaliate. And one of the means of convincing one's opponent that one "means business" is to take those defense measures which make sense. While cities cannot be protected through shelters nor their populations through evacuation plans, decentralization of urban centers and dispersal of industrial plant in peacetime would to some extent reduce the effects of nuclear attack and in this way discourage it. However, what seemingly amounts to indifference of government as well as public at large has so far prevented any kind of concerted, energetic action in the United States, even in this field where action is promising, indeed necessary.[48]

If the public thus is apathetic, or over excited and alarmed

48 See, for example, Coleman Woodbury (ed.), *The Future of Cities and Urban Redevelopment* (Chicago, 1953), pp. 173, 204. Similar criticism concerning general neglect of problems of dispersal and related "passive air defense" measures is given by K. Knorr, "Passive Air Defense for the United States," in Kaufmann (ed.), *Military Policy and National Security*, pp. 75 ff. (especially pp. 87 ff.).

in an emotional, unthinking fashion, or else simply confused, another factor has no doubt contributed to the development of such attitudes: excessive secrecy. This, again, involves the danger that a nation, instead of working out rational policies to cope with the situation, will be surprised by one international crisis after another and will react irrationally to each emergency. Surrender to nuclear blackmail or else rushing toward—possibly even forcing its leadership to rush into—an avoidable all-out war may be the result. Under policies of secrecy the public is denied essential facts—frequently even those which would not be of "aid to the enemy"— and thus remains unaware of possible policy alternatives. The issue of whether to be prepared chiefly for all-out war or to have in addition sufficient means for conducting conventional war vividly illustrates the danger of making vital decisions without prior disclosure of essential facts and before full public debate is possible.[49] Such secrecy is liable to create a dual trend: toward oligarchism in decision making, and toward irrationality in public attitude. Official secrecy, superimposed on the general complications and confusions inherent in atomic problems, makes those policy questions over which the public still has some measure of control, appear relatively unimportant when compared with the life-and-death problem of war and peace; but the latter now tends to be exclusively in the hands of a few, who alone make or influence decisions: "The institutionalization of secrecy has concentrated, in the hands of a few people, control over decisions of a great magnitude for the values of a larger number of persons than in all probability were ever affected by any old-fashioned authoritarian

[49] "Issues could be raised on the basis of precise information about the exact nature of Admiral Radford's proposals, but by the time such precise information is available the chances are that the policy will be set and public criticism then will do little good" (James Reston, New York Times, July 15, 1956). On the general problems see Robert A. Dahl, "Atomic Energy and the Democratic Process," The Annals, May, 1955, pp. 1 ff.

leader." [50]   To a degree this is inevitable. Dependence on nuclear weapons may make quick decisions of a vital nature necessary. These, in the ultimate event, can hardly be arrived at through prolonged democratic discussion of issues. But the ultimate decisions may be prejudiced by preceding military and foreign policies which, in turn, were formulated without genuine democratic participation or consent. There is no reason why the people, prior to "emergencies," should not participate in the formulation of these policies. It is here that excessive "censorship" (in the sense of withholding information for security reasons) hampers public knowledge of those facts and circumstances without which the people, called upon to decide issues or, at least, to give consent to policies, cannot judge situations. When more and more government activities, far beyond the original "atomic secrets," become "classified," limiting information to prefabricated official news handouts, the public remains in that dark which nurtures irrationality. Who, then, among the uninitiated can judge the requirements for defense and defense establishments, and the related budgetary or other legislation? Who can judge what measures are best fitted to counter an alleged or real aggression? A comparison of how different democracies have coped with related problems (for instance, Britain, as contrasted with the United States in its handling of matters of "internal security") reveals that there is no inevitability that liberties and democratic traditions must be sacrificed; but the threat is clear.[51]

[50] Dahl, "Atomic Energy and the Democratic Process," p. 2.

[51] In the long run, it may well be that loss of democratic control over the most vital policy realm, coupled with a general feeling of impotence in the face of an "absolute" weapon, will create a decisive turn in public attitude toward public life in general. In the place of a rational approach to the great questions of life and society a state of mind may emerge which becomes more and more like that of prescientific, animistic ages; a state of mind full of irrational fears and apprehensions, in which fate seems to depend on unpredictable and irresistible forces that deter-

Authoritarian trends like concentration of power at the top (especially in the executive and, possibly, in the military), broad mandates rather than checks and controls, and restrictions or suspensions of individual or group rights rather than their jealous protection thus may weaken Western democracy. By itself this affects primarily the competitive strength of the West in its ideological-political struggle, where it tends to render its professed belief system less credible, rather than in connection with nuclear relationships. These, however, are also affected, and in two respects. One is that the trends toward decision making at the top more often than not have meant confusion of power and jurisdiction rather than streamlining; the other is the prevalence of "preparedness" considerations over everything else, in particular, over considerations of substantial diplomatic settlement. I mentioned earlier the unresolved state of policy making and decision making in regard to such fundamental international (or interallied) problems as the ones referring to the use of nuclear weapons in NATO relationships. Similarly, secrecy, uncertainty, rivalries, and jockeying for position appear to affect the domestic situation in the United States.[52] The shift away from the people at large and even from Congress in favor of control by the executive and the military hierarchies is obvious. But where within those confines is it to be? Will final control become a

mine human destinies in an a-causal way, and to which they are irretrievably subjected. Beginnings of such an irrationalism have come to the fore in many places, and not the least has been one of the traditionally most rationalistic and democratic countries, America. A study of McCarthyism in its relation to the atomic factor might yield interesting results. For while its connection with the issue of Communism is clear, its concomitants of fears and hysterias, anti-intellectualism and similar obscurantism, its rumors and easy acceptance of fantastic stories, are more likely due to vague, suppressed fears of what the nuclear future may harbor; fear and hatred of an external danger with which one does not know how to cope tend to be deflected toward an imagined or vastly exaggerated danger of internal subversion or conspirary.

[52] We know next to nothing, of course, about the Soviet picture in this connection.

matter of more or less chance personal relationships, involving the President himself, his personal advisers, some high officers or officials in the military, the Defense Department, the Atomic Energy Commission?

One thing seems to emerge a little more clearly, however, namely, the shift away from the influence of foreign offices and others officially in charge of foreign policy making toward that of the military. The very fact that technical developments of weapons and armaments in themselves wield such a tremendous impact has meant that they have almost come to dictate policies instead of policies determining type and choice of weapons, their use, amount of armaments, and so forth. In other words, instead of weapons serving policy, policy is becoming the mere servant of a weapon that more and more constitutes its own *raison d'être*. Correspondingly, in the United States, influence and controls seem to have been shifting from the State Department to defense agencies and military establishments such as SAC. What happened in the summer of 1956, the determination to stress "nuclear preparedness" at the expense of the "conventional" military establishment, is a case in point. All American foreign policy, its alliances, its relation to the other bloc, to uncommitted nations, and so forth, depends on what the United States does by way of military preparation. But despite this enormous impact of strategic policies on foreign policies, these decisions were apparently taken (or proposed) by the military, and—more significantly—not opposed by the Secretary of State, who on that occasion declared that "defense matters" were not in his domain.[53]

Still more significant and fraught with danger is the effect of weapons and their operators determining policies on the nature of these policies. In the main, it has meant that the approach to world politics has become ever more "military for military's sake" rather than "substantive." That is, we have forgotten

53 New York *Times*, July 19, 1956.

that the building of "positions of strength" was meant to gain the power necessary to negotiate the outstanding issues with the opponent. Instead, building up strength has become its own justification. Armaments, as well as all other undertakings designed to add to preparedness—including political ones like alliance systems—are now mere steps in the race for superiority, or at least parity, and the original objective of it all, settlement of the great substantive problems of the world, has been lost in the scramble. Diplomacy itself tends to be ever less concerned with genuine foreign-"political" issues; it turns instead to procedural ones, and from there to the technical and propagandistic preparation for "the worst." The development of American-Soviet diplomacy since the Second World War may serve as a sad illustration. From the end of the war till about 1948 both sides made genuine efforts to solve the great outstanding issues (Germany, disarmament, etc.); talks, correspondingly, still revolved around the solution of real political issues. From that time on, however, with the issues deadlocked, there has been in the main a procedural stalling for position; conferences, if and when held, have been held with no intention of arriving at agreements as to substance; indeed, willingness on either side to come to an agreement would probably have been embarrassing to the other. Subsequently, the emphasis shifted entirely from the diplomatic to the military. The problem narrowed down to what kind of war to be ready for or to deter with: all-out atomic war, mixed atomic-conventional, nonatomic "localized" ones, or some other.

Whenever in the last several years some negotiation has "threatened" to come close to success—as has happened repeatedly in disarmament negotiations, for instance—some apparently inevitable factor has intervened, as if fate was determined to destroy any such opportunity. In reality, of course, it has been recalcitrance on one or the other side or on

both that has stalled any progress however slight. The petri-
fication of political positions and the very comprehensiveness
of military preparations have added to this rigidity. As if
hypnotized by their own words and formulations, the powers
have been staring at existing conditions as at so many finally
fixed and unchangeable situations. As if bound by their own
defense preparations, they have permitted these preparations
to lead them in one direction only. Policies in both fields—
strategy as well as diplomacy—once adopted become increasingly difficult to change. Even minor details become solid-
ified as if sanctioned by major principle. And the tendency of public opinion (manipulated in the East, and more
and more inclined to "conform" to set standards in the West)
to view whatever happens in the world and in its own country
as determined or influenced by the "conspiracy" of the other
side contributes to such rigidity.

It is therefore likely that the West will continue a policy
by which the threat of nuclear retaliation may for the time
being deter the East from more open and conspicuous ven-
tures, such as expansion through force of arms, while at the
same time it perpetuates the danger that a general conflict may
break out because of the very indeterminateness of the threat.
By the same token, with parity achieved or approaching, the
East is likely to try on its part to deter the West through
similar threats from what it may resent as Western policies of
"intervention." Mutual threats against vaguely defined "aggressive" or "interventionist" policies then will either result
in temporarily "stabilizing" an extremely unstable status quo,
or else will explode into localized or global, conventional or
nuclear wars.

Under these rather gloomy assumptions structure and policies in international affairs must for the present and the immediate future be described in somewhat somber and even in
partly contradictory terms. First of all, we shall continue to

have a constellation in which atomic penetration must perpetually be reckoned with and in which therefore permeability rather than old-style independence and protection is an underlying condition even for—especially for—the otherwise most powerful units of international relations. But on the other hand (as the word "otherwise" indicates) there will also continue to exist a preatomic, or extraatomic, level of power relations, the level on which powers will go on facing each other as territorial units. In so far as the traditional power factors will still count and determine relations among powers, with possibilities of balances, and so forth, to this extent the old concepts of sovereignty, independence, measurable power, etc., will remain valid, although considerably modified by the impact of bipolarity. We shall hardly be able to see from day to day which of the two levels is, or will be, the decisive one in a given situation, and this very unpredictability renders a clearer exposition of international politics and a redefinition of its basic concepts exceedingly difficult, if not impossible. Where underlying structure itself is fluid and contains (in the Hegelian sense) contradictory features, terms and concepts must likewise be fluid and possibly contradictory if they are to apply to the totality of the situation, and not only to one of its partial aspects. Thus power today, in one respect (the extraatomic one, in which atomic power merely adds to military power in the classical sense), is "territorial" power. In that respect it is so in the extreme, extensively (because it may comprise and organize entire "halves" of the world) and intensively (because it is immeasurably enhanced by new technological developments). But in another respect it indicates simultaneous exposure to pervasion by other power, then becoming synonymous with "absence of power," or impotence. It is "measurable" and "comparable," and no longer measurable and absolute, all at the same time. Everything else—the paradoxical character of sovereignty, independence and de-

pendence, balance and imbalance, security and insecurity—derives from this.   And ideological bipolarity adds to all this the
complexities and uncertainties in such concepts as aggression
and self-defense, war and peace, legality and illegality.   No
wonder that international politics, not only in its actualities
but also in its concepts and terminologies, is confused, and
that present-day man in the world exists as in a maze.   At no
time in modern history has security meant so much to him; at
no time has there seemed less hope of retrieving it.

PROSPECTS OF FUTURE

INTERNATIONAL POLITICS

If you do not hope you will not find the unhoped-for, since it is hard to be found and the way is all but impassable. HERACLITUS

9

Is There a Future for International Politics?

Has international politics as we have known it a future? International politics, *qua* politics, used to contain elements of rationality even at the worst times of "international anarchy" and "power politics." Power and power relations allowed for an amount of planning when reactions were to some extent foreseeable and events calculable. Systems of foreign policies could thus be maintained, policies themselves made coherent and consistent. Today, when the power of destruction has become immeasurable, when a common language of diplomacy —and the common terminology of simple human relations— seems to fail us, when we feel more and more at the mercy of uncalculable reactions and unforeseeable events, it becomes doubtful whether foreign policy planning can comprise more than "preparation for the worst." Indeed, our very obsession with the possibility of the worst tends to paralyze our capacity to think and act in any other terms of international relationships.

There is sufficient ground for despair, to be sure. Everything in this century seems to go wrong. One has the impression that the very progress which mankind has made in the "conquest of nature," with all its actual or potential blessings regarding a better life for the majority of human beings heretofore condemned to a life "poore, nasty, brutish, and short," has been granted us merely to turn against itself, to "backfire," to furnish more rewarding targets for eventual destruction. Indeed, one sometimes has an uncanny feeling that the very increase in the number of human being is somehow related to the number of victims of the great catastrophes of modern war, and that the fantastic rise of population figures the world over is merely proportionate to the tremendously enhanced power to destroy lives in a thermonuclear holocaust. The age-old dream of the mass-killers of history, which found a relatively modest realization in a Tamerlane's skull-mountains or even in a Hitler's gas chambers, now, thanks to the progress made in the technology of destruction, seems finally to be fully attainable. Small wonder, then, that even men like H. G. Wells, cheerful prophets of all sorts of utopias of the good or better life, in the end have declared that mind has reached "the end of its tether." [1]

Assuming that universal destruction should not materialize, it seems that a continual state of fear lest it materialize will be mankind's unhappy lot in the foreseeable future. And again, what was supposed to be an advance, namely, progress toward greater individualism, in the sense of respect for and development of personality and personal values and achievements, seems threatened by reverse tendency. In the shadow of the steady increase in numbers on the one hand, and the threat of mass annihilation on the other, regard for human life as something valuable is declining. It is as if the single human being, formerly precious within a smaller but needed number of humans on earth, now, within the billions, had disappeared, as if Life (a constant sum-total of it) had become "diluted" in these larger numbers so that less and less of its real substance remains, proportionally, for each individual. This "thinning

[1] See Wells's *Mind at the End of Its Tether* (New York, 1946), a book which, unfortunately, also indicates the decline of Wells's own brilliant mind. The way in which recent "utopias" have alternated between the utter pessimism of a George Orwell and the optimism of, for instance, a Morris L. Ernst (*Utopia 1976* [New York, 1955]) is perhaps illustrative of how people in general view the world's and their own future. Pessimism and despair alternate or coexist with euphoria, the former induced by fear of an apocalyptic catastrophe which may put an end to the human story, the other provoked by the endless vista of material progress opened up by technical achievements and potentialities.

out" of substance starts with people's concern, or lack of concern, for their own individual lives. It is one thing to be ready—in the classical spirit of *dulce est pro patria mori* or *in tyrannos*—to lay down one's life as a sacrifice for a close community or for a higher cause. It is quite another to value one's life so little as to be ready to throw it away for one hardly knows what. There is a strange apathy toward danger, as if in modern mass civilization and mass organizations individual life were no longer lived as a coherent and consecutive "whole," with an unfolding history, but rather as—in Sorokin's sense—a "sensate" and incoherent living from day to day in fragments.[2] And to this process of self-depreciation must be added the tendency to depreciate one's fellows, a tendency which in a way is natural considering the relative insignificance of a single human being in the mass, especially in a mass potentially perishable in one blow. Still, the equanimity with which, for instance, in discussions of nuclear attacks, prospects of survival in and defense against them, etc., entire metropolitan areas, populations, and countries are written off is appalling.[3] Indifference is understandable, to a degree, where ideology exalts individual sacrifice for the cause of a collective or for that of the better life of future society and where totalitarian rule tries to impress upon people a sense of their smallness and unworthiness as compared with the state or the community. But even in the case of Communism this approach loses its meaning in the face of the realization that universal destruction would leave no future generations for whom sacri-

[2] It is paradoxical that modern emphasis on "enjoyment" of life diminishes the feeling for the value of life, while concern with superindividual values and ideals enhances it.

[3] Equally appalling is the way in which the annihilation of the material witnesses of civilization past and present is taken for granted; it is as if future mankind (if any) were expected to start from scratch in this respect also. If all this was in the spirit of heroic sacrifice, it would be understandable. But people give themselves up, and things are given up, in the spirit of the slaughterhouse rather than that of the Thermopylae.

fice makes sense, or, at best, would leave them a globe so unfit for human habitation that it reduces any doctrine of progress and perfection to ridicule. In the nontotalitarian world, which calls itself the "free world" and claims to attach supreme value to each individual as a human being, such apathy is as unintelligible as it is in contradiction to the professed ideals.

In the face of despair or indifference, it is up to the humanists—that is, all those who esteem lives, their own and those of others—to see to it that the story of human endeavor and human accomplishment, that is, the story of humanity, does not end by default. For nothing justifies a belief that nature —the universe—as such is in the least concerned about the existence or disappearance of mankind. I therefore believe that in the present predicament it is everybody's, not only the "specialist's," responsibility to think about and work for the creation of conditions in which mankind has a chance to continue existing. It is in this sense that the final part of this study will be devoted to some of the problems concerning international prospects. First, the impact of one basic constellation, which is referred to as the "security dilemma," will be taken up in its capacity as an obstacle in the path of any proposal for "better" systems or policies. Because of the accentuated effects of this dilemma in the present world situation, I believe that only a sort of international "holding operation" can be practicable today and in the immediate future; the character and requirements of such a policy or operation will therefore constitute the second part of the remaining analysis. After that it will be legitimate to inquire into the prospects and chances for a "universalist" approach, which, I now believe, offers the only hope for a more permanent solution of world problems, or, to phrase it less grandiloquently perhaps, the only hope for something better than mere day-to-day attempts to avoid the abyss.

10

The Security Dilemma in the Atomic Age

The "security dilemma," or "power and security dilemma," referred to earlier in this study, is a social constellation in which units of power (such as states or nations in international relations) find themselves whenever they exist side by side without higher authority that might impose standards of behavior upon them and thus protect them from attacking each other. In such a condition, a feeling of insecurity, deriving from mutual suspicion and mutual fear, compels these units to compete for ever more power in order to find more security, an effort which proves self-defeating because complete security remains ultimately unobtainable. I believe that this dilemma, and not such (possibly additional) factors as "aggressiveness," or desire to acquire the wealth of others, or general depravity of human nature, constitutes the basic cause of what is commonly referred to as the "urge for power" and resulting "power politics."

This constellation and its effects can be observed at the primitive as well as the higher levels of human organization. As I have observed before, "the fact that is decisive for his (i.e., man's) social and political attitudes and ideas is that other human beings are able to inflict death upon him. This very realization that his own brother may play the role of Cain makes his fellow men appear to him as potential foes. Realization of this fact by others, in turn, makes him appear to them as their potential mortal enemy. Thus there arises a fundamental social constellation, a mutual suspicion and a mutual dilemma: the dilemma of 'kill or perish', of attacking first or running the risk of being destroyed. There is apparently no escape from this vicious circle. Whether man is 'by nature' peaceful and cooperative, or aggressive and domineering, is not the question. The condition that concerns us here is not an anthropological or biological, but a social one. It is his uncertainty and anxiety as to his neighbors' intentions that places man in this basic dilemma, and makes the 'homo homini lupus' a primary fact of the social life of man." And further: "Politically active groups and individuals are concerned about their security from being attacked, subjected, dominated, or annihilated by other groups and individuals. Because they strive to attain security from such attack, and yet can never feel entirely secure in a world of competing units, they are driven toward acquiring more and more power for themselves, in order to escape the impact of the superior power of others. It is important to realize that such competition for security, and hence for power, is a basic situation which is unique with men and their social groups. At any rate, it has nothing to do with a hypothetical 'power urge' or 'instinct of pugnacity' of the race, and even less, since the competition is intraspecific, with the biological 'big fish eats small fish' situation." [1]

The power and security dilemma, in principle, affects relationships between all groups, but how it does so within units

[1] *Political Realism and Political Idealism* (Chicago, 1951), pp. 3, 14. Reducing the "power urge" to "power competition," "power competition" to concern with "security," and the latter to a social constellation called "security dilemma" constitutes what has been characterized as "pragmatic realism," as distinguished from the "doctrinaire realism" (I would call it more politely "anthropological" or "metaphysical" realism) of the Niebuhr-Morgenthau school of thought, which bases power phenomena ultimately on the corruption of human nature (for this distinction see William T. R. Fox, "Les fondements moraux et juridiques de la politique étrangère américaine," in J. B. Duroselle [ed.], *La politique étrangère et ses fondements* [Paris, 1954], p. 288 f.). For a similar distinction of two kinds of "realism" see Arnold Wolfers, "The Pole of Power and the Pole of Indifference," *World Politics*, 4: 41 f. (1951–52).

where some sort of government exists does not concern us here. Rather, we are concerned with its impact on those relations which are characterized by the absence of any kind of "government" over and above the coexisting power units, and in particular, international relations since the dawn of the modern era. For it is in this area that the dilemma reveals itself as a prime mover in a more clear-cut—one is inclined to say, more brutal—way than anywhere else. "Because this is the realm where the ultimate power units have faced, and still are facing each other as 'monades' irreducible to any further, higher ruling or coordinating power, the vicious circle of the power and security dilemma works here with more drastic force than in any other field. Power relationships and the development of the means of exercising power in the brutal form of force have dominated the field here to the almost complete exclusion of the more refined 'governmental' relationships which prevail in 'internal politics.' Marxism maintains that political relations and developments form the 'superstructure' over the system and the development of the means of *production*. Within the sphere of international relations, it might rather be said that political developments constitute a superstructure over the system and the development of the means of *destruction*." [2] The elaboration in preceding chapters on the developments in the defense (or offense) systems of nation-states and on their impact upon the policies and relationships of "powers" has been sufficient, I hope, to illustrate the influence which considerations of "security," concern for protection from outside aggression and interference, mutual fear and suspicion, have exercized on their "power politics" as well as on their efforts to mitigate these effects through systems and organizations like the balance of power and collective security. But before inquiring how the

[2] *Political Realism and Political Idealism,* p. 200.

dilemma applies to the present situation in world politics, further clarification may be gained by reference to another author, whose analysis closely parallels my own.

When I first claimed primary importance for the security dilemma, I was not aware that a similar thesis had been powerfully put forth by a British historian and student of power politics, Herbert Butterfield.[3] What I have termed "security dilemma" is called "predicament of Hobbesian fear" by Mr. Butterfield, and for obvious reasons.[4] The "Hobbesian" dilemma, he states, constitutes "a grand dialectical jam of a kind that exasperates men"; indeed, he claims for it such fundamental importance as to talk of it as "the absolute predicament," the "irreducible dilemma," which, lying in "the very geometry of human conflict," is "the basis of all the tensions of the present day, representing even now the residual problem that the world has not solved, the hard nut that we still have to crack."[5] To illustrate this "predicament," Butterfield asks us to imagine two enemies, armed with pistols,

[3] *Christianity and History* (New York, 1950); *History and Human Relations* (New York, 1952). See also his essay "The Tragic Element in Modern International Conflict," *Review of Politics*, 12: 147 ff. (1950).

[4] My own book has been called purely "Hobbesian" by some reviewers. It is perhaps so in the first part and so far as the exposition of the security dilemma goes; it hardly is so in the less analytical and more constructive second part, which deals with what I have called "realist liberalism" and which, if historical antecedents are desired, is more indebted to Burke than to either Hobbes or Locke. Certain reviewers have thus charged me with neglecting what I meticulously dealt with in the second half of my book.

[5] *History and Human Relations*, pp. 19, 20. Similarly, in his essay quoted above, he terms it "a standing feature of mankind in world history" (p. 161). "Here is the basic pattern of all narrative of human conflict, whatever other patterns may be superimposed upon it later" (p. 154). I cannot go along with him quite that far. To consider the dilemma the basis of *all* past and present conflict seems to me an exaggeration. We shall attempt to show that there is a difference between "security policies" and policies motivated by interests that go beyond security proper. Consider the world conflict provoked by Hitler's policy of world domination. It can hardly be maintained that it was a German security dilemma which lay at the heart of that conflict, but rather one man's, or one regime's, ambition to master the world.

locked in one room. "Both of you would like to throw the pistols out of the window, yet it defeats the intelligence to find a way of doing it. . . . In international affairs it is this situation of Hobbesian fear which, so far as I can see, has hitherto defeated all the endeavor of the human intellect." [6] He then elucidates the role which suspicion and counter-suspicion, and the inability to enter the other fellow's mind, play in this respect: "You cannot enter into the other man's counter-fear. . . . It is never possible for you to realize or remember properly that since he cannot see the inside of your mind, he can never have the same assurance of your intentions that you have." [7]   And—it may be added, transferring this argument to the plane of international affairs—even if a nation could do so, how could it trust in the continuance of good intentions in the case of collective entities with leaders and policies forever changing? How could it, then, afford not to be prepared for "the worst"?

If mutual suspicion and the security dilemma thus constitute the basic underlying condition in a system of separate, independent power units, one would assume that history must consist of one continual race for power and armaments, an unadulterated rush into unending wars, indeed, a chain of "preventive wars." This obviously has not been the case. There have unquestionably been periods in which units have been less suspicious of each other than at other times, periods in which they have felt more secure and have been able to work out systems that gave them even a certain feeling of protection. The security dilemma, in its acute form, was then "mitigated." Thus, while it has confronted units of international politics throughout history, it has done so in various degrees of acuity, depending on the circumstances. Among these circumstances in particular are those which are con-

6 *Christianity and History*, pp. 89 f.
7 *History and Human Relations*, p. 21.

nected with the underlying structure of the units. Here we can return to what was said earlier about the structure of the "territoriality" of the modern state and about its transformations; for these have affected the security and the security dilemma of nations in a way closely resembling the manner in which power and power relations have been affected by them. In order to understand this impact, it is necessary to probe somewhat deeper into the changing meaning and role of "security" in the history of modern international affairs.

Systems are based on policies. Policies reflect interests. If we want to know how and why the security dilemma can be mitigated, we must know how the pursuance of nations' interests is affected by the varying feelings of more or less security which varying conditions inspire in them. "Security," in the sense of a certain felt condition of nations, has always been a rather elusive concept. It has at times been confused with or made part and parcel of an even more elusive and still more broadly conceived idea, namely, the "national interest." The "national interest" usually allows for a large variety of different objectives and methods of foreign policy, even where the basic interest in "security" is not lost sight of. This is what frequently has been overlooked by those who otherwise have given due recognition to the importance of "national interests." While it has been the great merit of students like George Kennan and Hans Morgenthau that they have reemphasized the importance of the national interest in the conduct of foreign policy, especially in a country which has at times (although not as persistently as it is sometimes believed) inclined toward "moralism" or "legalism," they have been prone to assume an unequivocal, so to say self-defining, "given" nature of these interests. Beyond the minimum requirements of "security" (which themselves are changing historically) "national interests"—in the plural rather than "the national interest" in the singular—not only are more ambiguous and indeterminate than is often assumed but are also liable to be shaped (and sometimes diverted from their proper direction) by "subnational" or "supernational" interests. There was a time (to which the present may be the reaction) when the influence of certain subnational groups on the determination of the national interest and the making of foreign policies was emphasized to the almost complete exclusion of everything else. But the extremism with which scholars like Charles A. Beard stressed the "relative" nature of national interests and the influence of economic and other subnational groups on foreign policies [8] should not blind us to the fact that the definition of a country's national interests, beyond the bare security minimum, may indeed range all the way from interest in maintaining and defending what it has (territorially and otherwise) to extreme economic and political "imperialism," and that the interests can be, and usually are, the expression of a great variety of party-political, personal, group, or "ideological" viewpoints and the composite result of many groups' attitudes. The German national interest, for instance, in the case of the same newly united, powerful, and prosperous Reich after 1871 seemed one thing to and under Bismarck and quite another one to William II; again, in the case of the defeated, less powerful, and less prosperous republic after 1919 Stresemann and the Republicans saw it one way, Hitler and the Nazis quite another. In such cases to define "objectively" (that is, without applying one's own preferences or value standards) what is (or was) in the interest of "the nation as such" may prove impossible, at least in so far as policies all aim at trying to safeguard a certain minimum of security. Even where, as in the United States, the national interest was for a long time identified with the basic security interests of the nation, and where security was rela-

[8] Beard's *The Idea of National Interest* (New York, 1934) may stand for the whole literary product of this school.

tively easy to define—namely, as protection from outside attack through the two ocean barriers and the existence of a strong and friendly British navy—from time to time it became enmeshed in expansionism of the "Manifest Destiny" variety,[9] when "frontiers had to be extended lest strong rivals get there first and use them to the nation's disadvantage." [10]

But how can one define that element of "basic security" which underlies the more elusive and variable "national interests" as their "minimum"? It must be conceded that even this "security" interest is not unequivocal. But one hardly has to go so far as does Van Alstyne who asserts: "The concept . . . . defies definition. It is an abstraction which finds concrete expression in policies far broader and subtler in their implications than mere defense programs." [11] I suggest that one gets to the bedrock of minimum security requirements by correlating them with the protective functions of territoriality. When "impermeability" was still a reality, and "sovereign, independent" hard-shell units were relatively small and self-sufficient, the range of their security interests was also limited. Usually, it would extend to the country's immediate neighbors or, at most, to the general balance of power in a limited area of Europe or (in the case of the "big powers") throughout the European continent. In the case of colonial empires it might, in addition, comprise specific overseas posessions and their surroundings, and possibly the sea lanes leading to them (including strategic points at straits, etc.). Even in the latter instance, however, it usually would not affect the "vital" security of the respective country whether a piece of territory overseas was gained or lost or, as happened so often, was traded for another one. The security interest of nations was thus identified with the maintenance of a certain, relatively stable,

---

[9] See Albert K. Weinberg, *Manifest Destiny* (Baltimore, 1935).

[10] R. W. Van Alstyne, *American Diplomacy in Action* (2d ed.; Stanford, Calif., and London, 1947), p. 48.

[11] *Ibid.*, p. 770.

balanced status quo, its protection from disturbance by more aggressive or expansionist units, and in exceptional cases (e.g., where, as in the case of Brandenburg-Prussia, fragmentation of territorial possessions rendered part of them undefendable) a usually moderate revision of a status in regard to the respective unit.

Under such circumstances, the security dilemma, while always existing, could be attenuated. There were always a number and variety of competing powers from which one could select allies and with which one could try to balance would-be hegemony powers; there was the possibility of shifting alignments; there were "balancers" and mediators; and there was a way out through overseas expansion when the security dilemma and resulting power competition became too acute "at home." Commonly accepted standards of behavior and "law" would also provide for mitigation of the fears and distrusts which the dilemma provoked. As we have seen, it all amounted to a system with such strongly "conservative" features that its members could feel relatively secure once certain minimum requirements of security—generally modest ones—had been satisfied.[12]

But there came a time when the factors which allowed for a mitigation of the security dilemma receded. During the nineteenth century, the "impermeability" of territorial state units lessened; the "security area," meaning the area in which whatever happened concerned the security interest of the nation in question, grew ever larger, until (at least in the case of the big powers) it comprised the entire world. The European balance had to be transformed into a world balance, and

[12] What in the political literature of the seventeenth and eighteenth centuries was discussed under the heading of "raison d'Etat," despite the frequently "machiavellian" ways and means of suggested policies, amounted to nothing more than the elaboration of what, in the cases of the different individual states, were these basic security requirements; in other words, it was the determination of the national interests in the sense of security interests.

thus, even prior to bipolar power concentration, the world as such emerged as the "security area" for the now so-called "world powers."

At that point a realization that attack upon the territorial integrity or political independence of any unit anywhere would concern every other unit in the world might have become the foundation of a working collective security system, had the powers been able to act jointly upon such a realization. As it was, they persevered in the traditional approach: trying to supply themselves with security individually, which meant that the security dilemma now confronted them naked and unmitigated. Security considerations and security motivations became all-encompassing. Whatever contributed (or was suspected of contributing) to the strengthening of any one power anywhere in the world was considered as of immediate security concern to the others, who therefore would try to oppose it or make up for it by their own increase in power or influence. This situation contributed as much to the emergence of bipolarity as it became accentuated into an ever sharper power competition once bipolarity had been established. What to the one side now would seem necessary to protect its security (e.g., a "protective" *glacis* of "friendly" peoples' democracies in the case of the Soviet Union, or a Western Europe, West Germany, Greece, Turkey, Formosa, Pakistan, or Thailand aligned with the West in the case of the United States) might appear to the other side, and with equal subjective justification, as evidence of "aggressive," hostile, expansionist intentions. It is likely that it was this divergence in the interpretation of the respective opponent's intentions, emanating from the security dilemma, that gradually resulted in the situation properly called the "cold war." That is, it has been fear of or concern with what the other side had in mind and might try to do, rather than policies or objectives of "world conquest" or "imperialism," which has motivated the attempts of the blocs to extend their spheres, or, in other words, fear of being "encircled" by "aggressive imperialists," fear of being picked up one by one through the Communist "world conspiracy." [13]   And it is one of the tragic implications of the security dilemma that mutual fear of what initially may never have existed may subsequently bring about exactly that which is feared most: actual "encirclement," actually "being picked up one by one."

Thus bipolarity has given the security dilemma its utmost poignancy. So far as the two blocs are concerned, little mitigates it. Competition for power now is chiefly between two instead of many. Values held in common have given way to ideological conflict, aggravating mutual distrust. The blocs touch each other everywhere, with few ways out into neutral or unoccupied ground. Whatever the security interest of one side seems to require increases the insecurity of the other side, and hardly any line can be drawn which would separate "defensive" measures and "security" policies from "offensive," "expansionist," and "beyond-security" action. Where previous alignments of powers occurred in order to protect the security of individual territorial state-units, today's alignments protect "areas" which, despite intended geographical delimitation, tend to circle half the globe and to encircle the other half.[14] Developments have reached a pass where almost everything in national and bloc policies resolves itself into security policies.[15]

[13] Such mutual fear, rather than genuine expansionism, was already at play in 1914 as the basis of the First World War. William II was more concerned with security than Hitler, who was a genuine "expansionist."

[14] NATO, for instance, which was founded to "maintain the security of the North Atlantic area," now, through direct membership or indirect affiliation stretches from Alaska through Europe to Pakistan.

[15] A keen critic of oversimplified security theories, according to which any and all "national interests" resolve themselves into security interests so that security is made to appear as the only or prime concern of all nations at all times, has rightly stressed that the policies of modern nations

The radical effects which policy decisions may have today and the suddenness and speed with which they may have to be executed still further accentuate the mutual fear. Nowhere, perhaps, has the compelling force of the security dilemma become more noticeable than in the sphere of armaments. No moral, religious, humanitarian, economic, or other considerations could prevail against the simple and brutal impact of a "they or us"; see, for instance, the statement made by one of the original developers of the atomic bomb:

We were driven not by hope, but by fear. We had to make the bomb, if it were possible to do so, because we knew that our enemies were trying to make it—and, in their hands, it could have meant the destruction of our own country. Most of us hoped—although we soon knew it was a vain hope—that the bomb could not be constructed, so that no one would be able to use such a terrific weapon. *But if it could be built, then we had to build it first.*[16]

And what was compelling in war has proved to be compelling in "peace," as, for instance, when the decision to produce the H-weapon was made. Indeed, as Pope Pius XII put it, "What is meant by 'cold peace' if not the mere coexistence of various peoples, based on the fear of each other and on mu-

---

used to cover the entire range from an extreme "pole of power" to the other extreme, "the pole of indifference" (Arnold Wolfers, "The Pole of Power and the Pole of Indifference," *World Politics*, 4:41 f. [1951–52], and "National Security as an Ambiguous Symbol," *Political Science Quarterly*, 67: 481 ff. [1952]). I agree that this could be so in a world of relatively "secure" nations, when a surplus or margin of security permitted units to concern themselves with non- or "beyond"-security interests of various sorts. But the situation has now changed, especially with the emergence of bipolarity. Today "security" has indeed become the overriding concern of all powers. Wolfers does not quite seem to realize this; he could still say in 1952 that "nobody can reasonably contend that Canada, for example, is threatened today to the same extent as countries like Iran or Yugoslavia" ("National Security as an Ambiguous Symbol," p. 487). Thus he was then still viewing the situation in a prebipolar, preatomic light. Today it is no longer a question of Canada's security from neighbors, such as the United States, but, as in the cases of all Western powers, one in relation to the East; and there Canada, because of north-polar strategies, is perhaps more exposed than other nations.

16 Interview reported in New York *Times*, August 6, 1951; italics added.

tual disillusionment? . . . The principal foundation on which the present state of relative calm rests is fear." [17]   Condition of "Hobbesian fear" if ever there was one!

The one, radical conclusion to be drawn from all of this would seem to be that nothing short of global rule can ultimately satisfy the security interest of any one power, and particularly any superpower. For only through elimination of the single competitor who really counts can one feel safe from the threat of annihilation. And since elimination without war is hardly imaginable, destruction of the other power in "preventive war" would therefore appear to be the only logical objective of each superpower. But—and here the security dilemma encounters the other great dilemma of our time— pursuance of the "logical" security objective is no longer practical. The means through which the end would have to be attained defeats the end itself. Since thermonuclear war would in all likelihood involve one's own destruction together with that of one's opponent, it "logically" precludes the end. Logical preclusion, of course, offers no guarantee against actual resort to all-out war in disregard of rationality. In that event, however, mutual annihilation, rather than one unit's global control of a pacified world, would be the probable result. Thus the aim, in the very interest of "security," must be mutual accommodation.

[17] Christmas Message, 1954, New York *Times*, January 4, 1955.

11

A Plan for a Holding Operation

In the face of desperate situations radical solutions appear appropriate. This, perhaps, accounts for the appeal of a "let's-get-it-over-with" policy of preventive war. Once it is realized that policies of this kind are likely to result in exactly that which one wants to avoid, the opposite extreme gains in attractiveness. May not the solution lie in one side's giving up the mad rush into "preparedness," thereby, so some say, setting an example which no other country could afford not to follow? May it not be found in finally setting up that world authority, which was perhaps unobtainable in ages when insistence on national sovereignty still made sense, but which is the only hope for mankind's survival now that territoriality has vanished and sovereignty has lost its very *raison d'être*, its function of protection?

Under an analysis of history and structure of international politics which calls itself "realistic" suggestions like these used to be ruled out as imbued with "utopianism"; and with good reason so far as the more ambitious plans were concerned, and so long as the territorial structure of nations rendered a minimum of international stability and "sanity" possible. But with the new, particularly the atomic, developments and a world clearly in danger of "getting out of hand," the question arises whether the most sane and "realistic" traditional attitudes have not led us to a dead end; and whether what used to appear as utopian does not now merit serious attention on the part of realists.[1] This, at any rate, is what will be given it here.

We cannot, however, realistically expect a radical change right away. It seems to me that we must proceed in two stages. An early—and quite possibly a lengthy and not very advanced —stage of development must precede any period of bolder advance in order to prepare its foundations. With the threat of war continuing and the security dilemma confronting the nations of the world more acute than ever, the best that can be expected for the time being would seem to be a continuation of the uneasy "peace" and "coexistence," which, as someone has remarked, is preferable to "no-existence." Even this somewhat dubious situation will not come unearned. All the resources of the mind, wisdom of scholarship, and skill of statesmanship, at best will be barely enough to find the tortuous way toward this temporary goal through what may be called a "holding operation." For there is a real danger that both sides may soon reach a "point of no return," where politically, ideologically, and, above all, strategically (that is, in regard to military planning for all-out atomic war) fronts will have become so rigid, attitudes so inflexible, thinking and feeling so synchronized in one direction that what now still constitutes one among several possibilities will by then have become "the inevitable." I have drawn attention above to the grave danger involved in an attitude of intransigence which, because of fear of being accused of appeasement, leads to a refusal to negotiate altogether. The United States, in particular, forgetting that "positions of strength" were supposed to be used for "negotiating from strength," may instead be faced with a situation in which the West will be forced to negotiate, and under much less favorable conditions. In the

---

[1] I plead guilty in having indulged myself in a somewhat cavalier attitude toward "utopian idealism" in my *Political Realism and Political Idealism* (Chicago, 1951). As an ameliorating circumstance I can only say that most of it was written prior to the atomic age.

meantime, rejection of whatever offers come from the East has merely provided the latter with a gratuitous propaganda advantage; we have neglected to find out whether anything was meant seriously, and, in case it was not so meant, to pin the label of insincerity on the opponent.

It is possible that rigidity was heightened by the disappointing results of the one experiment made in recent years with "top-level" negotiation, the Summit Conference at Geneva in 1955. But the lesson to be drawn from this experience is not that one should not negotiate but rather *how* not to negotiate. The "summit" can only ratify what in patient negotiation has been worked out before on the lower levels of day-to-day diplomacy. Without such preparation, to expect from the "top" over-all solutions of general problems can only result in failure and disillusionment. There is danger of expecting from *any* kind of negotiation today either too little or too much. The danger of expecting too much consists in anticipating a more than provisional solution of the basic problems now dividing East and West, a new "rule of law," or general standards for a lasting and—for both sides—genuinely satisfactory solution of outstanding world problems. Expecting too little, on the other hand, might turn the effort into just one more of the many tedious proceedings, all too familiar from cold war diplomacy, in which everybody knows from the outset that nothing will come of it and in which one engages chiefly in order to convince world opinion of one's own good faith and the bad faith of the other fellow.

Geneva has shown that a diplomacy that resolves itself into a mutual smiling contest cannot hope to achieve real results; nor can the belief that conferences, in order to be successful, must not have an agenda. Such renunciation of coming to grips with the real problems amounts merely to a confession of impotency. We have seen that some interpreted Geneva as signalizing a mutual if tacit agreement that all-out nuclear war was now outlawed. If this were true, policy using the threat of such a war as a deterrent against any kind of "aggression" would have lost its meaning and therefore been given up. But nothing has changed in this respect. All that —at best—was achieved was a constatation by both sides that they recognize the dangers involved in nuclear war. As for approaching—let alone solving—any of the more concrete problems dividing the powers, there was instead the customary subdelegation of tasks to the next lower level, that of the foreign ministers who, in due course, reported back their stalemate, as usual, and this failure, in turn, then became fertile ground for mutual recrimination. Diplomatic ball-playing, or buck-passing, of this sort has been a favorite pastime throughout the postwar era, whether it has involved referring matters from heads of state to foreign ministers, from them to "special delegates," and *retour*, or referring them from the United Nations to "powers concerned" and back, or other techniques of delay and inaction.

Is there anything which justifies expecting something better from a new effort? There is indeed, providing that at least a minimum of "reason" prevails over emotionalism and "ideologism" on both sides, and that there exists a genuine will to negotiate which people have been demanding with increasing urgency more recently. For one encouraging—though perhaps still modest—result of the shock that sputnik and weapons developments in the Soviet Union have created in the West has been the growing number of voices demanding accommodation or at least a serious attempt to arrive at it. It is true at the time these lines are written that the voices are still chiefly of those who, like George Kennan, are not in a position of responsibility, and that, at least in the United States, there still prevails "bipartisanship" in the accustomed sterile and exclusive concern with the armaments race and defense systems. And it is perhaps significant that Lester Pearson's clarion call for an East-West settlement has come from the *ex*-foreign minister who was not heard from this forcefully at all while in office. Can it then be that only "irresponsibility" indulges in hope for adjustment, while those responsible for policy are prevented from entertaining any such hope because of the security dilemma and the security interests entrusted to them? That, in other words, it is not a matter of "reason" versus "ideologism" but rather, of compelling interest versus "utopianism"?

I do not believe so. I believe that accommodation has a chance and therefore can—and must—be tried, for with almost everything dividing the blocs, there is yet one interest they have in common: to avoid mutual annihilation through resort to the forces now rampant in the world. In either side's view, therefore, a holding operation should rationally recommend itself as preferable to continuing the mad rush into what would more likely than not involve self-destruction together with the destruction of the opponent. In this overriding matter statesmen thus must act—and nations must allow them, even prod them, to act—as caretakers of a universal interest even while, simultaneously, they act as representatives of their own nations. Leaders in the Soviet bloc would have to realize that atomic war would write finis to any hope of future socialist plenty (while, of course, also destroying the basis of their present social and economic system); [2] Americans, that it would destroy their present "way of life" as well as any chances of the "American dream" of the better life; others, that it might lead to world rule by one of the two "big" ones

[2] Whether such minimal rationality in outlook and policy can be expected from Soviet leadership at all constitutes, of course, one of the fundamental uncertainties in the situation. Is it ideologically committed to one specific world-view to such a degree that what we consider rational cannot penetrate? And if so, what is that view? There have been so many divergent theories concerning Soviet behavior that a recent author could devote an entire article to their analysis (see Daniel Bell, "Ten Theories in Search of Reality: The Prediction of Soviet Behavior in the Social Sciences," *World Politics*, 10: 327 ff. [1957–58]).

under primitive and brutal conditions. In neither instance, on the other hand, need this realization and an ensuing readiness to try accommodation involve renunciation of ultimate ideals or more distant expectations. All we would have to aim at would be a temporary delimitation of spheres, adopting as a starting point for discussion a mutual *de facto* (not a "de jure") recognition of what each side now holds and of which it could be deprived only at the point of the sword. What this involves will be discussed in more detail below. At this point I shall mention a few more of the general prerequisites to successful negotiation.

Less preoccupation with ideology would be helpful. Should it be at all possible to get away from ideological obsessions and view conditions more coolly as involving interests in security, power, and avoidance of all-out war, both sides might even profit from the security dilemma itself, or, rather, from facing and understanding it. For, if it is true—as Butterfield has pointed out—that inability to put oneself into the other fellow's place and to realize his fears and distrust has always constituted one chief reason for the dilemma's poignancy, it would then follow that elucidation of this fact might by itself enable one to do what so far has proved impossible—to put oneself into the other's place, to understand that he, too, may be motivated by one's own kind of fears, and thus to abate the fear. This would not resolve the dilemma entirely, of course, for one could never be entirely certain; but it might at least take some of the sting out of it and insert a wedge toward a more rational, less fear-ridden, less ideology-laden, and less emotion-beset attitude through a kind of psychoanalysis in the international field where lifting one factor into the realm of the conscious might become part of the healing process.

All of this, as can be seen, requires some abatement of both sides' concern with the ideological elements involved in their

struggle and competition. To be sure, there is a great complication involved in so diluting the ideologies which presently
divide the world: though one cannot live with them since
they are likely to lead to atomic doom, one can also hardly
live without them, because they seem to give meaning to the
lives of humans who otherwise might become victims of complete "anomie." Stated as a paradox, one can no longer "afford the necessity" of a universal belief system. The only way
out here—a difficult one—is to renounce the universality of
one's ideology, that is, to accept that minimum of toleration
which consists in foregoing the missionary element in the
creed for the sake of the "holding operation."

In this connection, optimists have sometimes been fond of
citing certain periods and constellations in history as parallels
to the present situation—constellations in which, after a prolonged period of heated conflict and fight, the issues involved
eventually became less vital, indeed "uninteresting" to those
concerned, and adjustment followed. We have seen before
that parallels from history often lead to slippery ground. It
is true that there have been precedents for the present world
constellation: side-by-side "worlds" divided from each other
politically and ideologically and yet managing to "coexist" in
more or less uneasy adjustment. Examples most frequently
adduced are those of Moslem-Christian coexistence during the
many centuries when Islamic might was dynamic,[3] and of
Catholic-Protestant coexistence after the great schism in Christianity had occurred. There are indeed some encouraging
data here, but the flaw of the comparison is in the fact that
whatever "accommodation" there was in those instances was
either short-lived and in between major wars and conflicts or
the result, when it eventually emerged as a lasting relation,
of a stalemate following upon a long period of fervent strug-

[3] A recent summary and appraisal of relations between Christian and
Moslem states in the Middle Ages is contained in F. A. von der Heydte,
Die Geburtsstunde des souveränen Staates (Regensburg, 1952), pp. 274–71.

gle; both sides by then had tired of unending warfare, and the issues themselves had to some extent paled. We cannot afford to go through a period of "religious" wars.[4] We must start from the understanding that war, at least the "Big War," is "prohibited" (not, of course, in the sense of Kellogg-Pact legalism but in that of a self-denying ordinance). We must, to be sure, do so while continuing to be ready to engage in the supreme test if the other side should impose it on us. That attempts at accommodation will have to proceed in so little promising an environment constitutes their supreme difficulty as well as their supreme justification.

On the following pages only a few of the chief difficulties inherent in such an effort as well as some suggestions for grappling with them will be outlined. This adds to and, to some extent, supplements what has been said earlier in this chapter.

STARTING FROM THE CONCRETE SITUATION

In asking which "holding" policies may prove practicable and which not, I believe that under present circumstances problems should be approached and dealt with in their utmost "concreteness," that is, as they present themselves "here and there," wherever they may occur at any given moment, and not by trying to establish or maintain principles or fashion general, over-all systems of international relations. Stable and relatively "permanent" systems of international politics have been peculiar to certain periods of international relations, as we have seen earlier. Even in the interwar era there still existed a structural basis for establishing such a system, either in the traditional form of a balance of power, or in the more

4 This is what is perhaps somewhat neglected in arguments like those of Halle (*Choice for Survival* [New York, 1958], in particular, ch. 7), which place their trust in the "evolutionary process of history" that will, "in time", render Communism less revolutionary and this way lead to co-existence of two antagonistic worlds. If we are to survive we must do all we can to accelerate the process.

stable but more difficult form of collective security. Genuine collective security, as has also been pointed out before, is now impracticable because of bipolarity; and even if that impediment were absent, it is likely that the present ideological split of the world would outrule this approach. What, then, about the balance of power? Here, too, we would suggest that conscious pursuit of a balance *policy* might do more harm than good. If each side was preoccupied all of the time with trying to balance the other and pursued this policy as a matter of principle, the result would be unending quarrel over whether or not a "real" balance existed in this or another respect—militarily, economically, politically—or in this or that place or region of the world. Disagreement over the multiple factors which enter into the picture, inability to concur on the weighing of such items as the various types of armed forces and armaments to be compared (to mention only the most obvious of all factors, whose intricate nature the long history of futile disarmament efforts has amply revealed) might well exacerbate rather than assuage the present atmosphere of antagonism and hostility. It has been stressed earlier how rigid and precarious a bipolar balance is anyway. And if it were a question not of maintaining but of restoring an allegedly lost balance, it might even involve the danger of new conflicts arising over new claims.

On the other hand, deemphasizing balance of power policies *qua* general attempts at setting up a more stable system of world equilibrium need not—and cannot—involve disregarding balance considerations altogether. In a bipolar situation they are liable to guide policies to some extent anyway, and justifiably so, since any major imbalance would threaten the existence of the bipolar system, that is, through the demolition of one of the two superpowers and their blocs. But the fact that these blocs have now "coexisted" for over a decade indicates in and of itself that some kind of a rough balance does exist. Policies of a "holding operation" should not be directed toward giving that balance up or changing it substantially. The very impact of a delimitation of spheres rests on maintaining, roughly, the spheres as they are now. Starting from the given fact of an existing power equilibrium, a concrete delimitation and limitation of spheres might lead to an attenuation of tensions which otherwise might result in an overthrow of the balance. While over-all solutions, realization of higher and more general principles, building of stable systems and organizations may appeal more strongly to bolder minds and the ambition of statesmen, this is a time for more modest, though not less demanding experiments in the piecemeal solution of the concrete issue.[5]

This would mean beginning with Germany, China, the Near East, or similar issues, not merely by way of reacting to unanticipated crises—as has been characteristic of Western "policies"—nor, of course, in the manner of provoking such crises in order to promote one's own objectives—the policy of the Soviet bloc—but by starting out to find mutually acceptable solutions before crises occur, or at least during the more tranquil periods between crises, so as to facilitate a less tense and emotional approach on both sides.

One familiar objection is likely to occur in this connection: How can we expect to solve any specific problem so long as insecurity and fear are not abated through regulation of armaments? This is the time-honored argument concerning the alleged paradox of "no security without disarmament" and "no disarmament without security through prior solution of outstanding concrete issues." Raising the one objection during attempted armament negotiations and the other one in negotiations on concrete issues has time and again—in the interwar period, for instance—succeeded in stalling both.

[5] In this connection see George F. Kennan's pertinent suggestions (*Russia, the Atom and the West* [New York, 1958], p. 25).

The answer, of course, lies in trying whichever offers better promise. Since complete security cannot be obtained without solving both, we must be content with starting in an atmosphere of relative insecurity, striving thus to lessen the tension somewhat in preparation for further steps.

The issue of disarmament itself can serve as an illustration of what has been said here concerning the risks of too general an approach and the advantages of the more concrete one. It is quite clear—a clarity gained through painful experience of more than a dozen years—that a general and over-all system for the regulation of armaments—even "only" one for abolition or internationalization of atomic weapons—cannot be had at this point. An agreement of such far-reaching nature would, indeed, be a major step for the second phase—that which would follow upon the period of the "holding operation"—and its implications will be discussed later. An even more radical approach which has occasionally been suggested would consist in unilateral disarmament. Its advocacy is related to the general theory of integral pacifism (or Gandhiism in the form of nonviolent resistance), which suggests that nations unilaterally scrap their bombs in the realization that war in the atomic age has become suicidal and in the expectation that no remaining nuclear power would be in a position to wage war against a world which would subject it to universal moral condemnation.[6] Realists are perhaps tempted to reject this sort of proposal offhandedly as "utopian," but it may not actually be quite so utopian as it would appear at first view. Supposing the United States destroys its nuclear arsenal unilaterally, calling upon all to follow suit. Would the Soviets attack, or use atomic blackmail to subject the West to its control? Probably not. The power advantage might be canceled

[6] For this attitude see, for instance, the characteristic letters to the Editor of the New York *Times* by A. J. Muste and C. Rajagopalachari (October 8 and December 26, 1954).

by the universal antipathy raised in such an event. And yet one comes to the reluctant conclusion that such a policy would be impractical, for what is more likely to happen in such an event is this: The Soviet bloc would continue a policy of expansion through "peaceful penetration"; at some point wars fought with conventional arms would ensue, and any such war might easily degenerate into all-out war, which then would be one-sidedly nuclear; for in such circumstances the Soviets would hardly be ready to entertain defeat, if it seemed a possibility to them, by foregoing the use of available nuclear force, which in that event, of course, would no longer be balanced by deterrent nuclear force on their enemy's side.

Discussion of overly general disarmament projects merely detracts attention from what is perhaps feasible. To this the story of over a decade of disarmament efforts bears testimony. No detailed study of the attempts to arrive at an international agreement on regulating atomic armaments need be made here. Nothing is more illustrative of the urge to obtain "security" in the face of the all-pervading insecurity created by the new weapon developments than the long drawn-out, forever failing but ever renewed efforts to get out of the new insecurity through some international arrangement involving prohibition of the use of the weapon, destruction of existing facilities, or whatever other measures have been suggested. It is quite obvious that no feeling of genuine security can be expected unless existing weapons are destroyed or otherwise taken out of the hands of individual powers, and future production of atomic energy, whether for peaceful or other purposes, is so supervised that a violation of the respective international agreement is for all practical purposes excluded. The same sort of ironclad guarantee is necessary in case of agreed-upon reduction in stages, limitation of manufacture to certain agreed-upon types or levels of armaments, time limits, etc. But the history of a decade of efforts in this direction has been one of frustration. It has closely paralleled that of general superpower diplomacy. Beginning with some genuine efforts involving debatable and debated plans, the attempts soon ran into a stalemate during which "negotiations" have been used largely for propaganda and jockeying for cold war positions, with a United Nations fig leaf, as it were, covering up the nuclear armaments race and the forever progressing, fantastic technological development of the new weapons system.

It is the sad story of missed opportunities. For what is at least technically feasible at one point may no longer be so at some later point of development. During the first years of the atomic age, so the majority of experts assured us, supervised destruction of existing weapons and control of the manufacture of new ones through a safe inspection system was within the realm of the possible. But this chance was not used, first during the period of the American atomic monopoly, due to Soviet apprehensions, subsequently, when the monopoly was broken, due to American fears. Despite the warnings of the experts the opportunity to control nuclear weapons was again allowed to pass when such new and increasingly dangerous developments as the emergence of the hydrogen bomb and the beginning of the missile age occurred. In each instance—close students of the problem believe—the vast increase in the number of bombs, other weapons, and installations, rendered impracticable the functioning of any safe system of discovery and inspection once a certain period of grace had been allowed to go unused. How, for instance, could any power be prevented at this point from hiding stocks of fission or fusion weapons where so many exist—to mention just one of the numerous and apparently insuperable difficulties? It has even been asserted that there would not be enough qualified persons in the entire world to supervise the kind of inspection system which would be required today (supposing inspection was still feasible at all). The result, in the words of one nuclear scientist, has been that

we may have to add, to the appalling knowledge of the material and biological damage of an atomic war, the recognition that time for an effectively controlled atomic disarmament has irretrievably passed . . . . Mankind will have to live, from now on, with unlimited and unchecked stockpiles of atomic and thermonuclear explosives piling up, first in America and the Soviet Union, then in Great Britain, and later in other countries as well.[7]

In view of this we may well query whether plans of the sort so far proposed (whether by West or East) now retain any degree of practicality.

Does this imply that nothing can be done in the field of control, that more and more powers must simply go on piling up more and more weapons capable of destroying the world twice or a hundredfold over? Here, as in other respects, an "all-or-nothing" kind of approach would be disastrous. Concrete—albeit, compared with the over-all issues, relatively small—problems could and should be tackled. Thus an agreement on the cessation of hydrogen weapons' and similar tests, while surely not solving the larger problem of thermonuclear armaments, would constitute an important advance—and this not only because it might prevent the development of even more frightful weapons, nor primarily because of its effect on radiation pollution of the air, but, so far as future prospects of East-West accommodation are concerned, primarily be-

[7] Eugene Rabinowitch, "Living with H-Bombs," *Bulletin of the Atomic Scientists,* 11: 6 (1955). A fairly realistic and balanced picture of what at this point appears possible and impossible in regard to atomic inspection and disarmament emerges from a number of technical experts' contributions to Seymour Melman (ed.), *Inspection for Disarmament* (New York, 1958). It is, in the main, a rather somber picture, much more so than would appear from the editor's own, overoptimistic conclusions concerning the possibility of "inspection by the people" (pp. 38 ff.).

cause of the psychological advantage of creating an atmosphere of lessened tension. Objections raised by the American and British governments in this respect have been less than convincing, since an agreement of this type would be self-policing, and experiments for testing less powerful weapons than the existing ones (e.g., bombs for "tactical" use, or "clean" bombs) might be licensed by an international agency of supervision (since this is an area where, fortunately, supervision is practical). Here, as has happened so often before, it seems that the underlying cause of negativism lies solely in the suspicions raised by the fact that it is the other side which has taken the initiative. But the fact that something feasible and desirable is suggested by the "wrong" side (possibly for mere propaganda reasons and in the expectation that the opponent will reject it without consideration) should not preclude its discussion. The Soviets' advocacy of "peace" and "coexistence" must not be allowed to make of the West a supporter of war and "no existence"!

Even at this very moment we may be in danger of missing new opportunities in regard to weapons developments. As we have already seen, whether or not more powers become nuclear powers may have a decisive effect on future international politics. Agreements by the present nuclear powers on withholding the weapons (or their secrets) from others should now be on their agenda (provided it is not already too late in view of the technical factors indicated). And, space technology, now in its infancy, may still offer a chance to regulate military uses of outer space by an agreement which a few years from now may no longer be enforceable or supervisable.[8] There has been and might continue to be real tragedy in what Henry Kissinger calls the American "lack of tragic ex-

[8] As these words were being written, President Eisenhower made his proposal to this effect. "The time to move is now in the infancy of this art of penetrating the atmosphere and reaching outer space" (John Foster Dulles, see New York *Times*, January 17, 1958).

perience" if it produces again and again that "absence of a sense of urgency" [9] which prevents solutions when there is still time.

DELIMITATION OF SPHERES

Any holding operation which is intended to lessen tension and make adjustment of concrete issues possible must be based on a provisional delimitation of spheres which the two opposing camps would have to recognize—tacitly or otherwise—as circumscribing the Communist and the non-Communist worlds. And this demarcation must, in turn, be based upon the existing status quo. For, if one would insist on drawing more "equitable," "fair," or "advantageous" lines first, this demand by itself more likely than not would provoke new or rekindle old conflicts rather than establish foundations for accommodation. It would require the conclusion of exactly those agreements which the establishment of provisional spheres would be designed to facilitate, and which therefore can only follow upon them.

In embarking on such policies, however, it would be of the greatest importance for leaders to clarify to themselves and to their publics what such a delimitation would imply and what it would not. An agreement on maintaining the status quo would by its very nature not involve the surrender of anything either side now holds. Yet, in an age of ideological obsessions, it may be expected to run into difficulties connected with the suspicions of the opposing systems and the emotionalism of the clashing world views. Thus we have to expect an objection to the effect that the agreement would involve the renunciation of objectives and policies of "liberation," and therefore constitute "appeasement"; or, that any delimitation involves "recognition" and would therefore amount to lending moral or even legal approval to existing conditions.

[9] *Nuclear Weapons and Foreign Policy* (New York, 1957), pp. 426 f.

A public opinion expected to back a holding operation of the kind indicated must be made to realize that such arguments are spurious. Renouncing policies of "liberation," for instance, would not involve "giving away" anything we have or can reasonably expect to have without paying the price of all-out war. Second, nothing in a *de facto* accommodation need be interpreted as "recognition" or "approval" in any legal or moral sense, or as sacrifice of any moral or ideological principle, exactly as in the case of "recognition" in the technical sense (recognition of states or governments); mere establishment of relations on the basis of *de facto* control of territory does not grant moral or political approval. It is the identification of such recognition with such approval that has so often caused confusion in the past.[10]   Third, we must realize that any "renunciations" and sacrifices we might consider involved in such an agreement would be mutual. If the West would permit the—provisional—continuation of Soviet controls, the "oppressive" rule of Peiping Communists, the "ill-gotten fruits of aggression," etc., the East would—provisionally—sanction "colonial exploitation," "oppression" of racial or similar minorities (or majorities), and, quite generally, the continuation of what in Communist ideology constitutes the rule of the "wealthy few" over the "exploited masses."

Neither does the standstill agreement here suggested imply that there can be no changes whatsoever in the status quo; all it does require is that the superpowers abstain from making change their major policy objective. Both sides, therefore, could continue to entertain hopes. For nothing would prevent nations or populations, underground or above-the-ground movements, present or exiled rulers and governments, from

[10] The illusionary nature of doctrines and policies of "nonrecognition" à la Stimson, unless accompanied by or followed up with policies of actual "liberation," must by now be clear to all who have studied the effects, or rather, the absence of any effects and the resulting inconveniences of the League of Nations' and Stimson's nonrecognition policies in the thirties.

persevering in the hope that internal changes, breakdowns, upheavals, or revolutions will one day bring about liberation of whatever and whoever, according to their various and diverging views, is entitled to it.   Thus the West may hope that another seventeenth of June in the Soviet Zone of Germany may bring about a situation with which its present rulers are unable to cope and thus lead to the liberation of that now enslaved portion of the German people; the East may hope that an election victory of the Italian Communist Party will free the Italian toiler from the yoke of capitalism and the country from being a NATO satellite; or that the West will be defeated in Malaya or Laos or Indonesia, and that these will join the Peiping-controlled new Greater East Asia Co-Prosperity Sphere.   Delimitation of spheres would merely imply renunciation, in such events, of open military intervention; that is, each side would leave it to the other to deal with the situation in their respective spheres as best they can and as they see fit.   If one side manages to cope with its difficulties, the other side must postpone realization of its hopes.   If it cannot, it has to take the loss in stride; it cannot, then, assert with any amount of plausibility that what happened was due to intervention on the part of the other.   That such charges could no longer be leveled would by itself serve to alleviate tension.   The West, then, would have only itself to blame if, let us say, Burma were lost because too feeble an economic assistance program left the population to misery exploited by Communist propaganda; and the East would have only itself to blame if one of its satellites were lost because an overemphasis on building heavy industry resulted in lowering living standards and driving its population to despair.

A couple of thorny problems would still remain, however, under *de facto* delimitation.   Despite the emphasis one might put on the *de facto* nature of the delimitation, a certain discouragement of those groups and forces in the world whose hopes are placed in essential change would be inevitable. Chinese all over the world, and especially those in South-East Asia who are now still siding with Nationalist China, might turn to Peiping. In addition, the West might lose its "silent allies" behind the Iron Curtain. The same consideration would appear to apply to world Communism. In the long run, however, the advantages of maintaining unrest or of nourishing hopes may well be outweighed by the grave dangers in keeping alive expectations without being able to satisfy them. Disillusionment created when hopes remain unfulfilled, resentment incurred after an unsuccessful uprising during which help from abroad was not forthcoming, may be ably exploited by one's opponent, as witness what happened in East Germany after the failure of the revolt in June, 1953, or in Hungary when the West failed to intervene in the bloody suppression of the revolution of 1956.

Lastly, there is the problem of distinguishing permitted from prohibited interference. If a delimitation of spheres rules out open military interference—as it clearly must—what about indirect means, such as propaganda or economic assistance? It would probably be asking too much to rule them out too. It can hardly be supposed that the West will agree to cease telling the Poles how much better the free world is, or even asking them to demand more independence; the East, by the same token, will not forego the chance to inform the French or the Pakistanis how much they are enslaved and exploited, and to call on them to join the camp of peace and democracy. There should be nothing amiss with ideological competition per se in the eyes of those who believe in the higher value of their respective ideals. And even if such competition should be coupled with competition in economic assistance, it would seem that the people concerned could only benefit if, say, American assistance to India provoked the Soviets into inaugurating their own Point Four program for the "exploited" Asian nations, as they have already begun to do; or if a planned rise in Rumanian living standards were met by increased Western efforts to establish trade relations with satellites.

This still leaves open one problem closely connected with modern totalitarianism and its techniques: What about an attempt to modify the agreed-upon demarcation line through "subversion"? How, we may ask, can a clear line be held if powers or regimes are permitted to assist—or even to instigate —in any manner at all opposition forces, subversives, revolutionaries, underground movements, or liberation groups on the other side of the Divide; provided, of course, that such assistance proceeds not in the form of pure economic assistance to the country in question, or as general ideological appeal, but through shipping military or strategic supplies to specific groups, or through sending out propagandists or "advisors," or possibly saboteurs, or openly inciting to insurrection? Such Trojan-horse tactics, most of them originally invented by the Nazis and subsequently perfected by the Communists, are no longer a monopoly of totalitarian regimes; their opponents likewise, if only in self-defense, have learned how to make use of them. It has been remarked in another connection that classifying them as "indirect aggression" serves only to muddy efforts toward drawing clear distinctions between that which calls for nuclear "retaliation" and that which does not. Here we meet the same problem again. Is it possible, and desirable, to arrive at a clearer definition of "aggression"?

A SIMPLIFIED "AGGRESSION" TEST

What constitutes "aggression"? Can we hope to arrive at an agreement on what it means and implies, so as to be able to agree on what has to be renounced or foregone in the interest of delimiting spheres and maintaining a provisional and "cold" peace?

The vagueness of present aggression tests [11] stands in sharp contrast to the overriding role which the notion of "aggression" plays as criterion and determinant in the most vital foreign policy decisions. The word has become an all-purpose slogan, enabling policy makers to slur over the difficulties inherent in devising clear lines of decision making. Whether it is a question of defining the *casus belli* (or *interveniendi*) for an alliance, or the problem of drawing a line between what is permitted and what is forbidden to members of a collective security organization, whether it is a matter of announcing in which cases "massive retaliation" with thermonuclear weapons may be expected or a matter of deciding under which circumstances some other means of force will be resorted to against another country, it is a safe bet that at one point or another the word "aggression" will make its appearance like a *deus ex machina* as the supposedly clear and unambiguous *terminus technicus* for decisive distinctions.

But in this lies the great deception (either of others or of oneself). For the term "aggression," as it is commonly used, cannot possibly serve the purpose of clear distinction. Its "moralistic" or "legalistic" overtones themselves indicate how far we have traveled from "classical" times and attitudes, with their frank and unashamed use of terms like "war," when the use of force was the permitted though ultimate means of conducting international politics. Under the impact of "the bomb" nobody cares or dares any more to claim a right to make "war" as he pleases; indeed, it is generally not even claimed any longer as a legitimate means of enforcing one's "rights." But not much is gained by the renunciation of the right to wage "war" so long as one insists on his right to use force "in self-defense" (individual or collective) against "ag-

---

[11] The details of legal and other attempts to define aggression need not detain us here; a survey of recent literature on aggression is to be found in Julius Stone, *Legal Controls of International Conflicts* (New York, 1954), pp. 330 ff.

gression," when the latter term is left undefined and thus denotes whatever one wants it to denote. In the end, then, it becomes practically identical with whatever is deemed to threaten one's "vital interests" or "security." "Aggression" then is whatever one wants to impute to the other fellow as "bad" or 'unjust" or "evil."

Under opposing ideologies this results in complete confusion of language and concepts. What to the one side appears as "aggression" to the other constitutes the sum-total of those trends and tendencies that arise "naturally" out of given conditions in the different parts of the world. Thus, in the eyes of Communists, social revolutionary trends in any region outside the Soviet-Chinese sphere appear as the natural outgrowth of "objective" conditions prevailing under capitalism, imperialism, or colonialism, even though the "socialist motherland" of all "toilers" may consider it a duty imposed on it by history to assist and stimulate these trends (the "vanguard" role of Communist parties). In Marxian parlance, one plays the role of "midwife" to that which is bound to be born. But to the other side the "midwife" is the "conspirator," the "aggressor" or world enemy responsible for whatever is so "born." Contrariwise, in Western interpretation, freedom and liberation trends in the totalitarian world (which, if the West is sincere, should also include fascist-controlled countries) emerge as the natural outgrowth of conditions under which the free life of individuals and groups is stifled. And, in turn, the free world reserves the right to lend assistance in a way that may well appear menacing ("aggressive") to the other side.

Thus the unsophisticated as well as the cynics on both sides "know" what constitutes "aggression"; to them any and all things and concepts, be they ever so complicated, are simple because they always know what they believe in or what they want: "We'll know aggression when we see it." [12] They re-

[12] See quotation above, p. 192, and other references there.

fuse to take cognizance of the fact that there are not only two opposing camps but that their notions, "knowings," or ideas are bound to be diametrically opposed, too. To them, the term "aggression" is merely a verbal weapon to be used to legitimize policies and justify the eventual use of force; both sides, in the latter event, would apply it in "self-defense against aggression." Traditional wars, likewise, used to be fought "in defense of" rights or "legitimate" interests on the part of *each* of the contestants. Thus we are back to where we started, except that wars, "in defense" or otherwise, may now be mutually annihilative.

Is it possible, under these circumstances, to agree on a definition which is not vague or mutually exclusive? In the protracted history of efforts to arrive at an internationally agreed-upon test Soviet and Western suggestions have been in sharp conflict. The Soviet attitude,[13] contained in what is still known as the "Litvinov proposal" (also known as the "Politis proposal," after its chief promoter at the time of the League of Nations), takes so-called "objective" factors as yardsticks, defining, in an enumerative way, as "aggressor" that country which invades the territory of another country or otherwise subjects it to military attacks (bombardment from the air, etc.). It goes only slightly beyond such "direct" criteria by including in its definition of aggression also the "support of armed bands" invading another country and using the territory of the supporting country as a base of operations. To the West, this has not seemed to go far enough toward including in the definition "indirect" methods of aggression, but, despairing of incorporating all the imaginable cases of indirect aggression into general formulae or provisions, the United States and her allies have been inclined to give up trying to define aggression by international agreement altogether for fear of becoming entrapped by words.

[13] On it see W. W. Kulski, in *American Journal of International Law,* 49: 532 (1955).

These attitudes clearly reflect interests. What the West is most afraid of is expansion through indirect means, like subversion, fomenting of civil strife, etc., of which the Soviets are most likely to be guilty, while the East fears direct attack more than the indirect approach. The West, of course, is right in its realization that means outside direct attack may serve the policies of the other side, possibly even better than military means. But for this reason, to oppose any attempt at arriving at a definition of aggression altogether is the counsel of despair. A court, faced with the task of interpreting what "due process of law" means, cannot refuse to do so because the expression is obscure, or because definition might show the would-be lawbreaker ways to circumvent the law. In the absence of definition each side is completely free; any agreed-upon definition is therefore better than none. Thus, the choice is between a narrower one, with emphasis on the more easily verifiable "objective" criteria, and a broader one which would include a larger number of "indirect" techniques and policies. Since the chief virtue of defining aggression today lies in providing the countries of the world with clear standards for knowing when they might expect warlike "retaliation," the simpler test would seem the more practical one, whatever the various interests of the powers may otherwise be. Under the "indirect" standards, whatever their other merits, definitions tend to be so broad as to become practically meaningless and thus to defeat their purpose of delimiting the *casus belli*.

Would this imply an unwarranted disadvantage for the West? Not necessarily. All it implies is foregoing the use of force against an outside country as a reaction to attempts at "boring from within." But war would seem to be a poor way to counter such attempts anyway. Countries affected by foreign-instigated subversion or similar "indirect aggression" remain, of course, entitled to take, within their sphere, whatever measures they see fit to resort to. That is, they may outlaw or otherwise combat subversives, Communist parties and organizations, and whatever else seems dangerous; they may prevent the import of weapons or other supplies, arrest saboteurs and propagandists, restrict propaganda from abroad by closing the channels of communication; in short, they may, in retaliation, do all that which totalitarian regimes do whenever they deem it necessary. Additionally—and this would be an indirect but in many respects a more effective approach—they might try to strengthen that which prevents totalitarian subversion from taking root in the first place: economic opportunities and living standards; racial and social equalities; a sense of freedom and security. If the West despairs of doing this, if it loses faith in its ability to give the people and nations on its side the "better life," or at least as good a life as the totalitarian world can promise, it deserves to be defeated.

Opting for "objective" aggression tests does not imply acceptance of the Litvinov definitions without qualification, however. But the objection raised here does not concern their "rigidity"; the trap lies elsewhere. The simplicity of the "objective" criteria is deceptive. Any definition of aggression in terms of "crossing frontiers," "invading foreign territory," etc., if it is to work, has to be predicated on a system in which the units of international relations are well circumscribed geographically and well defined politically. In other words, there has to be general agreement on standards for recognition and on similar legal-political criteria of statehood. But, as has been pointed out before,[14] an agreement on standards and principles of statehood is frequently absent today among the two chief protagonists; and with the evanescence of clear-cut international units and unambiguous frontiers the possibility of applying the simple criteria of "violation of territorial integrity" has vanished too. It is therefore not surprising that East-West conflicts have been apt to break out at exactly those

14 Above, pp. 161–63.

neuralgic points where such an agreement has been most conspicuously absent. It has been in Korea, Berlin, Indo-China, that what appeared as "aggression" to the one side could and did most easily seem "defense" to the other. How, indeed, could one speak unequivocally of "crossing international boundaries," or of "armed invasion of another country's territory" in those instances? What in the Korean situation constituted "foreign attack" in Western eyes, to the East meant "outbreak of hostilities within one country," that is, "civil war." This proves the uselessness of the Politis-test in some of the most crucial recent or present-day situations, unless it is supplemented with something else.

It is here that mutual bipolar accommodation might be of assistance. If such an adjustment, as its first, basic step, proceeded to draw lines around the globe delimiting the respective spheres of the blocs and defining the units which they were both prepared to recognize within clearly defined boundaries, there might then be a common understanding that these units and these lines would be the ones to which the criteria of an objective aggression test would henceforth apply. In other words, one would here have demarcations which could not be crossed without risking counteraction. Again, it should be understood that such demarcations would not imply concessions regarding what each side considers as "legitimate" or "fair"; neither would they constitute definitive settlements conferring unequivocal title, as European settlements following upon general wars used to do in the classical era of international relations. All that seems required and practicable now is an agreement concerning a one-purpose line: the line which divides two spheres and whose crossing implies crossing the line from peace to war. Whether North and South Korea, then, are considered "legally" one country or "de facto" two, whether crossing from East Germany into West Germany means crossing a "real" international boundary or not, whether attacking Formosa from the mainland of China "juridically" involves attacking foreign soil or "liberating" part of China then would no longer matter. What would matter is that the Thirty-eighth Parallel or the zonal boundaries in Germany, or the Formosa channel are defined as those "provisional," "truce," "armistice," or "compromise" lines whose violation constitutes "aggression." What, in that event, is to be regarded as "crossing frontiers," etc., in the technical sense may then be defined in Politis terms. The thing that counts is to agree upon where and how to draw the lines.

Can the East, which by its very nature is more "dynamic" than the West, be expected to agree to such a self-denying ordinance? According to its doctrine of the "just war" (any "war of liberation from capitalism and imperialism"), drawing of lines might preclude it from the "rightful" prosecution of its "liberation" efforts, or from intervening in the struggle of "oppressed classes against their oppressors." [15] But, first of all, such a renunciation would constitute a *quid pro quo* for the West's foregoing the "indirect" aggression test; both sides, after all, must make concessions if there is to be adjustment. And second, any accommodation of this kind presupposes that the participants in the present conflict or contest realize their overriding interest in the prevention of at least the "Big War." [16] If, in addition to the drawing of the lines, there

[15] It should be noticed that, despite this doctrine, the emphasis in Soviet legal discussion has been entirely on a static rather than a dynamic interpretation of international law; that is, on "sovereignty" and the "sovereign rights" of nations, on duty of nonintervention, on delimitation of jurisdictions, and, last but not least, on "objective" aggression tests. All of this lends itself more easily to a policy of "peaceful coexistence" than does the doctrine of the "just war," and thus would seem to favor a policy of mutual accommodation.

[16] Those who like historical parallels may perhaps derive some comfort from the practice of another "expansionist" movement with a "just-war" theory. I refer to the Moslems who, according to recent investigations, once they had concluded a treaty with a Christian ruler, were generally

could be agreement on not using the atomic (or at least the thermonuclear) weapon first,[17] the danger of the "Big War" would be further diminished. Without such an agreement, even an objective aggression test would still involve grave risks. Suppose a border clash at the Thirty-eighth Parallel or at the border between West Berlin and the Soviet Zone in Germany is reported as "invasion by armed forces" and interpreted as the beginning of the "real thing" by the West (or the East), which thereupon starts retaliating with nuclear force. It may then appear—too late—that it was only a minor skirmish for which only local authorities were responsible. It requires some time to verify—possibly with the aid of international organizations, through Security Council investigations, or in similar ways—what actually is happening or has happened. To assure avoidance of all-out war, therefore, nothing less than the combination of three things would seem necessary: clear delimitation of spheres ("demarcation lines"); agreement on "objective" aggression standards; commitment not to use the nuclear weapon first.

A RETURN TO "LIMITED WAR"?

Adoption of the three measures mentioned above would be likely to reduce somewhat the chances of war breaking out in the future. But it would mean erring through that combination of overoptimism and legalism which in the past has often been the hallmark of plans for world peace and world organization to assume that wars—whether permitted under those standards or not—then would no longer occur at all. And it is therefore still necessary in any plan for a holding operation

---

more faithful in the observation of the agreement than the Christians, although, theoretically, they considered themselves in a state of perpetual war with them (see Arthur Nussbaum, "Forms and Observance of Treaties in the Middle Ages and the Early Sixteenth Century," in G. A. Lipsky [ed.], *Law and Politics in the World Community* [Berkeley, Calif., 1953], pp. 191 ff.).

17 As suggested above, p. 197.

to devote some attention to questions concerning the prospects of war, of avoidance of war, and of limiting its effects.

Any discussion of "what to do about war" in terms of future international relations must start from the transformation of the underlying structure of territoriality and the impact it has had on power and power politics, in particular, on the "security" and the "security feeling" of the units of international politics. It has been shown in the first part of this study that in the classical age of modern international relations the structure of statehood was such that a comparatively high degree of impermeability and defensibility of hard-shell units provided nations with a correspondingly high degree of security, and that the ensuing feeling of safety was enhanced by additional factors, like economic self-sufficiency, trust in a relatively stable power balance, standards ruling out the political annihilation of members of the "family of nations," and so forth. This situation allowed for a clear distinction between "peace" and "war," not only through the somewhat superficial criterion of existence or absence of "hostilities," [18] but also on the basis of genuine security feelings.[19] "Peace" prevailed whenever a feeling of security permitted states to pursue their "national interests" by other than forceful means, and "war" signified that condition in which power units would try to remove threats to their individual "security" (or, beyond this, to satisfy other "national interests") by attacking the hard shell of other units and in this way compel them to yield to their demands. It was thus a situation in which, despite the security dilemma in which power units find them-

[18] See Fritz Grob, *The Relativity of War and Peace* (New Haven, 1949).
[19] A. A. Berle has made a valuable contribution to this problem by pointing out that peace throughout history has always been "somebody's peace" (the "king's peace," the Roman peace): "peace is a result, not a condition" (see his *Tides of Crisis: A Primer of Foreign Relations* [New York, 1957], pp. 240 ff.). This corresponds to my view on the importance of a unit's "pacification" for its territoriality and hence its security and protection.

selves in *all* "anarchic" societies, a relatively strong sense of security ordinarily prevailed over long stretches of time and among many of the units within that society; this "normal" condition could legitimately be called "peace."

Then came the time when impermeability and the concomitant reliance on the state's own power was more and more undermined by factors like the increasing economic interdependence of nations and the increasing range and destructiveness of arms. Today, with impermeability gone, insecurity is the all-pervading feeling. Even in the absence of actual hostilities, therefore, "peace" in the classical sense can no longer be said to prevail; rather, we live in that continual uncertainty that lies between "war" and "peace" and that already existed in the period between the two world wars. Then it accounted for the widespread conviction that there was merely a prolonged "armistice"; now it has become known as the "cold war," a situation of insecurity and uneasy truce interspersed with occasional "little," localized wars and similar uses of force or with periods of "good" or, at least, "better" feeling called "cold peace." We have, perhaps, not yet quite reached the acme of insecurity feeling, at least we in America, a country which until recently enjoyed "atomic superiority" and which, moreover, has remained uninvaded for more than a century and unbombed even in the Second World War. Consequently, it is still difficult for most Americans to realize what "permeability" with its menace of instant annihilation entails. But it is safe to predict that, once the fact that nuclear parity through atomic "saturation" leaves the country wide open to devastation has penetrated, war scares are likely to be more frequent and war crises, more violent, thus rendering the "pursuit of happiness" and the "peaceful life" which we have known more and more precarious. What this may do to a society which lately, in contrast to a more daring approach to life in the past, has put prime emphasis on individual security and "living standards" should be the object of somber reflection. It is evasion of the issue to approach the problem in that frequent spirit of bravado which takes for granted that the American people will be able "to take it"; conditions likely to follow nuclear attack are unprecedented.

In its effects, as in other respects, thermonuclear war would be "the ultimate." In respect to time: the entire battle would be concentrated in the initial stage when minutes may decide everything; as for numbers: millions, or tens of millions, may be destroyed, together with most of the material products and witnesses of our own and of past civilizations (the cities and their present life, the works of art, the libraries, the museums, the archives). In regard to mechanization and de-humanization of warfare itself: war used to involve "human" relations, even in the fight. The fight was once hand to hand, then weapon to weapon, where the warrior would see the blood, hear the moan. With firearms, the enemy became more remote, and fighting more mechanized. But even with long-range artillery, or the dropping of bombs from planes, some result of personal action—the flames of cities, the smoke of battlefields—would still be visible, and thus a minimal connection between act and destruction, actor and victim remained. The pinnacle of de-humanization was reached with Hitler's *Vergeltungswaffe* (the V-2 rocket). There is not much difference, except in degree, between this and a "push-button" war fought with intercontinental ballistic nuclear-warhead missiles. This can be called the bureaucratization—or reification—of fight. A decision reached in some office, arrived at in office-like manner, and implemented in office-type surroundings, has its effects a couple of hours, or minutes, later somewhere half way around the world, destroying that world; this is likely to release a counterdecision "effectuating" a corresponding result in the "initiating" part of the world. The "transaction" produces mutual annihilation, neatly and according to plan. Paradoxically, it is imaginable that, with neither side capable of assessing the effect of its action on the other right away, both will surrender immediately and unconditionally! It is more likely, however, that sheer anarchy will ensue. If all-encompassing, the "third war" may turn out to be the "ultimate" end in that it may spell finis to the human story on earth.

On this realization some have been inclined to build what may be called a "theory of the vanishing war aim" and to draw too optimistic a conclusion from an all-out war's impracticability. War, so one says, is no longer practical because it denies its initiator that reward which used to be his incentive, namely, the "loot" which he hoped to gain. Thus Churchill, in his speech of March 1, 1955,[20] suggested:

Major war of the future will differ therefore from anything we have known in the past, in this one significant respect that each side at the outset will suffer what it dreads the most—the loss of everything it has ever known. The deterrents will grow continually in value. In the past an aggressor has been tempted by the hope of snatching an early advantage. In future, he may be deterred by the knowledge that the other side has the certain power to inflict swift, inescapable and crushing retaliation.

In a similar vein, Arnold Toynbee has said:

In the past, war has seemed to make sense because it has seemed reasonable to make two assumptions: *a)* that the soldier, by risking, and, if necessary, sacrificing his life at the front has at least a chance of being able, at this price, to defend something behind the front effectively; *b)* that it is better to win a war than to lose it. But the invention of atomic weapons looks as if it may obliterate the formerly valid distinctions between soldier and civilian, front and rear, victor and vanquished.[21]

20 New York *Times*, March 2, 1955.
21 New York *Times Magazine*, February 20, 1955. See also B. H. Liddell Hart to the effect that "victory has no point if its purpose has disappeared—from the face of the earth" (*The Defense of the West* [London, 1950], p. 132).

This theory, like similar deterrence doctrines which we discussed at another point,[22] is open to similar objections. Such a war's lack of "practicality," which as such is incontestable, does not exclude all possibility of its occurrence. For one thing, we cannot rely on absolute rationality in the behavior and calculations of nations, and, above all, there is the security dilemma, which, even in the absence of incentives such as "snatching" an early advantage, may become a motivation for "preventive war."

Our age has been fertile in producing other attempts to prove that war is becoming less likely under certain, attainable conditions—attempts which testify to the power of wishful thinking in an age of anxiety. Thus the realist Churchill himself at Teheran cogitated that general satisfaction with a status quo might ensure a stable peace:

I answered that . . . the government of the world must be entrusted to satisfied nations, who wished nothing more than they had. If the world government were in the hands of hungry nations there would always be danger. But none of us had any reason to seek for anything more . . . . We were like rich men dwelling at peace within their habitations.[23]

The opposite conclusion from this "rich man's," or "powerful man's," doctrine has been drawn by Leopold Kohr, who asserts that, whenever a nation transcends a certain size and volume of power, it "detonates in spontaneous aggression"; he calls this the "atomic power theory of aggression." [24] Peace may be more certain in the situation envisaged by Churchill; war may arise out of developments envisaged by Kohr. The trouble with both is that they are theories of the "single fac-

[22] Above, p. 184.
[23] *The Second World War*, 5 (New York, 1951), 382.
[24] See his letter to the editor of the New York *Times*, December 5, 1950, and, in addition, his volume *The Breakdown of Nations* (London, 1957), in which, however, he wavers between considering absolute size and relative superiority in power the decisive thing.

tor," [25] and that they both neglect the impact of the security dilemma. Churchill's expectation that "satisfied" superpowers would remain satisfied with what they had gained was, unfortunately, not long in encountering refutation in the postwar era through the very developments of the cold war. Kohr's doctrine, in its generality, is disproved by the *pax Romana* and similar peace situations established from time to time by aggrandized and powerful nations.[26]

One might, perhaps, raise another question, or expectation, also connected with conditions of "satisfaction," in particular, economic satisfaction, but referring to individuals rather than nations as such. There are those who see the most significant developments of our times in the steady and vigorous rise of general standards of living. This rise has produced, and is bound to continue to produce, increasingly an almost exclusive interest of people in their personal well-being, and, consequently, a decrease in their ideological and political involvement. Indifference to whatever may be at stake in a war, coupled with ever closer attachment to the goods one may lose in war, the argument concludes, thus renders war obsolete.

In reference to this argument, or theory, too, the skeptic will have his doubts, among them these: (*a*) Despite distaste for war and appreciation of the good things of life, the world may run into war because of insufficient influence of this kind

25 Kohr admits unashamedly that he has "tried to develop a single theory through which not only some but all phenomena of the social universe can be reduced to a common denominator," namely, size, with "only one cause behind all forms of social misery: bigness" (*The Breakdown of Nations*, p. ix). For all its exaggeration, the idea merits attention, possibly more in the field of general societal relations and of internal affairs than in the realm of foreign policy.

26 Kohr's positive suggestions likewise make little sense. He suggests, for instance, the division of Europe into small regional or provincial units. But has the disintegration of British India decreased tension in South Asia? Or that of the Ottoman Empire the tension in the Near East?

of public attitude on policy makers—who may be motivated by ideologies, see the security dilemma more clearly, etc. (b) Even though this attitude might influence policies in Western countries, in the East it is likely to be less strong or less influential, and it might be used by the East to blackmail the more complacent West. (c) While living standards are on the rise in the advanced countries of both East and West, they may not rise sufficiently, or they might even decline, in the vast "underdeveloped" part of the world faced with the vicious circle of the population-resources problem,[27] where the age-old causes of war thus would continue to play their part.

A realistic approach has therefore still to reckon with war as a possibility, and the important question thus is: With what kind of war in preference to what other kind? We have already seen that under nuclear conditions, instead of the classical, clear-cut distinction between peace and war, we have, realistically speaking, this dichotomy. On one hand, something threatens which should not be called "war" at all any longer, because, although it may still be intended as a "continuation of policy by other means," in its effects it now negates, or contradicts, any imaginable policy aim; "all-out war" is a process of mutual annihilation. On the other hand, we have that product of pervasive insecurity, the cold war, a "peace" which may be called a "continuation of war (namely, the Second World War) with other means," seemingly peaceful ones, which, however, all reflect the underlying tension, and which occasionally warm up into "conventional" and more or less localized hostilities.

A holding operation of the kind here contemplated cannot be expected to bring about a change in the structure which undergirds this cold war situation. Efforts designed to prevent the outbreak of the annihilating type of war, therefore, are hardly promising if directed toward the outlawry of all

[27] On this see below, p. 316.

use of force whatsoever. Trying to establish "genuine" peace would at this point be a utopian venture. All that can be undertaken with a prospect of success is to try to see to it that conflicts which, despite accommodation efforts, lead to hostilities be limited to a "conventional"-type small and localized war. This kind of "limited war" can, and should be, kept limited not only in respect to area and weapons but also in objective. Thus, the way to keep the Korean war limited was to aim not at the unification of Korea by force of arms—desirable as this seemed to the nations joined as "United Nations"—but merely at restoring the status quo ante, i.e., at throwing the opponent's armed forces back behind the previous dividing line, the Thirty-eighth Parallel. Going beyond this involved the risk of transforming the localized war into an all-out one between the main powers as such.

More recently, the problems of "limited war" have been ably and extensively debated, but it would be too much to assert that very much has been clarified. What must be realized first of all is the difference between "limited war" in the classical era of international politics and what rendered that type of limited war possible, and limited war in the present situation. In the eighteenth century war was conducted according to what powers were able to do, and "limited" war then simply reflected their limited economic and military capabilities. Today, limited war does not indicate the limit of capabilities, and the powers face a choice among different possibilities, of which limitation of war is one. Nuclear power in principle being unlimited, the application of power is annihilative when all-out; it can be, as in prenuclear times, regulatory when less than all-out. As in so many other fields (for instance, in that of speed or of space), man today is confronted with a novel situation. Where in former times attainment of "more" meant unequivocal gain (more speed: easier reaching of distant places; more destructive power of weapons:

easier achievement of one's war aims), now for the first time it may lead to yields which are useless or even negative in character (whether you reach Los Angeles from New York in two hours or in one hour and forty-five minutes hardly matters any more; nuclear weapons destroy what you want to obtain—plus, probably, yourself). Thus, since everything in the present situation—weapons developments, power concentration in superpowers, the ideological split—is the opposite of the conditions prevailing throughout the classical period of limited war and seems to drive the powers toward the most unlimited of all imaginable conflicts, limitation of war today really involves something akin to conducting "war against nature," involving as it does deliberate restraint from that "which comes naturally"; in one student's words, "a deliberate hobbling of a tremendous power that is already mobilized and that must in any case be maintained at a very high pitch of effectiveness." [28]   And he continues, correctly, "no problem like this has ever presented itself before." [29]   Somehow, technology has led man into situations that are beyond his measure,[30] and his survival may depend on whether he will be able to exercise self-restraint and avoid making use of that which he can technically achieve.

But self-restraint in international affairs runs into (among other things) the security dilemma, and the chances for war's limitation, therefore, depend on the observance by both sides of certain minimum conditions dictated by reason.   This minimum of required rationality has been summed up by Henry A. Kissinger as demanding: (a) limitation of actual conduct and means of warfare (for instance, as to weapons, area of combat, targets), that is, that *both* sides try to avoid the

---

[28] B. Brodie, "More about Limited War," *World Politics*, 10: 114 (1957-58).

[29] *Ibid.*

[30] This discrepancy and its consequences have been stated powerfully by Guenther Anders, *Die Antiquiertheit des Menschen* (Munich, 1956).

devastation of all-out nuclear war; (*b*) limitation of objectives, that is, foregoing aiming at unconditional surrender or all-out destruction of the enemy, so that the side that gains the upper hand utilizes its advantage to offer peace on moderate (i.e., limited) terms; (*c*) conveying to the opponent whatever particular limitations one is willing to observe, this being necessary to avoid degeneration of an initially limited war into all-out conflict by inadvertence or through misinterpretation of the opponent's intentions.[31] Convincing the opponent that one means to keep war limited seems particularly vital, and doing so requires corresponding action and attitude prior to actual hostilities. It has been emphasized before how essential it is to avoid a military policy of preparing exclusively or chiefly for all-out nuclear war, in order to be able still to cope with situations in which all-out war can neither deter nor achieve actual results (except senseless destruction). But maintenance of establishments for fighting other than all-out wars is needed equally to give the opponent convincing proof of one's readiness to fight limited war. This requires a capacity to wage both nuclear and limited war. An establishment to fight all-out war must, as we have seen, be maintained for deterrence. What does the additional required capacity to wage limited war imply?

In this question those who oppose the use of *any* kind of nuclear or atomic weapon in limited war have clashed head on with those who favor "limited nuclear war." The latter are divided among themselves over the kind of nuclear limitation they advocate or believe feasible: relatively small atomic weapons for "tactical" use only; "graduated deterrence" depending on what the opponent does; or "counterforce strategy" under which nuclear attack would be carried to the enemy's military installations avoiding deliberate attack on cities, and so forth. One lay reader of the various suggestions has arrived at the skeptical

[31] Kissinger, *Nuclear Weapons and Foreign Policy*, especially chs. 5 and 6.

conclusion that whatever each side to this dispute marshals against the other by way of argument sounds equally convincing. Thus, what James E. King [32] says to show that "minor" use of atomic or nuclear weapons cannot be expected to be kept minor once hostilities have started seems as sound as do some of Kissinger's arguments concerning the danger that it may be exactly *non*readiness for limited nuclear war that may eventually lead to all-out war, because there is no preparation for anything in-between. One thus arrives at the somewhat disheartening conclusion that any kind of *general* limited war, whether purely "conventional" or "limited nuclear" in character, involves almost equal risks of eventual all-out war. The thing to aim at would be keeping hostilities not only small but as localized as possible. This involves two different efforts: first, to see to it that the cold war does not degenerate even into "small" local wars; second, if it does so nevertheless, to keep such a contest from degenerating into war involving the superpowers directly, even though initially they might use only conventional weapons. There is too great a risk of such a general war, once begun, to be transformed into nuclear war when one side weakens and sees no other way out ("war of desperation").

Efforts to keep the cold war "cold" or actual war localized are endangered by an inclination to tie up every situation, event, or incident with the over-all antagonism of the two blocs. Doing so is, in a way, understandable because of the interconnectedness of situations and happenings with practically all other events and situations in our shrunken world. But oversensitivity to this fact may result in a loss of the ability to discriminate between the really important and the minor issue, policy, or position. Incidents involving a few nationals of a country then loom so large that they can ob-

[32] "Nuclear Plenty and Limited War," *Foreign Affairs*, 35: 238 ff. (1956–57).

struct settlement of the really big issues; conflicts over the possession of tiny, strategically worthless islands threaten to degenerate into major war.   There is a real danger that policies of prestige or provocation might build up an atmosphere of crisis to such a heat that "preventive war" in the end appears justified.

But the limitation of military conflicts to local wars is the best we can hope for now.   It would mean that "marginal" or "fringe" wars, local in their restriction to limited areas of the world where the more specific conflict is located, and "peripheral" in that they happen remote from the "hearts" of the superpowers, by common if tacit agreement would substitute for the big blowup.   Paradoxically, "war," not "peace," would thus be the alternative to another type of war.[33]   From the viewpoint of the perfectionist, this implies much that seems intolerable.   For instance, it would mean recurring devastation of "fringe" areas, with all the sacrifices this demands from countries and populations concerned, in order to enable the superpowers, and the world as such, to survive.   Something which George Orwell, in his *1984*, depicted as a perpetual bleeding of mankind, a very somber prophecy, now appears as a relatively desirable objective, a policy aim worth striving for in order to avoid worse things.   This shows how far mankind has traveled toward an abyss unforeseen even in 1948 by one of the most perspicacious of observers.

"Fringe" wars thus loom as the "minor evil."   In this they can be likened to other devices and techniques we may have to resort to in order to escape world-wide conflict and which, like-

[33] Strangely, this other type of war, the "big," all-out nuclear war, would be the opposite of such local war not only in a general sense but more specifically in that there now looms the possibility that the two superpowers would kill each other off by shooting from "heart" to "heart" without pulling in or touching the regions and nations outside and between them.   Indirect effects, of course, such as fall-out and other radioactive pollution as well as economic decay, would in all likelihood affect the others too.

wise, may require sacrificing legitimate interests or aspirations of populations or nations to enable the big ones to maintain a *modus vivendi*. Partition, dividing nations like Germany, Korea, Indo-China (Vietnam), comes to mind. "Unjust" and seemingly insufferable as they may be to the people concerned, "solutions" of this sort have so far proved the only practicable ones in a cold war; they may prove inevitable even under over-all accommodation.

Might not something, at least, be done to ameliorate this situation? I do not refer here to the possible ameliorations for countries, regions, populations condemned to suffer vicariously for the benefit of all. It should be a matter of course that the remainder of the world's nations do all in their power to "repay" them to the limits of their power to wipe out the ravages of war, lend economic assistance, resettle refugees, etc., although this will not revive the dead or restore the maimed to health. I rather have in mind the question of how to make sure that the cold war does not explode into the real one.

In this respect new legal rules or novel techniques, organizations, or "systems to preserve the peace" may prove to be less useful than certain diplomatic practices. We should not try to be pretentious. After all, we are dealing with the phenomenon of war, that process into which all the concerns of men, their fears and passions, their apprehensions and even their hopes, have gone since the beginning of time. And if we consider that even under conditions of relative security legal commitments and organizational setups to enforce them had less of a chance to safeguard the peace than had old-fashioned "power politics" and diplomacy, the present *condition humaine,* characterized by total insecurity, loss of common value standards, and a rigid, uneasy two-bloc balance, can hardly be expected to lend itself better to that kind of safeguards.

Some guidance as to what is perhaps possible can be gained from the practices of the cold war, including its localized "little" wars. The Korean war, for instance, did not involve the interruption of "normal" diplomatic relations between the two major powers. Such "incidents," therefore, should be treated as "incidents" rather than as "wars" in the traditional sense, which were accompanied by the rupture of diplomatic, political, and economic relationships. Continuation of diplomatic contacts, besides rendering the outbreak of general war less likely, also facilitates the eventual settlement of local issues. Korea, moreover, resulted in a kind of *de facto* recognition of so far "nonrecognized" situations and regimes: of North Korea by the West, of the Republic of Korea by the East, and even (quite "naturally," because "unavoidably," through armistice negotiations and sitting down at conference tables) of the Chinese "People's Republic" by otherwise nonrecognizing powers like the United States. Such recognition on a *de facto* basis of what exists *de facto* could, as we have seen, become one of the procedures for the more general, overall adjustment of relations between the two power blocs. It would enable these blocs to deal more realistically with those who actually have control over the respective issues and situations. By the same token, it would prevent groups not having such control from pursuing policies—or influencing policies of the major powers—which in the absence of such control must remain illusory.

Korea also proved that observation of certain limiting rules of warfare is still feasible so long as war is fought with conventional weapons. Observation of these rules was tacitly agreed upon by the Korean belligerents. Something may be gained by a more official agreement, in the process of over-all accommodation, on rules to be so observed.[34] This kind of agreement, or a companion agreement, might also contain the

[34] Possibly by mere reference to or enumeration of the respective conventions on rules of war which the powers still want to consider valid and applicable.

rules concerning renunciation of the use of nuclear weapons and the conditions under which the renunciation would become operative, or the rules concerning restriction of their use in regard to types of weapons, targets, etc., in the event the desire is to agree on "limited nuclear war."

It is clear that such kinds of agreements will have a chance of being negotiated only under conditions of a *détente* created by preceding settlement of more concrete and specific issues now dividing the blocs. In conditions of unabated tension and arms competition, such as we now have, we are indeed far away from agreement—tacit or otherwise—on armament renunciations or limitations. As a matter of fact, it seems that the Soviet line has now hardened into ridiculing the very idea of "limited war," in particular, "limited nuclear war," insisting on an all-or-nothing approach to the problem; while Western, and in particular American, policy is inclined to make the too easy assumption that war can be limited at will by mere (and, moreover, unilateral) reference to "tactical uses of nuclear weapons" or similar declarations of intent. But, as has been stressed earlier, it will take more than mere words and optimism to arrive at reliable restraints of what the development of technology and power has placed within our capabilities. Even in the "mere" material realm of expenditure and economic sacrifice—to take an obvious example of what is required—policies for effectively combatting Communism without banking exclusively on deterrence through the "big" weapon would seem to call for three types of expenditure, each of which would amount to something like the present, full-size American-type budget for defense: first, for continuation of the present defense effort, which is chiefly devoted to the "big" weapons and corresponding establishments; second, and paralleling this, for a conventional (or combined conventional-limited nuclear) establishment, for reasons already indicated; and third, for economic and similar assistance to the underdeveloped world of a dimension hardly conceived of at present, in order to have the merest chance to deny vital areas to the East. Whether any economy—"free enterprise" or "socialist"—can bear such burdens is questionable, and this by itself might produce increased readiness to find some kind of accommodation in time. And even supposing it is feasible economically, it remains to be seen whether a nation like the United States, unused to regulation and still basically living by the standards of a business society, will be able to exercise the tremendous self-restraint required and thus to compete successfully with a society "restrained," that is, manipulated, from the top.

Finally, any policy of limitation of war or of the conduct of war requires patient effort to find ways and means for the solution of the concrete political issues. Are there any, besides those already discussed, which lend themselves to the abatement of tension and the facilitation of accommodation? We shall now discuss certain devices and procedures which may prove suitable for mitigaing the trends toward all-out war and for promoting the chances of "coexistence."

SPECIFIC PROBLEMS AND PROCEDURES

Charles B. Marshall, in his witty little study, *The Limits of Foreign Policy*,[35] reflects on how easy it seemed from the vantage point of a study room, or even an editorial office, to devise patent solutions for the world's outstanding problems, and how difficult their solution seemed when the burden of responsibility weighed upon the policy maker. It would appear advisable to learn from the experience of the experienced and to forego the tempting game of proposing solutions for the pressing problems of today or tomorrow. What today may be pressing may no longer be so tomorrow, and tomorrow may have new pressure in store. Furthermore as pointed out be-

[35] New York, 1954.

fore, the problems dividing East and West should be approached through the concreteness of individual situations, and one would arrogate to himself the business of teams of statesmen and diplomats were he to delve into such concreteness. All that can be done here is to point out the usefulness —or the lack of it—of certain devices and procedures, and to elucidate certain more general problems which an attempt to arrive at accommodation through negotiation of concrete issues may present.

It is possible, perhaps, to distinguish between two different kinds of "arrangements" in international politics: one where the issue concerns "quantitative" matters, as it were, and the difference, as in a business deal, can be "split" or similarly made the object of a "give and take"; the other one where the object of the conflict is, for one or all parties, a matter of principle or of such vital interest that no concession as to this particular point seems possible. In the latter case, in so far as it is such an important matter for one side only, there is still the possibility of arrangement through compromise if a *quid pro quo* can be found somewhere else, outside the specific matter. To the first category belong those issues of economic "imperialism," for instance, in which the conflict is over how much profit and similar benefits foreign investors should be entitled to, and how much of the total yield should remain in the respective country (in the form of wages and salaries, taxes, reinvestments, etc.). Such issues have frequently been the cause of heated international conflict, particularly since the rise of nationalism in the colonial or "backward" regions of the world. The "honor of the nation" has seemed to conflict with the "sanctity of private property" or the "sanctity of contract," principle has seemed to clash irreconcilably with principle; but for anyone approaching the problem rationally, that is, without ideological or emotional involvement, it is easy enough to look at it as a case open to potential bargaining in which the difference can be split, so as to leave a "reasonable" profit to the investor and a "reasonable" amount to workers, population, and the country in general. Contrast with this a case in which no concession in quantitative terms is possible, one, for instance, in which the issue is over the delivery (extradition) of persons desired by a hostile regime. The West could not, for instance, without betraying its highest principles, hand over to the East a political refugee seeking protection from persecution. This was the reason why the West could not yield in the issue of the repatriation of prisoners at the time of the Korean armistice negotiations. It does not, however, imply that in such a situation a stalemate is inevitable; it is quite possible that, in return for getting satisfaction in the issue of principle, one may yield to the other side in another matter.

Since "compromise" involving mutual concessions is the only present alternative either to the continuation of a more or less "cold" war or to settlement imposed by force, interbloc accommodation may well involve the necessity, or the advisability, to tie up one issue, problem, region with another, in other words, to put them on the bargaining counter and offer one in exchange for another. Let us suppose that both East and West consider it to their advantage to conclude a "deal" in which Western control of or influence in an area or region would be given up in exchange for a similar Eastern concession; let us assume that such a deal has its advantages from the point of view of drawing clearer lines of demarcation between the blocs. This would then be a deal in the best (or worst) tradition of classical diplomacy, possibly involving the bartering away of populations and territories which do not even belong to the "barterers," in short, a Machiavellian, power-political "sellout." Or so the moralists would charge. Here, of course, we encounter the problem of the relation between "international morality" (or ethics) and international politics.

I do not believe that international politics—thus far always "power politics"—can, or should, always proceed in absolute conformity with what, at any given time, is accepted as "political morality." On the other hand, politics should so far as is possible proceed within its limits and so far as is feasible should strive to pursue not only the minimum aims of security and other national interests but also, and beyond these, to realize goals and standards of ethics, for instance, humanitarian ones. I have called this policy "realist liberalism." [36] It implies the distinction between lesser evil and higher (or more universal) goal. Reference has previously been made to the cold war situation in which a precarious balance between East and West has been found by drawing the demarcation line right through the hearts of certain nation-states. There, a precedent was set for sacrificing legitimate claims to national unity or unification to the maintenance of "cold peace." The populations concerned, and the moralists or ideologists abroad, can hardly be expected to be enthusiastic about this. Realists, however, may find that the over-all gain was worth the sacrifice involved.[37] But if they were "realists *liberals*," they would not be satisfied with the finding but would go on trying to devise means to alleviate the situations at least so far as individuals and groups of individuals are concerned. Thus, in the imaginary example of trading territories, no deal should be contemplated

[36] See my *Political Realism and Political Idealism*, pp. 129 ff., 200 ff.

[37] Strangely enough, cold war "solutions" such as the partition of countries, although originating in unpolitical (i.e., military) decisions (such as the one concerning the Thirty-eighth Parallel), have since turned out to be the only practicable ones from the point of view of an East-West balance. Thus Korea, while dangerous to the West when in Eastern hands in its entirety ("dagger pointed toward the heart of Japan"), would be a dangerous wedge into Eastern possessions if West-controlled. In the case of Germany, adding the West German industrial potential, including the Ruhr, to that of the East might tip the balance in favor of the East and would thus be intolerable to the West, while a unified Germany in the Western camp might be considered an intolerable addition to Western strength by the East. Division, in both cases, has served as a *modus vivendi*.

which would not safeguard the interests of the people affected at least to the extent of giving them an option to leave their homes if they so desired and to take part of their properties along. Although this might involve evacuating entire populations, it should not present insuperable technical difficulties in our "advanced" age. The Geneva agreements on Indo-China (Vietnam) might serve as a precedent in this respect.

Possibly there are other devices through which the harshness of exchanges, partitions (new and presently existing ones), or similar accommodation "deals" could be mitigated. In looking for them, it should be borne in mind that under present conditions they are likely to be based on, and implemented by, "diplomacy" rather than by any novel institutions or organizations. Indeed, they may even reflect what to modern international lawyers and students of modern trends in international relations must seem "old-fashioned" if not "retrograde" ways.

If there be any way to bridge the gap between the opposing camps, diplomacy, that is power-to-power negotiation, must be among the primary means. This merely implies that powers, now in one sense more powerful than ever before, must take it unto themselves to settle issues; the job cannot be left to supposedly self-enforcing standards (rules of international law or international morality) or to superior organization. Both, however, rules as well as organization, may well be utilized by diplomacy to serve its aims. Despite the absence of moral or ideological principles common to the contesting blocs, rules of international law, for instance, may still serve today or tomorrow, in a manner similar to their classical role in times of national territoriality,[38] to delimit and stabilize the respective, agreed-upon jurisdictions of the two blocs. They would thus fulfill "merely" a pragmatic purpose, to be sure, rather than any higher purpose of "right" or "rightfulness;" but in this

[38] See above, ch. 3.

humbler role they would provide standards for actions and behavior of powers otherwise liable to slip into conflict situations. Some new (or reconfirmed old) rules concerning such things as the approach of planes to the air space of other powers, the kind and amount of propaganda one side would be allowed to direct to the other, or the definition of "political" crime in connection with extradition, or even the still (or newly) applicable rules on conduct of conventional (or "limited nuclear") war might all serve such a purpose. And with the advent of the "space age," rules on jurisdiction in outer space, urgently needed, may also help.

We may recall in this connection the theory of international law propounded by the Soviet author E. Korovin in the first decade of Bolshevik rule in Russia.[39] Korovin's doctrine was for a long time thereafter in disfavor in the country of its origin as not consistent with a forever changing ideological "party line." More recently, however, it seems to have found new favor,[40] a turn which would be in line with the general trend today of Soviet legal doctrine mentioned earlier—namely, to stress the role of international law as a factor for stabilizing relations between the Communist and the non-Communist worlds. Having this emphasis, Korovin's approach, beyond the needs of Soviet doctrine, could actually meet those of a bipolar world in its "transition period." For it contains what seems to be a correct appreciation of the function which international law as "interbloc law" can play in a period of "transition" (whether transition toward a politically and ideologically

[39] *The International Law of the Transition Period* (1st Russian ed., 1924; German trans., 1929). A more detailed analysis of Korovin's earlier doctrine is to be found in E. Bristler (pseud. of J. H. Herz), *Die Völkerrechtslehre des Nationalsozialismus* (Zurich, 1938), pp. 207 ff. See also Hans Kelsen, *The Communist Theory of Law* (New York, 1955), pp. 156 ff., and Wesley L. Gould, *An Introduction to International Law* (New York, 1957), pp. 86 ff.

[40] See G. M. Mason, "Toward Indivisible International Law?," *Social Research*, 23: 57 ff. (1956).

homogeneous all-Communist world, as Korovin and the Soviets expect, or transition toward an equally homogeneous world of free, democratic, and self-determining nations). Korovin stated that in addition to the legal systems prevailing among the units *within* each of the two worlds (capitalist and Communist, respectively), there could be legal rules regulating the relationships between the two worlds. The fact that the two existed side by side in one actual world and were, willy-nilly, involved in various relationships, provided the "social basis" for the rules. True, this "common law" would apply to specific and limited fields only and, in the absence of common moral or political standards, would express contractual rather than customary, bilateral rather than multilateral relationships, stressing national sovereignty, independence, noninterference, and delimitations of jurisdictions rather than majority voting in international organizations, or authority and decisions of international agencies or courts. Yet, he asserted, it could within these limitations yield effective guiding standards for both worlds. Thirty years after this doctrine was first enunciated the world faces a vastly increased range of Soviet power, including additional numbers of Soviet-type countries. Apart from this, however, it is still the same split world, and what Korovin described as the chief function of the "transitional" international law seems still to be what international law, as law between the two blocs, can be expected to achieve.

Similarly, international organization offers opportunities to interbloc diplomacy which, if not overrated but reduced to what is practicable, may prove useful. First of all, it presents a "neutral" meeting ground where hostile powers can get together and discuss issues. This it has in common with ordinary diplomacy; what it offers in addition is an opportunity for organized mediation and the use of certain institutional and procedural devices.

In appraising such devices and procedures one must not

lose sight of the two contradictory aspects of power today: the extreme developments of power-means, especially in the case of the superpowers, and the extreme of powerlessness, again especially in the case of superpowers in view of their "exposed" condition. This, as we have seen, has an impact on "third" powers. Compared with the power concentration in the superpowers their power seems lessened; compared with the superpowers' exposedness, they may be better protected. In certain circumstances, this gives them leeway for maneuvering and also for playing a mediating role in superpower relations. Indeed, since they are, or should be, interested in the avoidance of the "big" clash (in which, in all likelihood, there would be no "innocent," unharmed, or profiteering "bystanders" any more), they are the natural mediators. Their services in this capacity can be important, whether as supervisors of plebiscites or elections, or, in war, of the observance of rules of warfare, whether as initiators or supervisors of a cease-fire, a truce, an armistice, prisoners' exchange, or what not. Through them, also, regimes not "recognizing" each other may speak to each other. While it is understandable that bloc powers, under bloc competition, compete for the alignment of still uncommitted countries, they should realize that the commitment of all would deprive them of services not easy to get along without so long as they are not unalterably committed to all-out war.

If countries, like India, Sweden, and Switzerland in this way and in this sense can perform a kind of buffer function, to what extent, we may ask, can buffer areas in the more specific, geographical sense still be useful? The utility of buffer-states in the classical age of territoriality and power politics is obvious, but can buffer areas of the size of Sweden, or Austria, or Yugoslavia still serve to keep hostile nations apart in an age of "space-conquering" planes and missiles? Would they not simply be overflown, or overshot, or, if it is a matter of armies, overrun in no time? It is indeed likely that such would be their fate in the event of major war, especially nuclear war, but the function of a buffer would lie primarily in reducing the chances that such a war would occur. Since incidents or conflicts are liable to arise in spots where the blocs touch each other geographically, existence or establishment of buffer areas between them can be a way of eliminating grave risks. Whoever studies the crises which have been provoked thus far through a too-intimate contact between the two bloc spheres (planes transgressing, on purpose or inadvertently, into "enemy" air space, nationals abducted, even uncertainty about where, exactly, the boundary line runs) will appreciate the potential blessings of distance and of keeping one's distance.

Some more enthusiastic adherents of the idea of territorial separation have therefore advocated the establishment of a belt of "neutralized" countries insulating the "fighting cocks." In Europe, this area might extend from Sweden (Norway, unfortunately, is contiguous to the Soviet Union) through a reunified and neutralized Germany, and through Austria, to Yugoslavia, with a couple of satellites—perhaps Poland and Czchoslovakia—added; in the Near East, the Arab nations and India are (or were) "neutralist"; for the Far East there is a variety of suggestions, from "neutralization" of all of Korea and Japan to more modest proposals such as providing for a United Nations trusteeship over Formosa, or the "internationalization" of the Chinese offshore islands of Quemoy and Matsu.

Apart from the problem of the political feasibility of the more grandiose among these suggestions, there is a danger here of "internationalist" pitfalls which can serve to illustrate the thin line dividing the realizable from the utopian in thought and action. Despite the growing realism noticeable in recent years, a naive belief in the magic of certain "internationalist" solutions persists. One can be sure, for instance, that the terms "internationalization," "neutralization," "trusteeship," and so on will turn up whenever the status of some contested area raises problems. In practice, "trusteeship" or like "solutions" may become (and have often proved to be) a cover-up for politics; they cannot help being so in the absence of genuine "international," that is, collective, power and authority located in the United Nations or elsewhere. Attempts of this sort then either break down or they result in a sham setup. They break down if a transfer of actual control to an international organ or power holder is intended—as in the case of the "Free City of Trieste," where it was not even possible to agree on the selection of the governor who was to act under the control of the Security Council. Or they result in a sham as they did in the case of "trusteeship" in areas deemed of strategic importance (for instance, the Pacific island groups administered by the United States), which, supposedly, are under the Security Council but actually are under no such organ, being in effect part and parcel of the security system of the respective "administering" power. One could hardly expect this to turn out differently in the case of a "trusteeship" for Japan, or Germany, or Formosa, or the city of Jerusalem, even if the powers concerned were willing to agree to such a solution.

Skepticism regarding "internationalist" solutions in cases where the major powers clash or major power interests are at stake does not imply rejection of internationalization or similar devices in any and all cases, however. Genuine internationalization of areas, for instance, whether through "trusteeship" or otherwise, might be practicable in these two instances: (a) when the area is quite small and international control is more in the nature of supervising a tiny "truce" area than in governing a country; (b) where it is not a "cold war" issue but one occurring *within* one sphere, in particular within the Western sphere. In the first instance, such a way out might be practicable for Quemoy and Matsu, as it was in the case of the "no man's land" between the lines at the time of the Korean armistice negotiations, or as it still is in the border areas separating Israel and the neighboring Arab states. In the second, we have (or had) Tangiers, established by "classical" diplomatic devices, as we had the Saar, or Danzig, or the "international" sector of Shanghai. However, as the last-mentioned examples indicate, even these relatively minor or "easier" cases are disappearing, under the dual impact of two present-day forces: the new nationalism of the formerly colonial or semicolonial countries which no longer tolerate even minor international or multipower "enclaves" in their "sovereign" jurisdictions; and bipolarity, under which one or the other big power tends to rush into any "power-empty" area, if only in order to forestall the opponent.

Trusteeship proper offers an example of what an international organization like the United Nations can do and what it cannot be expected to do under present conditions. It can —and has done so quite successfully in the genuine trusteeship areas—ameliorate the effects of colonialism through supervision and related activities of the Trusteeship Council and the General Assembly. It cannot be expected to place a—nonexisting—power into an area of mutual power competition.

If internationalization does not work, what about "neutralization"? The latter is distinguished from the former in that it does not involve international agents, control, or supervision but instead relies on a country's voluntary abstention from siding, politically and militarily, with any power or group of powers—a policy which may be reinforced by agreements with and commitments and guarantees by other powers. There are advantages as well as pitfalls in this sort of policy too. Genuine neutralization implies freedom from foreign troops and bases and absence of political agreements such as alliances, "security pacts," or similar alignments. It thus creates a neutral space, which, however, may also be a "power-empty" one if neutralization is coupled with demilitarization or insufficient military strength of the unit. In that event, it may invite rather than prevent conflict of powers, which may be tempted to move in, militarily or through "political infiltration," commitments to the contrary notwithstanding, in order to forestall suspected moves by the other side (the "security dilemma" again). On the other hand, if the neutralized country possesses sufficient power to fend off such intervention, it might use its power to line up with one or the other side, a move that would in practice terminate its neutral status and thus cause new tension, if it did not create a new conflict. Supposing a reunified Germany, "neutralized" by East-West agreement and permitted some military power of its own, subsequently decided to join the West, the Soviets would have to intervene, and vice versa. Everything then would seem to depend on the determination of the country in question to stay neutral, on the model set by Switzerland and more recently by Sweden and Austria, and on the trust the powers place in such a determination. Even so, the danger of "subversion" would persist, with one or the other bloc's trying to replace a neutralist regime with a government which it could control. Powers on both sides must therefore remain prepared to intervene "for the protection of neutrality," and the mere disagreement over whether there was a genuine threat to the neutral or not could well enhance the chances of conflict instead of diminishing them. The alternative is the continuation of a situation in which the powers clash over the policies toward a partitioned country with a demarcation line running right through it, and where partition itself makes for continued unrest and agitation. Which of these alternatives is preferable is for statesmen to decide.[41] What does not work in a case like Germany's is to stand firm for all or nothing—as both sides have been doing, at least for the record. Realistic choice lies only between continuing the present state of affairs and achieving some sort of neutralization coupled with unification. The difficulties involved in the choice are a—perhaps not untypical—illustration of the difficulties inherent in the weighing of the pros and cons in any "concrete" problem of accommodation.[42]

[41] Keeping these pros and cons in mind and weighing them against each other is necessary in the discussion of plans, such as the recent projects for military "disengagement" of the powers in Central Europe, thinning-out of troops along the Iron Curtain there, and "denuclearization" of the area à la Rapacki or otherwise. Again, it should be the merits of the respective plan that count, and not whether it is initiated by East or West respectively.

[42] In the effort toward accommodation no device which in the past has proved useful should be overlooked—be it ever so "outmoded" or seemingly inapplicable today. Thus we might ask whether the time-honored device of exchanging hostages might not find application to ensure the observance of commitments mutually entered into by superpowers. Although we are not usually aware of it, the factor of "personal safety" of leaders does play a role in today's policies. Supposing, for instance, that top Soviet leaders travel in the United States, or that an American President pays a state visit to the Soviet Union. Neither side would be likely to resort to war during the stay of its leader(s) in the power sphere of its opponent. Yet trying to "institutionalize" this factor through exchange of hostages would hardly be promising. We are no longer used to "personalizing" international relations to the extent that it was done when nations were more or less identified with their ruling dynasties. At that time, danger to the life of a member of the ruling house might actually deter a ruler from breaking a stipulation or even from waging war. Today, less personalized regimes would be hard put to find somebody whose fate would be considered important enough to have an impact on the respective country's treaty fidelity or vital policies. Dictatorships, on the other hand, where personal connection between hostage and ruler can be established more easily, would hardly be influenced by what might threaten the hostage. Can one imagine a Stalin, or a Hitler, foregoing vital policy steps out of consideration for a relative's or a friend's life?

12

Universalism as Alternative

to the Power Dilemma

What matters is to learn how to hope. ERNST BLOCH

Some time ago the newspapers reported what they referred to as "a bizarre accident": "JET SHOT DOWN BY ITS OWN GUNFIRE AS IT SPEEDS FASTER THAN SHELLS" (New York *Times,* October 10, 1956). Substituting "MANKIND" for "JET," and "NUCLEAR WEAPON" for "GUNFIRE," could one have a more apt description of the potentiality inherent in the atomic situation? Mankind has become destructible in toto through the extreme development of its own capabilities, "speeding" so fast that what used to serve for protection now may reverberate to its annihilation. And sometimes an uncanny foreboding persists that man will be unable to forego making use even of his self-destructive potentialities. Throughout history it has always been his highest endeavor to rise higher and higher by stretching himself to the utmost of his capacities; his boldest aspirations, as symbolized in his heroes (Prometheus, Faust), demanded this from him as the price of ever greater achievement; even war, with all its destructive implementations, seemed ultimately to serve constructive purposes. But now the bomb is here, waiting to be used. So one uses it. One kind of "logic," at least, would point in this direction.

To continue with this trend of attitude and action would indicate an insufficiency of man, as historically shaped and presently construed, to provide for his own survival. The insufficiency is both intellectual and moral. Man would prove intellectually—or imaginatively—defective because unable to grasp in time the apocalyptic implications of his product. The present attitudes of his leaders provide ample illustration. For instance, Khrushchev contends that the Communist world would survive the apocalyptic war, for, although such a war would involve "great suffering" for the Soviet people (the understatement of the century), Communists are apparently not as killable as others. And in the West, the boast of "Sunday punches" to be delivered to the enemy by SAC (or whatever may replace it in the future) betrays the same poverty of imagination (or of the will to imagine). And so, in Lester Pearson's words,[1] "we prepare for war like precocious giants and for peace like retarded pygmies."

Morally, we are equally ill-prepared for a situation in which what formerly appeared justified—for instance, war conducted in self-defense—now necessarily, and performed with the best of "conscience," results in such immeasurable evil (the slaughtering of defenseless millions) that no imaginable "provocation" would seem to justify or even excuse it. For even the least destructive use of the bomb (let us say, that of the "baby bomb" at Hiroshima and Nagasaki) compared with or transgressed that which constituted the ultimate of immorality in the entire preatomic history of mankind—the Nazi "extermination camps." The latter atrocity appeared so utterly depraved because it denied to the victim that which international "morality" still considered then a minimum condition for the justification of killing: a minimum chance to survive, in the armed forces or at home, through defensive or protective action. Exactly this, however, is denied the victims of the bombs, that is, all of us, as it was denied the victims of Hitler's

[1] From his Nobel Peace Prize lecture, December 11, 1957 (New York *Times*, December 12, 1957).

death camps. And thus our traditional standards and attitudes can no longer measure up to man's present potentialities.

THE ATOMIC BOMB AS ATTITUDE MAKER

Must we not ask, then, whether a different approach and a more commensurate attitude are possible? This has to be done, not in a utopian spirit of "what must be will be," but in agreement with this "syllogism":

a) The present approach endangers human survival.
b) An attitude of "universalist concern" may save us.
c) Therefore we must inquire into the possibilities of such an attitude.

We must, indeed, start thinking now, not only because of the more or less imminent danger of nuclear war, but more so because even at this very moment what we are doing may affect all future generations (if there are any), through, for instance, nuclear tests or similar experiments which pollute the atmosphere, water, and soil, with as yet scantily known effects on human bodies and genes, world supplies and resources. The urgency with which a man like Albert Schweitzer has addressed us on this point cannot be disregarded. The necessity for a "universal concern" is as urgent as it is novel.

To study the nature and prospects of "universalism" as a new attitude would seem to be at once more urgent and more profitable than to engage yet again in the more traditional and common discussion of a future world order. Plans and proposals for world government abound, and the details as well as the arguments pro and con any one of them—whether they concern the views of the "maximalists' or the "minimalists," the "functionalists" or those who believe that "security" should be the prime objective first, the adherents of partial, for instance, "Atlantic," organization or the world integrationists—can be looked up in any convenient treatise on the subject.[2] I have previously voiced skepticism in regard to overly high hopes entertained at this point of bipolar and nuclear developments so far as international organization is concerned, and indicated the rather modest role which must for the time being be attributed to the United Nations and related institutions even under developing accommodation of the superpowers. Any discussion of the details of a more integrated world structure, such as problems of representation and voting procedures, jurisdictions and organs, must of necessity remain rather theoretical and detached from present realities. Any more concrete features are not foreseeable now. Moreover, most of the plans in this field either antedate the nuclear situation or are conceived without much attention to the newness of the new.

Our task is more basic; it concerns the conclusions to be drawn from the unprecedented condition that has befallen mankind. And the first thing to realize is that the situation confronts for the first time the whole human race as one group, negatively, it is true, for it is the menace rather than the promise, the destructive rather than the constructive and creative potentiality of atomic energy that concerns the group as such by placing its very continuance in doubt. But even though negative, it constitutes the root basis for a new attitude and approach. For in an objective, although not yet necessarily a subjective, conscious sense, the situation makes everyone and every group on earth, whether "East" or "West," whether "powerful" or not, whether international-minded or isolationist, part of what Reinhold Niebuhr has recently called "the minimal community of the fate of the common threat of

2 See, for instance, Frederick L. Schuman's *Commonwealth of Man* (New York, 1952); also the very incisive although extremely critical survey by Harold D. Lasswell in his *World Politics and Personal Insecurity* (New York and London, 1935), pp. 237 ff.

nuclear annihilation," [3] because it creates what a German
author has referred to as "the interdependence of doom." [4]
It thus involves the necessity to think in terms of the interest
and destiny of the whole, since partial action motivated by
partial interest will no longer merely "affect" but possibly will
doom the group in its entirety. It requires thinking in terms
of and in the place of one's opponent, since he cannot be permitted to take risks which, by dooming himself, may pull
everyone else into the abyss with him. The new realism of
universalism thus puts the common weal—in the elementary
sense of the common interest in survival—before the traditional interest in seeing one's opponent commit mistakes, because his decisive mistake "would not only mean *his* perdition; it would be *my* perdition too." [5] That behavior pattern
which the great religions of the world have preached since
ages past as "altruism," a new "religion" of humanism, that
places the preservation of human kind in the physical sense
above all else, now perceives as indispensable to each individual's own interest if the entire race is not to perish.

What are the chances of such an attitude emerging under
conditions of a holding operation such as was outlined in the
last chapter? Supposing that a holding operation of this kind
resulted in inaugurating a reasonably lengthy period of
"peace," a period of time, that is, which extended over a
couple of decades and during which, though localized "little
wars" might flicker here and there, no major war among
major powers occurred; should we obtain such a period of
grace, where might it lead?

It is of course possible that despite serious and partly successful efforts at accommodation the underlying tensions

[3] In a paper read to the American Political Science Association, September, 1957.

[4] "Die Interdependenz des Untergangs," in W. W. Schütz, *Wir wollen
überleben, Aussenpolitik im Atomzeitalter* (Stuttgart, 1956), p. 162.

[5] Schütz, *Wir wollen überleben*, p. 13.

would remain unabated; that the ideological abyss separating the two worlds would leave the security dilemma confronting the powers more vexing than ever; and that, with further perfection of destructive weapons and with nothing done about a continuing race for "preparedness," the "power dilemma" would reach its pinnacle; probably with the additional complication that, by then, others, including thus far "minor" powers, would have become nuclear powers, so that all would face each other in an utterly destructive and simultaneously utterly exposed fashion. New attitudes would then be submerged, and there could be little doubt that sooner or later the worst would happen and mankind, most of it or even all, be destroyed. Mind, and Man, would have arrived at "the end of their tether," and there is little point in wrecking one's brains over what a surviving remnant-world would look like. It might be that there would survive, or revive, something resembling "international politics," but in that contingency it would seem to matter little whether ultimately one or the other "power" would rule more or less "hegemonically," over the remains of a shattered world or—as seems more likely— whether scattered tribalized hordes of people would "coexist" in an utterly barbarized existence.

As things stand now, this dismal view seems to have a better chance of coming true than do more appealing ones. I grant the skeptic the great likelihood that it will be so, and yet—if there remains the slightest prospect that things might be different, I believe that it is worth while to explore the nature and conditions of the new and better. Let us then do so, remembering throughout that it is not wishful thinking or utopianism that leads us on, but an ever so faint ray of hope that that which is not entirely impossible will emerge as real.

It will do so only if something like the holding operation here envisioned has been successful. Let us then assume that prolonged coexistence and successful accommodation result in a state of greatly reduced tension. Experience with how to prevent smaller or local conflicts from breaking out or, at least, from developing into big crises and all-out war over the years has led to some such thing as an accepted tradition of "living with the bomb" as well as "coexisting" with different ideologies. As in the case of rival religions, none of which has been able to conquer all and which, therefore, have learned to tolerate each other, respect each others' spheres (without giving up their hope ultimately to prevail), and which no longer try to impose their creed by force of arms, the present antagonism of ideological creeds and political-economic systems has somewhat abated. At the risk of sounding heretical, one might even surmise that the two primary opposing systems—advanced capitalism and industrialized communism—have become rather alike in certain respects, even more so than are the respective mass-societies in West and East today with their technological organization of life. In the West, the spheres of political freedom and general "privacy" left to the individual person, caught as he is in the large-scale apparatus of mass organizations, tend to shrink, while it is imaginable that within the coercive machinery of Communist totalitarian organization fissures may in time open up, which will allow for some personal leeway, some individual opportunity to deviate from an official "line" which may tend to partake of the nature of magic incantation rather than coercive force. The two major systems, in other words, may come closer to each other by meeting on some middle ground. Such a meeting, to be sure, would neither satisfy the convinced followers of today's two systems nor look pleasant to a present-day adherent of the values of freedom and personality; but from the viewpoint of survival it would not be without its merits.

All of this, then, may produce a heightened feeling of security or, to put it less daringly, a somewhat diminished feeling of and preoccupation with insecurity. But any inclination to feel more safe would be bound to conflict with the still unchanged structure of international society and its basic characteristic, the power of "sovereign," although no longer "impermeable," powers mutually to destroy each other. It would therefore not be surprising if, across the dividing lines of countries and blocs, and even of systems and creeds, a realization grew among men that something new had to replace the very foundation of existing international relations. And it is likely that the problem would appear first and foremost in the form of the armaments question; that is, in the form of a demand that the "absolute" or "super"-weapons, whatever forms and types they may have assumed by then, be removed from the sovereign control of the powers.

This might involve nothing less than the establishment of a genuinely supernational authority with the monopoly to possess these weapons; it might then proceed to destroy them and set up an inspection system to enforce upon the atomically disarmed powers prohibitions to manufacture or otherwise have nuclear armaments. I cannot foresee, and venture even less to discuss, the technical problems which a transaction of this nature and these dimensions would entail. It may well be that the technical difficulties, some of which were mentioned before, by themselves would already be insuperable. But perhaps not. The dynamic nature of the "new" is such that venturing to guess what in a few decades will be feasible or not is itself impossible. Thus, the present apparent impossibility of discovering concealed atomic weapons or hidden nuclear material may by then have been overcome. If so, what about the "political" problem? Have we not dwelt sufficiently upon the vicious circle which mutual fear and distrust create among independent powers and the dilemma of security and power which at this point seems to have reached its peak? How, then, can we suppose that the gap between a situation where power is concentrated in the hands of powers and one where it suddenly would be monopolized by a new "superpower" (in the sense of "supernational" power) could be bridged? The difficulty is only too real. "Logically" there seems to be no solution. The question is whether pure logic will prevail. The life of politics, like that of the law, in the words of the sage from Washington and Beverly Farms, may be "not logic but experience." Is it not at least imaginable that, supposing tension has lessened and distrust diminished, a new pattern of attitude and behavior becomes possible? That, once accommodation and abatement of ideological conflict enables nations and their leaders to view conditions less subjectively, they might even be able to put themselves into the place of their opponent and to understand, to some degree, the "other fellow's" fear and distrust? Assuming that distrust has actually proved unwarranted over some length of time, might this not lead to a situation where the security dilemma is felt less urgently and the means for coping with it, armaments, considered less vital, while at the same time more dangerous than ever because of their "being there"? Under such circumstances, might one not envision a situation in which, without actual establishment of a supernational atomic monopoly and with weapons remaining in the hands of "powers," the weapons would gradually no longer be looked upon as real threat because their use would have become implausible? This might resemble somewhat a situation within a country in which the poisoning of the water supply or similar vital installations materializes as little as the doctors use germs to infect the population. One might even envision a solution to the problem of how to transfer weapon power, that is, a solution to what has been described as the "Hobbesian dilemma" of the two enemies, armed with pistols and locked in one room, unable to get rid of their weapons. Might they not find a way to hand them over simultaneously, perhaps in stages, to a group of third "persons" present and acting for a "super-agency" to be set up gradually? Might not, this way, the atomic bomb, after having played its role as "policy maker," finally come to play that of "attitude maker" for peace?

I do not mean to ask all this in the spirit of utopian expectation. Just the opposite: For still competing powers to give up what constitutes the very core of their strength, to do so not under direct compulsion but more or less voluntarily, would certainly involve a most radical transformation of attitudes and approach. And, if history teaches anything, it would seem to teach that people learn (if at all) only from "experience," so that they would be ready for the transformation here envisioned only after first having once "experienced" the impact of nuclear war. But then, of course, for all we know now, it would be too late. For the first time in history, there would not remain a world (or much of one) where people could apply what they have "learned." Only if we grant an ever so slight chance that it will be different this time will the following discussion of the nature of the approach that must underlie such a transformation make sense.

THE NATURE OF THE UNIVERSALIST APPROACH

Universalism is that comprehension of mankind as a group, or entity, which imposes itself on those aware of the absolute peril in which the atomic weapon has placed mankind as such. Once the possibility of the absolute end of mankind is apprehended, not as something almost imaginary in some remote future, but as a concrete, hard, imminent threat, that "dread of annihilation" which is said to beset individuals about to die is bound to engulf them in regard to the group, a feeling the more horrible because anticipating such an end renders all previous life and achievement of human beings on earth, retroactively as it were, meaningless.

Having experienced that feeling, however, we shall then be capable of translating it into something more positive: a sense

of concern which will urge us to be alert to chances to prevent extinction. At this point, concern for the fate of the
group merges with something familiar, because it recalls the
concern individuals have always had for something or somebody beyond mere self. The new "universalist" concern can
thus be considered as the expansion of something existing and
known; it then no longer appears so radically novel that it
seems impossible of achievement. Rather it can be conceived
of as a human potentiality which, if acted upon, can be utilized to counteract that other, death-bearing potentiality of
utter destruction.

In this way "universalism," with all its emphasis on mankind as a group and its common interests, need not be idealistic "sentimentalism.' On the contrary, one of its foundations
must be a solid, cool-headed realism, which takes into account
the transformation that has occurred in the traditional relationship between what used to be referred to as the "true"
interests of nations, on the one hand, and "internationalist
ideals," on the other. "National interests" used to be involved
with nation-states as units of power, their security, and their
power interests beyond security proper; "internationalist
ideals," while possibly recognized as ethically valid, at the
same time ran counter to what nations were able to afford if
they wanted to survive and prosper. Even more progressive
students of international affairs would at that time not go
further than to assert that the interests of nations might be
reconcilable with certain "sacrifices" of sovereignty—with international arbitration for instance, or with collective security
commitments. It is my thesis that this dichotomy between
"national self-interest" and "higher," that is, supernational or
international "ideal," however valid it was in an age of protected national units possessing "territorial" power, no longer
fits a situation in which neither "sovereignty" nor an ever so
absolute power can protect nations from annihilation.

A vague idea that the *interests* of people, and not only a moral law, demanded the outlawry of war had occasionally touched the thoughts of philosophers, pacifists, and internationalists even in the time of classical international relations; but in practice this realization could not take hold of men's minds so long as they could put trust in national power as the chief guardian of "life and liberty." Anything which would detract from this power was naturally liable to be considered a threat to one's immediate interests; at best, it might be an "idealist's dream," and possibly a bad one at that. Until recently, therefore, advocacy of policies based on internationalism instead of power politics, on substituting the observance of universal interests for the prevalence of national interests, was considered utopian, and correctly so. In an age of absolute interpenetrability of powers, on the other hand, the "ideal" is bound to emerge as a very compelling "interest" itself. In former times, the lives of people, their goods and possessions, their hopes and their happiness, were tied up chiefly with the "internal" conditions, the "domestic" affairs of the country in which they lived. "Foreign" affairs affected most of them only in so far as the successful pursuit of national interests might add to the power and prosperity of the nation collectively and of the people in it individually. Occasionally, it is true, some of them would have to go out to the "front" and even lay down their lives, but this was to ensure the continued life and welfare of all the others. "Interests" thus all centered around the nation and internal, or at best, collective national issues—nationalism, power, and power politics.

Now that destruction threatens everybody, in every one of his most personal, intimate interests—the businessman in his possessions, the worker and employee in the continuation of his job, everybody in the peaceful pursuit of his daily life and the planning of his and his family's future—"domestic" as well as "national" issues and interests are bound to recede behind—

or at least only to compete with—the overriding interest of all in sheer survival. And while survival, together with all one's other interests and concerns, still seems to be predicated upon national power—even power raised to the utmost—it appears, on the other hand, more and more bound up with the maintenance of peace through renunciation of the atomic weapon and similar policies that seemingly contradict the pursuit of power interests in the traditional ways.

What used to be a dichotomy of interests and ideals thus emerges as a dichotomy of two sets of interests. And the struggle between the two is liable to proceed right in the minds and attitudes of the average person. For instance, depriving individual countries, including one's own, of nuclear weapons, or devising other means of coping with the danger of nuclear war are likely to cause stout and stern opposition on the part of the "unreconstructed" nationalist; but to others, or sometimes even to the same, tradition-bound person, they may no longer appear now as the objective (or "scheme") of the starry-eyed idealist but as a policy for restoring the lost paradise of lives and goods and for making it once again secure. For once the danger of absolute destruction is averted, something like the traditional territoriality of nations, including their (relative) impermeability and protective function, might thus be restored, on a "higher plane," to be sure, but in essence still—or again—the accustomed condition of a minimum security, without which life becomes a nightmare. This is thus an issue, and an interest, which tends to affect the individual person within each national society directly. And because there is now a conflict between two sets of interests, the traditional, nation-centered interest and the new international, or rather universalist interest, the latter may have a better chance of prevailing than it had when hard-boiled interest clashed with lofty but "unrealistic" ideal.

That universalist attitudes can and do issue from realistic appraisal of interests is apparent in many recent utterances, by the naive as well as the more sophisticated. See for instance, the touching "Declaration by Mayor and Councilors on Behalf of the People of the Community of Sein" (France), in which we read:

While declaring our island symbolically world territory, we renounce nothing of our attachment, duties, and rights with regard to our native land or France. The security and well-being of our population are linked with the security and well-being of all the towns and communities of the world today threatened with destruction by total war.[6]

Or read the statement of a "hard-boiled" student of military strategy: "A realism that fails to see the need of world order is more unrealistic than any idealism." [7] Or that of the nuclear scientist:

It is a practical thing to recognize as a common responsibilty, wholly incapable of unilateral solution, the complete common peril that atomic weapons constitute for the world, to recognize that only by a community of responsibility is there any hope of meeting the peril . . . . It would seem to me visionary in the extreme, and not practical, to hope that methods which have so sadly failed in the past to avert war will succeed in the face of this far greater peril. It would in my opinion be most dangerous to regard, in these shattering times, a radical solution less practical than a conventional one.[8]

Or even a "nationalist" general:

[6] From New York *Times*, March 31, 1950.

[7] B. H. Liddell Hart, *The Revolution in Warfare* (New Haven, 1947), p. 118. It is true that he goes on to say: "Yet a sense of realities shows all too clear the unlikelihood of its early fulfilment in a common government." But we are here concerned with the emerging "universalist" attitude rather than with the chances in specific plans and projects of world federalism.

[8] J. Robert Oppenheimer, "Atomic Weapons," in *Proceedings of the American Philosophical Society*, 90: 9 f. (January 29, 1946). On the problems connected with the "internationalization of responsibility," touched upon in this statement, see below.

The tremendous evolution of nuclear and other potentials of destruction has suddenly taken the problem away from its primary
consideration as a moral and spiritual question and brought it
abreast of scientific realism. It is no longer an ethical equation to be
pondered solely by learned philosophers and ecclesiastics but a hard
core one for the decision of the masses whose survival is the issue.[9]

So far I have stressed the danger of physical destruction
which derives from the new weapons and the new methods of
warfare. This, indeed, is the strongest basis on which a universalist attitude can arise, but if it were its only foundation,
it might still be too narrow, too isolated, and too negative a
basis. Fortunately, there is much more than this in the world
picture today. And the most important among these phenomena is this: In all previous periods of history the world
presented itself to man as mere segments of an immense whole
extending beyond his range of vision, knowledge, and planning. Problems, therefore, could only be approached as partial ones, and solved as such. In contrast, the world today is
"one" in that it now can be grasped, comprehended, and sur-
veyed as an entirety. Human problems thus can likewise be
understood in their reference to mankind as one group and
approached as universal ones.[10] In the past everything appeared—necessarily—under particular views, and this not only
in politics ("power politics") but in almost every other field,

[9] General Douglas MacArthur, speech at Los Angeles of January 26,
1955 (New York *Times*, January 27, 1955).

[10] Imagine that some superhuman authority or being had to pass on
mankind's future, its continuation or its doom, and that it had to judge
us from our achievements and failures; imagine that we looked for what
we could present in our defense. We could offer a vast and varied testimony: Latter-day saints like Gandhi or Schweitzer; the systems of Einstein and Planck; Figaro at Salzburg, and Shakespeare at Stratford-on-
Avon; the Balinese dancers and a Japanese motion picture, the cities of
Paris and Venice, the pyramids and the Alhambra, the Golden Gate and
the Taj Mahal—but we would now know that it was not limitless, and in
the finite nature of these contributions we would discover one of the
roots of universalism, a feeling for the one-group nature of the race,
which in due course may bring about an awareness that what fate has in
store—whether it be doom, survival, or development—concerns us all.

whether it was a question of population (effects of emigration, immigration, changes in birth rates, etc.), or of resources (use and development of the soil, opening up of new mines), or what so ever it might be. Only in those exceptional instances, where the phenomena as such refused to let themselves be so isolated or limited, could problems be seen and approached in a more universalist manner, for instance, when it was a matter of combatting epidemics. Now, with mankind itself a finite, surveyable entity, other world problems have become surveyable too. Thus they are liable to be viewed in dual, and often contradictory, fashion. One of them is the traditional parochial way, to which people throughout history have become so thoroughly accustomed that it is sometimes difficult for them to comprehend the existence of another approach altogether, but the other one now does exist. Whether it is a matter of exploiting a new iron ore resource, for instance, or a subsoil or submarine oil deposit, or whether it is one of exploiting—and quite possibly exhausting—the fishing supplies of part of the seas, the universalist, "general" view not only asks whether this lends itself to the profits of individuals or benefits a nation or group of nations but also, and above all, what it means in regard to the future availability of the respective resource in terms of global needs. How much of a given material is there, exploited or still unexploited, and will the present rate of exploitation lead to exhaustion? What does the present rate of population increase in a given country or region signify, not only to the economy or manpower situation of that country or area or the "bloc" to which it may belong, but to mankind as a whole, its over-all economy, its food supplies, its living standards? For the universalist, that is, it is not a question whether and how this or that event, attitude, or policy benefits the United States, or India, or China, but what are its likely effects on mankind as a whole, present and future.

It is easy to see how particular and general views are bound to clash here. The security dilemma itself may play its role again to complicate matters. One of the most conspicuous consequences of interbloc power competition has been the acceleration of the exploitation and use of all imaginable raw materials and resources to build up and strengthen the blocs' respective economic and industrial systems and, if possible, to overtake each other; or to stimulate the birth rate so as to form an ever more "invincible" bloc of humanity. Under global views this involves irresponsible overuse and overexploitation of irreplaceable treasures, the impoverishment of future mankind, and, under present population trends all over the world, the threat of soon raising the world's total population to so many billions that the entire future of mankind may be jeopardized. Indeed, there are many who believe that the combined population-resources problem (rapid increase in population, sometimes referred to as "population explosion," coupled with exhaustion of food supplies and depletion of mineral and other resources) already constitutes *the* other big threat to the world, no less deadly than that of the atom bomb and possibly even more so because it is less obvious and less spectacular. It is a menace which grows gradually and almost imperceptibly, a bit every day, and thus permits the unenlightened, if they perceive it at all, to postpone serious consideration and concern to a never-faced "next day." We now have in principle the means to understand and deal with these problems as they present themselves to mankind as a whole. But the question remains how, in the face of the "particularist" state of mind, a universalist attitude can be made to prevail; who, in particular, can be relied upon to embrace and promote it?

There is in the universalist approach simplification and complexity all at once. Matters have become simplified because we know now that there is only a limited amount of land, water,[11] space, soil, and materials on earth, that there exist the present nations, populations, races, their problems, and no others. We can thus deal with fixed and surveyable data. But the complexity has grown too, since the sum total of all these data and of all these problems may have to be brought to bear on each single question that arises. Problems had already grown enormous within the confines of the traditional nation-states. Who, for instance, quite apart from the different "interests" that come into play, is in a position to visualize and comprehend the "general interest" of a nation like the United States in a given connection? Consider the difficulty involved for the man who is President of the United States to gain a genuinely comprehensive view of its ramifications—even if he devotes himself twenty-four hours of the day to the task. But he, at least, has the "national interest" to guide him. How then can a universal "comprehensive view," a "world's-eye view," a *Gesamtschau,* be obtained for the world and mankind as a whole? Who "speaks for man"? How can a "planetary mind" be developed? Division of labor itself, that ever growing specialization which has enabled modern, industrialized civilization to develop the "oneness" of

[11] Reference here is not only to the "water" beneath and on the surface of the "land" but also to that in the vast and seemingly inexhaustible expanses of the oceans. Nothing, perhaps, illustrates better the necessity for a universalist approach than the fact that even here the world is getting too small for the expanding and clashing interests of separate nations, whether this is reflected in conflicts over fishing grounds, or in claims to territorial sovereignty over "coastal waters" extending hundreds of miles into the ocean; in unilateral extension of sovereignty to the so-called "continental shelf" areas comprising whole portions of the high seas, or in the use of large parts of the oceans for nuclear weapons tests or as similar "new weapons" proving grounds. All of this is, of course, incompatible with the traditional uses of the seas by all nations, and with their respective rights under classical international law. Indeed, one "internationalist" suggestion has been to the effect that the United Nations be given jurisdiction over all of the so far "masterless" high seas (plus, incidentally, the terra firma of the last remaining masterless land area on earth, the Antarctic continent), not only to enable nations to cope with the problems just mentioned but also as a means of providing a basis for incipient world government.

the world, has become an obstacle to the formation of an over-all world view. It tends to confine the individual mind within its own field of interest, so that one is inclined always to leave it to the "other fellow" to be concerned with the more remote effects and consequences of one's action. But the "other fellow" is likely to be a specialist too, and thus the problem of "generalization" is deferred *ad infinitum*.[12] It has been pointed out earlier how, in the present confusion about handling the atomic problem, almost everbody concerned tends to look for somebody else to provide answers and solutions: the multitude for "experts" or "governments"; these for "specialists" in this or that field; the specialists for subspecialists; scientists in general for nuclear scientists; these, since they have no special concern with the "social" effects of their discoveries,[13] for social or political scientists; and so forth. Somebody has pointed out how in a more "primitive," that is, less specialized, age restraints concerning the practical application of inventions entailing increased infliction of pain and suffering (new weapons, etc.) were more effective, not only because moral inhibitions were stronger, but also because inventors themselves still had a more general comprehension of the over-all effects of their discoveries. Occasionally they would even withhold them from the public.[14] Now they are "specialists," usually working with others in teams and large-scale establishments, and are thus no longer in a position individually "to do something" about the effects of what they are doing, even if they want to. There is even the problem of how to be heard. In an interdependent and labor-dividing so-

[12] Herein lies one of the most dangerous consequences of our turning away from "general" education, be it "humanistic" or in other ways at least "coherent" and "generalist."

[13] With the exception, be it expressly stated, of a few broad-minded and frequently "universalist" atomic scientists, such as the ones who express their views in the admirable and responsible *Bulletin of the Atomic Scientists*.

[14] See J. U. Nef, *War and Human Progress* (Cambridge, Mass., 1952), pp. 113 ff., 364 f.

ciety few, if any, are at liberty to remain members of a "free intelligentsia," [15] that is, a group which, free from pressures and interests, could freely give voice to the "general interest." If there be such a person, he is liable to get into trouble, domestically and internationally, as a citizen and in relation to competing powers and ideologies. The objective mind—like the traditional "neutral" in world politics—is likely to have two enemies.

But all may not be quite so gloomy. The underlying facts of "globality" must, and do, have their impact on minds and attitudes. Read any of the annual reports of the Secretary-General of the United Nations to the General Assembly, and there you will find a good many examples of a universalist approach. Even the General Assembly itself occasionally acts "as if it were an entity charged with responsibility for promoting the long-range interests of the world community." [16] Read the minutes of the Scientific Conference on the Conservation and Utilization of Resources, convened in 1949 by the United Nations, when "veteran observers of United Nations and League of Nations activities were frankly amazed at the cooperative spirit with which the discussions were undertaken. Personalities and national interests were laid aside." [17] It is true—and no realist should belittle it—that a genuinely universalist spirit reigns more often in what is called "technical" fields and problems than when it comes to politics; in the

[15] Karl Mannheim's *freischwebende Intelligenz.*

[16] I. L. Claude, *Swords into Plowshares: The Problems and Progress of International Organization* (New York, 1956), p. 171. Claude goes on to say: "This is no more mysterious than the phenomenon of a collection of party politicians, sectionalists, and interest group representatives who constitute a Congress which sometimes gives expression to the national interests of the United States." There is, however, in the international field the problem of the security dilemma, adding one more difficulty to those existing in the domestic field.

[17] New York *Times,* September 7, 1949. It was similar when atomic scientists met in a conference on "peaceful uses of the atom" at Geneva in the summer of 1955; this meeting also included scientists from both East and West. And so again in 1958.

latter case a "Geneva" or like "spirit" is easily submerged. But the "technical" problem may be vital (as it is, for instance, in the case of the "conservation and utilization of resources" and, possibly, in that of atomic inspection and detection). Solution of some technical problem, hampered though it may be by political factors, *if* it can be arrived at, may, in turn, facilitate the solution of political problems. Even in the technical fields, however, universalist solutions presuppose a universalist approach and thus require universalist minds. Where, we must ask, do we find this state of mind? Is it possible more specifically to define groups or classes which represent the "universal" rather than the "particular," which speak for "man" rather than for nations, classes, races, or others of mankind's multitudinous subdivisions?

THE PROBLEM OF A "UNIVERSAL CLASS"

There have in the past been doctrines concerning a "universal class," and movements which claimed to act in the name of groups or classes representing not merely their own particular class interest but the interests and needs of all, that is, of an entire society or nation or even of mankind as a whole. Examples are furnished by Marxism and by the Hegelian theory regarding the role of officialdom; they clearly illustrate the pitfalls of a self-styled universalist approach. Marxism, of course, proferred the thesis of the "proletariat" as the "universal" class, that is, a class which, in contrast to all classes that had preceded it in history, would be free from "class interest" in the sense of particular, ego-centered concerns. According to Marxism, the proletariat, even prior to its own, socialist revolution, embodies the interests of all. It represents "mankind" and "humanism," and after a final class struggle will do away with "history" as "class rule" and establish a society free from the narrow concerns of specific groups or classes. In a similar, though less chiliastic and more restrained, vein, Hegel and some Hegelians, looking for a group which, beyond the interest-centered sphere of "civil society," would have as its function the representation of the general interest, professed to find it in a civil service that was trained in the idea of the "State," and thus used to upholding the cause of that super-individual and supergroup organization—or organism—against any and all personal, estate, or class interests.[18] Here, therefore, the caste of "officials" or "functionaries" emerges as the "universal" class.

Performance, of course, has fallen short of expectation in both cases. Officials, or civil servants, even where (as in Prussia-Germany) they were steeped in a strong tradition of disinterested service to the state, could not help issuing from, and representing, classes and groups holding power. They thus became defenders of particular interests almost by necessity. Moreover, no country, perhaps, demonstrates better than Germany that officials tend to develop interests and "vested rights" as a caste of their own and in this sense too fall short of being a true "universal" class. The proletariat, on the other hand, wherever it is still one among several classes in a nonsocialist society, has discovered that it has more to lose than its chains and thus has tended to stand for its own, plus possibly allied groups', particular interests; and wherever it has assumed power in the form of Communism—or, rather, where Communism has assumed control in its name—we know that, far from representing the "universal" interest of mankind or even that of the nation in question, it has fallen victim to totalitarian rule by a closed group which controls the proletariat exactly as it controls everybody else.

But Communist leaders are presumably convinced that they exercise their control in the "true" interest of all and that in

---

18 I do not mention Hegel's theory of the monarch as the guardian of the common weal, since this is an ideology he shared with many preceding theorists, while that concerning officialdom was more peculiarly his own.

their world policy they represent and promote the true "general" interest of mankind. We have here a supreme illustration of an ideologically distorted pseudo-universalism which mistakes its own particular interest for that of "all." Self-identification with universal ideals and objectives has been characteristic of most of the religious, political, and other "movements" which spread more or less militantly over various parts of the world. Islam, Christianity, and other creeds have laid claim to being depositories of the universal truth, but their fight to impart the truth to all has usually degenerated into a power-conflict, in the course of which they would feel compelled to organize themselves for power competition. Political movements like the liberal-democratic ones that attacked prebourgeois societies and regimes have also claimed to act in the interest of all but subsequently have turned into class rule as of yore.[19] That socialism as a movement is liable to take the same turn has just been demonstrated through the example of Marxism. Even fascist-type regimes, such as Nazism in Germany, have asserted that they represent "the community of the people," and that they integrate diverging groups and clashing interests into the entirety of a nation. On the other hand, where idealism of this sort (whether genuine or fake) has tried to avoid being corrupted through participation in power conflict, it has tended to become a somewhat abstract defense of individual rights against established authority. It is then usually carried on by isolated individuals or small groups. One should not belittle the efforts of an individualistic liberalism of the kind that organizes itself in "ligues pour les droits de l'homme"; but it can hardly claim to be "universalist" in the sense of standing for the universal interests of mankind as such. For these latter interests are not merely a sum-total of individual "rights." True uni-

[19] Note the use of terms like "humanity," "mankind," "posterity" by the French revolutionaries. A more detailed analysis of these developments may be found in my *Political Realism and Political Idealism* (Chicago, 1951).

versalism of the sort now required and beginning to emerge goes beyond traditional cosmopolitan liberal international-ism, out of which these more individualistic efforts grew. Only those who are ready to care and plan for the needs—both present and future—of humanity as one collective entity are "universalists" in the broader sense.

Thus we return to the question whether there is a group in the making which, by understanding the "needs of man-kind" as a group, would identify its interests with them rather than with any partial interest, thus constituting a true uni-versal class. For the first time in history we have not only a world-wide economy, world-wide communications, etc., but also the possibility of global organization and of planning for the implementation of universal needs. In the last chapter I referred to the increasing threat to all that derives from the depletion of the world's resources and the simultaneous rise in world population. Is it possible that growing awareness of this and similar perils might make a new, genuinely uni-versalist class out of those concerned with the future of the human race and determined to find new means and procedures to cope with novel and challenging tasks? Such a group would have to rise above partial interests and consider those of man-kind as a whole; it would have to rise above the needs and interests of the present and give consideration to those of the future. In either case one set of interests is liable to be op-posed to another: those of powers, power blocs, and "interest groups" to that of the whole; those of the present generations, inclined to say "après nous le déluge," to that of the yet un-born. Only those who are apprehensive about what may hap-pen to the whole—a whole conceived in terms of present *and* future generations—would deserve to be called "universalists."

A group now commonly referred to as the "international civil service" may be scrutinized in this respect. The grow-ing number and widening range of international agencies, especially those of a more technical, or "functional," character, has led to the growth of a particular group of people employed by these organizations as such and devoted to agency tasks rather than to the pursuance of policies and objectives of the nations whose nationals they are. The "universalist" spirit which often informs members of that group has been commented upon before. "International organization is slowly acquiring its vital minority of men who view its evolution in terms of the general needs of humanity rather than the particular interests of nations." [20] Two factors favorable to the development of truly universalist attitudes merge here. One is the establishment of permanent international bureaucracies, as distinguished from case-to-case delegation of nationals by their governments to perform functions in international organizations. The other one is the prevalence of experts among the members of this service. "Civil service" of any kind, whatever else its drawbacks, tends to foster a sense of responsibility for the units in whose name and for whose needs it acts, an urge "to take care of" those entrusted to its jurisdiction (in this case, the "family of nations"). It is true that the danger of "bureaucratism" (in the sense of addiction to "red tape") lurks here, as does that of authoritarianism or paternalism, but, to balance these, experts, unless they become corrupt, are wont to develop a habit of dealing objectively and impartially with "what the situation requires," and of doing so with some degree of independence from personal or group influences.

One should of course beware of uncritical overestimation of what the "international civil service" [21] is and can do. We have to recognize the fact that there are a couple of major obstacles to the successful functioning of the group as a "uni-

---

[20] Claude, *Swords into Plowshares*, p. 170.

[21] I use this term throughout in a generic sense: there are strictly speaking, of course, only "civil services," in the plural, of the various international agencies so far.

versal class." One is the influence of "partial" groups and interests, in this instance primarily that of powers, in particular the nations whose nationals the individual civil servants are. This kind of influence is certainly real, especially in the case of nationals of totalitarian or other dictatorial regimes that demand loyalty to their respective ideologies or interests from their citizens regardless of status or position; but it is equally insidious where "loyalty investigations" are used to establish similar "national" control over international officials on the part of otherwise nontotalitarian states. On the other hand, nonexistence of a world government or world state in whose employ the international officials would be constitutes an asset in this connection; it implies the absence of those centralized interests which in the case of national officialdoms often subject bureaucracies to group pressures. Since in the international field such influences and pressures are diffused among a plurality of nations, they are less powerful and tend to neutralize each other.

Another threat arises from the group itself: it consists in the danger that it might turn into a caste concerned chiefly with protecting and promoting its own vested interests. As in every field of administration and bureaucracy trends of this kind have been noticeable here too. There is, in particular, interagency competition, there are "jurisdictional conflicts," there has been "empire building," all of those phenomena which are well known in national administrations. As in the case of the first danger, however, the absence of one government behind the international civil service, and the fact that available funds are small, have so far operated to keep this threat in bounds.

The third obstacle is more fundamental. To what extent are these "universalists" given a real chance to implement their approach in the teeth of all the forces and interests which stand for and defend the particular against the general approach? Reference here is not to a specific national influence over nationals but to the general impact of power politics. Are these people not powerless to achieve anything essential precisely because of the universalism of their attitudes? It would be quite unrealistic, indeed, to believe that the future of the world is safe because of the existence of—relatively speaking—a mere handful of men and women in New York, Geneva, and other places scattered around the world, whose services are devoted to problems of world food supplies, health standards in underdeveloped areas, and similar tasks. For instance, if one would tackle the world food problem effectively, probably nothing short of conferring on FAO (or some other agency) powers comparable to those of the opium-control organization, i.e., jurisdiction including enforcement of measures within nations themselves, would do. What might be required to really start solving the population problem would be to give WHO (or some other body) powers to deal with birth control, again within the respective countries.

It would be sheer utopianism to expect an easy and early realization of such requirements. A widespread "functionalist" approach to world affairs errs through excessive optimism in this respect. "Functionalism" assumes that through "a spreading web of international activities and agencies" in the "functional" fields (as distinguished from the field of power-political and ideological conflicts) "the interests and life of all the nations would be gradually integrated." [22] Politics and ideologies divide, interests and working together to implement them unite. Functional activities will render political frontiers unnecessary because the latter will become "meaningless through the continuous development of common activities and interests across them." International

[22] Quotations here and in the following sentences are from one of the chief "functionalist" manifestoes, David Mitrany's *A Working Peace System* (London, 1944).

government will be "co-extensive with international activities"; it will be "federalism by instalments."

A personnel which would be largely technical and permanent is likely to develop both a professional pride and a vested interest in good performance . . . . This line of action would help to develop also another factor that is needed for the good working of any such experiment, namely, an international outlook and opinion.

One can agree that "functional" activities will develop this kind of personnel and this kind of outlook, even that they have already done so; but to jump from there to the conclusion that they will render power politics, and even the facts and factors of power, such as existing powers and their frontiers, "unnecessary" reminds one of the rationalist-utopian logic of certain "world planners" who have postulated that world government will be real because it is necessary.[23] It is somewhat strange to find "functionalism," which prides itself upon the pragmatism and practicality of its approach, in this company. Cynics, in contrast to such naivete, might even define functionalism as the theory that defends the power positions of international bureaucracies. This would not do it justice. On the other hand, it is only by keeping in mind the realities of the actual, power-divided and ideology-torn world as it exists today (including its security dilemma) that we can appraise the prospects and impact of functionalist activities; only then can we fairly appraise the almost superhuman efforts demanded from those who would work and fight for universalist objectives and under universalist viewpoints. Functionalists must realize that the very factors which have caused international "interdependence," instead of mitigating power accumulation and power conflicts, may even stimulate them.

[23] See, for instance, one of the four basic "assumptions" of the famous *Preliminary Draft of a World Constitution*, by Robert M. Hutchins and others (Chicago, 1948), to the effect that "World Government is necessary, therefore it is possible" (p. 41).

Dependence of a power on foreign resources, for instance, may cause it to seek extension of its control over the areas where they are found. Such universalist policies as providing for "fair" distribution of resources or for their protection from overexploitation must therefore often proceed in the face of power trends which are accentuated by the very developments which give rise to universalism itself. This is its basic "dialectic."

Moreover, unless functionalism proceeds in truly universalist fashion, that is, by keeping in mind the relation of specific types of policies and action to the over-all problems confronting all mankind, there is a recurrent danger that it will make matters worse instead of improving them, exactly because of humanitarian or purely technical considerations. Supposing, for instance, that a major health program is directed toward stamping out a disease that accounts for a high mortality rate in some region. The very success of such an enterprise might be responsible for an increase in population which, unless some action is simultaneously undertaken to improve the economic conditions of the country or countries in question, might entail increased misery and, possibly, starvation. Or, an industrialization program, undertaken without due regard for the food basis of a country, can have an adverse instead of a beneficial effect on the population in the long run. Therefore, a health program that deals, not with a killing, but with a disabling disease, an economic plan for irrigation of land instead of, or at least prior to, developing heavy industry are preferable. In other words, we must operate under priorities, even though to the "partial" view this may appear biased or cruel. Attributing low priority to the saving of lives where such saving is possible may seem inhuman, but only to those who cannot perceive the broader or long-range consequences of the program concerned as compared with other, equally beneficial programs. For a humanitarianism that is not coupled with a clear vision of the total situation defeats its own purpose.[24]

On the other hand, if a functionalist approach proceeds in such a way as to recognize the interconnectedness of problems, it can contribute a good deal to the solution of problems in truly universalist fashion, since today, in so many fields, the technical prerequisites for success exist, frequently for the first time in history. To say this is not merely a verbal realism. I have not forgotten what I emphasized before concerning the impact of power and power conflict and the interference of partial interests and pressures. But techniques can be developed to meet pressure with counterpressure. In the field of international organization, for instance, this becomes apparent when one studies the role played by the so-called "NGO's" (nongovernmental organizations) admitted to counsel the Economic and Social Council of the United Nations (under Article 71 of the Charter). Those familiar with their role know how these organizations can be utilized to function as "universalist pressure groups," as it were, so as to facilitate action on some UN program or another. They function as transmission belts between UN organs or other international agencies, on the one hand, and governments on the other hand, mobilizing public opinion in the countries or regions concerned, enlisting support of the program by groups or influential persons, and bringing the necessary pressure to bear on parliaments, national bureaucracies, or delegations to international agencies which have to vote on programs on the international level. These are matters of detail, but they serve to show that not all that which is internationalist or universalist is unrealistic in an age when—as has been stressed

24 If that which Adlai Stevenson once called "the revolution of rising expectations," in the meantime, according to the same statesman, has often turned into a "revolution of frustrated hope" (see his Commencement address at Michigan State University, June 8, 1958, New York *Times,* June 9, 1958), neglect of such priorities may frequently have been a cause.

before—it is no longer a matter of "mere idealism" opposing "interests," but when universalism can rally one set of interests against another.

It is clear, however, that whatever success can be expected from "functionalism" and from the functioning of the international civil service as a "universal class" must be based upon a broader foundation of public support and public attitude. When mentioning the NGO's as "pressure groups," it was noted that a growing number of more or less important and influential "private" groups and organizations in the world can be enlisted for the support of universalist principles and policies. They may comprise the less self-centered portions of labor and labor movements—whether organized as trade unions or as political labor parties—and the more liberal portions of enterprise, churches that subordinate dogma to a realist appraisal of world problems as well as nonreligious organizations interested in education, housing, or birth control. But number and identity of organizations matters less than a favorable attitude basis. For all of the groups mentioned can also—and in the past often actually did—endorse policies in the partial (for instance, the national) interest. It is therefore of great importance to assess prospects for the emergence of what I have called the "universalist attitude" among people at large (in contrast to specific groups like international functionaries, or students of international affairs, or atomic scientists). And here some cautious optimism can, perhaps, be based on a seemingly growing awareness of what universalism is and what it requires. True, mere wishing is not enough, and the inverted Hegelianism of "what is necessary is therefore possible" is thoroughly misleading. But the father of modern dialectic, Hegel himself, stressed the importance of thought and attitude in bringing about changes in the actual world: "Die theoretische Arbeit bringt mehr in der Welt zustande als die praktische; ist das Reich der Vorstellung revolutioniert, so hält die Wirklichkeit nicht stand." [25]   If this be so, if ideas and attitudes can have such a "revolutionizing" function, everything would seem to depend on the emergence of a universalist "groundswell," from which the feeling for the necessity to act in a common world interest would impose itself with compelling force upon people and people's minds.[26] Can we perceive at least the beginnings of such a groundswell?

Ever since man as an individual emerged from the primitive collectivism of tribal communities he has been faced with the problem of responsibility; responsibility, that is, to others in regard to his actions and his behavior.   If, in a laisser faire society, everybody is out for himself alone, who is to take care of the "general interest"?   We know now that there is no "invisible hand," no preestablished harmony guaranteeing the permanent identity of individual and general welfare.   Even laisser faire individualism never went so far as to excuse from "caretaking" and, in this sense, "responsible" action the most intimate groups, such as the family.   What Thorstein Veblen once called the "parental bent," involving as it does "an unselfish solicitude for the well-being of the incoming generation," [27] contradicts a selfishness which even under the most individualistic systems and conditions has never been absolute (except for borderline cases of "abnormality").   The problem now is how to extend this feeling of responsibility to larger entities and, since conditions demand it, to mankind as a whole?   In this connection the same dilemma which renders "powers" competing units in "power politics," even where no additional "selfish" or "aggressive" motive exists, frequently

25 Like all of Hegel, this can be translated only approximately: "Thought achieves more in the world than practice; for, once the realm of imagination (ideas, the mind) has been revolutionized, reality cannot resist."

26 In "up-to-date" social science parlance, the "myth" of universalism must become "operative."

27 See *The Instinct of Workmanship and the State of the Industrial Arts* (New York, 1914), p. 46.

prevents individuals who act "in the name of" specific groups
or entities (their family, or a business enterprise, or their nation) from feeling responsible for units that are larger and interests that are more general than the ones they represent.
That same feeling of "altruism" which may spur them on in
assuming responsibility for "their" group may make any concern for other units appear to them as "irresponsible." [28]
Here, too, the dilemma presents itself in terms of "security,"
that is, in terms of the individual group's "survival" vis-à-vis
its competitors. In these terms an urge toward competition
and conflict has been common in the life of societies within
state borders exactly as it has been so in their "international"
relations.

But just as within countries the general concern, the interest in the welfare of the community as a whole, gradually
asserted itself in the face of the interests of partial groups, concern for mankind as a whole has spread despite prevailing
concerns with welfare, survival, and power of the political
units into which it is divided. Its strongest root is, perhaps,
in man's concern for the future. It is a strange but very real
fact that this concern generally extends beyond the individual's life span and for an indefinite period; or, to put it
differently, one acts as if one were immortal. But if this be so,
why should concern for the future be restricted to the future
of any particular unit or group? It was indeed natural to
think in terms of such groups so long as they were the ultimate
ones beyond which one seldom directed one's gaze; a nation
then was a sufficiently large receptacle for anybody's cares and
concerns. But today our vision easily encompasses the globe.

[28] This phenomenon is familiar to students of Reinhold Niebuhr's so-
cial philosophy, in which the problem of the interaction between in-
dividual idealism and group egoism has played a prominent part (cf.
John C. Bennett, "Reinhold Niebuhr's Social Ethics," in Charles W.
Kegley and Robert W. Bretall [eds.], *Reinhold Niebuhr: His Religious,
Social, and Political Thought* [New York, 1956], p. 53).

And thus our "parental bent," which in Veblen's own words is connected with the future of the group,[29] may now, in the words of one of his critics, be defined as "a kind of generalized solicitude not only for one's young but for the future of mankind." [30]

There are signs indicating an extension of this kind of concern to a universalist, that is, world-embracing feeling of responsibility in many fields, but at present its strongest motivation seems to be the threat to the physical survival of the race presented by the new weapons of war. I have frequently mentioned the concern which statesmen and students of foreign affairs have recently voiced in this respect. With specialists in international affairs, this is not very surprising. More significant, perhaps, is the fact that this specific concern is now found increasingly in more esoteric fields in which little attention used to be given in the past to the concrete issues of politics and military technology. It is found, for instance in the utterances and doctrines of theologians, or philosophers, or writers, and is no longer merely a repetition of those general and ancient universalist verities which we expect from representatives of universal creeds or from the elaborators of ethical systems. Rather, it is something informed of a sense of concrete urgency and a realization of the utter practicality of world-mindedness that distinguishes these more recent statements from the traditional "love-thy-neighbor" type of admonition. In a slightly cynical vein, one might assume that it is the "love-thy-neighbor-if-you-love-yourself" argument implied in the nuclear threat to the world that has been the compelling element in the new approach, but there is no reason to

29 "A bias for the highest efficiency and fullest volume of life in the group, with a particular drift to the future" (*The Instinct of Workmanship*, p. 46); a "concern entertained by nearly all persons for the life and comfort of the community at large, and particularly for the community's future welfare" (*ibid.*, p. 27).

30 See David Riesman, *Thorstein Veblen* (New York, 1953), p. 52.

doubt the moral sincerity of the statements we are about to refer to.

Niebuhr, who has made recent reference to the "minimal community" of mankind formed by the "common threat of nuclear annihilation," had already said a couple of years ago:

Enlightened men in all nations have some sense of obligation to their fellow-men, beyond the limits of the nation-state. There is at least an inchoate sense of obligation to the inchoate community of mankind. *The desperate necessity for a more integrated world-community has undoubtedly increased this sense of obligation.*[31]

Thomas Mann, in his very last publication, which can perhaps be considered his philosophical legacy to mankind, has given this concern moving expression:

A universal approach is the demand of the hour . . . . It is precisely this feeling of comprehensiveness that is now required, all too much so; for, unless mankind as a whole becomes aware of its oneness, its honor, and the secret of its dignity, it is lost not only morally, but even physically.[32]

Others, like Eduard Spranger, have emphasized that genuine morality is defined as—and only as—standing for and being concerned with the most comprehensive group.[33] True, the distinction between the morality of the narrower group and the higher ethics of the universal group goes back before the atomic age, specifically to Henri Bergson.[34] But it now has a more tangible and more realistic underpinning by virtue of developments, atomic as well as others, as for instance, those in the field of communications. Thus Karl Jaspers elaborates

[31] Reinhold Niebuhr, *Christian Realism and Political Problems* (New York, 1953), p. 28 (italics added).

[32] *Versuch über Schiller* (Berlin, 1955), p. 102.

[33] See his article "Wesen und Wert politischer Ideologien," *Vierteljahrshefte zur Zeitgeschichte,* 2: 118 ff. (1954).

[34] *The Two Sources of Morality and Religion* (New York, 1935). For instance, "The open society is the society which is deemed in principle to embrace all humanity" (p. 256). In a similar vein Ralph Barton Perry spoke of the "morality of inclusiveness" which "gives to the total aggregate of the members of all nations a priority over the members of one of its constituent nations" (*Puritanism and Democracy* [New York, 1944], p. 602).

an entire new approach to the theory of cognition, as well as to that of ethics, on the basis of universalism as an attitude, defined as "the meeting of men in the spirit of universal communication," which only now has become possible as a result of global intercommunication.[35] The compelling force of the argument is vividly illustrated by the line of thought of one of the foremost present defenders of "the national interest" and an opponent of "moralism," Hans J. Morgenthau. According to Morgenthau, universal moral principles, when guiding foreign policies, may lead to moral crusades which, by identifying national interests with the respective moral principles, add ideological furor to power conflict. He therefore recommends a pursuit of national interests undeflected to universal concerns. On the other hand, he recognizes the insufficiency of traditional "national interest" considerations when he states that "none of the traditional objectives of foreign policy can justify war any more, except national self-preservation itself; and even then, the nature of modern war being apt to defeat the end of self-preservation for which the war is being waged, the choice is really between two kinds of national destruction." [36] The choice is, I would add, however, between various kinds of national destruction, on the one hand, and survival through temporary accommodation and eventual prevalence of a moral-political universalism, on the other. Natural and justified as concern with national interests was in an age of independent nation-states with their separate sets of interests, it can no longer be the only legitimate standard when no particular national interest is on a level with the common interest in the avoidance of universal destruction.

In casting about for further sources of universalist attitudes

[35] *Vom Ursprung und Ziel der Geschichte* (Zurich, 1949). The same author's new book on the impact of the atom bomb on man's future, announced for publication in late 1958, was not available when this book was written.

[36] Hans J. Morgenthau, *In Defense of the National Interest* (New York, 1952), p. 58.

we should not limit ourselves to "Western civilization," to which all of the aforementioned authors belong. "One world" contains several civilizations, some of which, although outwardly dominated by Westernism, in their deeper attitude patterns may be closer to universalism than the individualistic West. The culture of India, and particularly Hinduism, has long been imbued with a feeling for the oneness of mankind, and with a sense of "participation" in other human beings, their life and their fate. Chinese culture has been characterized by a profound feeling for the connectedness of past, present, and future generations, and this feeling, while thus far expressed chiefly in traditionalism and ancestor worship, might in the future be directed toward placing greater emphasis on the future with a corresponding "descendent worship." China, with its traditional inclinations now being corrupted in the service of Communist "exclusivist universalism," may have to be counted out for the time being. The Indian approach, however, may be made serviceable, not in its more mystical aspects, but for sober, practical purposes, of which some have been mentioned in connection with "neutralism" and the role of international mediation. We should, to be sure, beware of an "alien-culture enthusiasm" which easily leads to neglect of the practical political problems facing *all* cultures. A mystical "world feeling" [37] or the most intimate comprehension of the peculiar "spirit" and "uniqueness" of the various civilizations of the world [38] will not, by itself, solve world problems or even contribute much to universalism in practice, unless there is added a comprehension of the practical problems and the real difficulties with which the world (a world of powers, not

[37] As it pervades Arnold Toynbee's work, for instance.

[38] As it appears in F. S. C. Northrop's work, for instance. That author's belief in the possibility of solving major world problems through the mutual recognition, on the part of these civilizations, of their respective "spirits" and "worth" reminds one of the utopian assumptions concerning peace and harmony made by the early representatives of "idealist nationalism" (see my *Political Realism and Political Idealism,* pp. 67–77).

only of cultures) is beset. What may be called "UNESCO utopianism" errs through a similar simplification of problems. If it is true that "war starts in the minds of men," it is also true, unfortunately, that peace is not ensured by preaching international understanding, no matter how emphatic and sustained.[39] This is not meant to belittle the more sober efforts and the more realistic objectives of UNESCO or of any other group or organization engaged in bringing the peoples of the world closer together. True universalism in its fight against ingrained older attitudes and traditional parochial interests needs every bit of support from whatever quarter it may come. But a "realist liberalism" must also fight an excessive optimism which—as history with its graveyards of utopian hopes and movements shows—may do as much damage to the cause of realizable ideals as does a cynical realism that denies the validity of such ideals altogether.

A universalist attitude is therefore likely to emerge here and there, in different regions and within different groups, by a kind of "natural selection" or "self-selection" on the part of those who are gripped by a sense of responsibility and concern for the future and who, at the same time, possess the

[39] The doctrine of one forerunner of such a utopianism is perhaps characteristic of the overoptimism inherent in this approach. According to Benjamin Kidd (*The Science of Power* [New York and London], 1918), children (and women), in contrast to male grownups, have a capacity for altruism and sacrifice which after adolescence weakens and gives way to self-centered combative actions. But, Kidd argues, since attitudes and ideologies are not inherited but transferred from generation to generation, the world, by implanting the ideal of peace instead of war, can be remade in one generation: "Universal peace can only be secured in one way—by raising the mind of civilization through the emotion of the ideal conveyed to the rising generation by the collective inheritance, to a plane where the barbarism of war would be so abhorrent to it that the degradation of engaging in it would take away from a people that principal motive of self-respect which makes life worth living" (p. 154). Similar "biological utopianism" is reflected in another, more recent appeal to set up, after the catastrophe of "masculine violence," the feminine element as the supereminent one (see Thomas Baty, *International Law in Twilight* [Tokyo, 1954], p. 300).

broadness of vision which is required to grasp the common survival interest of mankind. Unlike most of the great ideological, political, or religious movements in the history of the human race, the universalist attitude probably will not come in one fell swoop; it will hardly arise somewhere as a powerful "movement," thence to engulf the world. This may turn out to be to its own and the world's advantage, because it may save it from the common fate of world-sweeping movements, namely, turning into power movements deflected from their idealist objectives by the necessity to fight for victory or for mere survival. And, in as much as universalism partakes of a quasi-religious element of "creed," a sense of knowing what is needed and an urge to communicate this sense to others, its advantage over traditional religious movements may lie in the fact that moral demand now coincides with reason and with interest in self-preservation, so that it can appeal to the "unconverted" in the name of the highest in man, his idealism, as well as of that which is of lower ethical order. But in doing so, it will have to cope not only with the powerful material forces which now oppose it—all that which is concerned with individual nations' power and security, the "national interest" narrowly conceived, and possibly also subnational interests. Even more important as an antagonist of universalism may be a certain form of idealism which, by nature, is the opposite of universalism: that idealism which in the past has been strongest in the form of a feeling closely connected with the existence of separate and independent statehood and "sovereignty," that is, national allegiance. Some problems raised by the relation, or conflict, between these two loyalties will be discussed in the following section.

UNIVERSALISM AND NATIONAL ALLEGIANCE

What is the universalist to reply to the seemingly conclusive argument that what he advocates runs counter to the vital interests of the nation to which he belongs, that its very survival is incompatible with universalist policies, and that advocating them, therefore, implies disloyalty to his country?

One argument with which he can counter is that in the vital field of security the old reliance on power is no longer valid, that survival now involves at least renunciation of "total" war, and that this renunciation will ultimately mean divesting nations of their nuclear power. Such a divestment would not, however, diminish the status or stature of nations in the world. On the contrary, it might imply the restoration of some degree of territorial "impermeability," which, in turn, would mean the reestablishment of something like that traditional "sovereignty" which powers have lost under nuclear conditions of permeability. Contrary to what is commonly assumed—and sometimes advocated—the realization of this objective would render the "world state" unnecessary and give a new lease of life to nation-states. Once they have regained their previous protective functions, they can also protect themselves from those more far-reaching encroachments on their independence which the more enthusiastic world planners envisage. Realistic universalism, far from being the deadly enemy of the nation, thus emerges, paradoxically, as its best friend, and quite possibly its last one.

It cannot, on the other hand, be friend to that form of nationalism which is exclusivist and, allied to one or the other "crusading" ideology, now one of the most powerful motors of extremist power politics.[40] For, if nations are to survive in the age of world integration, they can hope to do so only by recognizing what their common interests demand, whether this be in the field of resources, trade, population planning, migration, or in the field of ideologies and attitudes toward each other. It has long been apparent that many of the smaller

[40] This is what Hans J. Morgenthau has called "nationalist universalism" and which, of course, is the opposite of the supernationalist universalism here advocated.

and weaker nations have lost their economic and military viability in an age of ever larger economic and defense regions. But we have seen [41] that despite their apparent obsolescence the older ones among these units have obstinately insisted on persisting—and even on being resurrected after a temporary demise. Nationalism, in these instances at least, is based upon a strong subjective foundation of loyalty feelings and sentiments of patriotism, and no believer in the principles of self-determination and freedom can afford to belittle its role when it comes to rallying forces against totalitarian subjection—as witness the stubborn resistance of European nations to Nazi-Fascist domination, and now to Communist control. But nationalism becomes doubtful in its functions as well as in its credibility in the case of many of the more recent nations (or those not yet born but planned). With the spread of nationalism to Asia, the Near East, and Africa and the application of the principle of national self-determination to these areas, it has become obvious that nationalism in many respects has become outmoded at almost the very time it has reached those parts of the world. Nationhood as such often lacks credibility there. The units themselves and their boundaries are often matters of coincidence, and not (as in the case of most of the old and established nations) of ancient and deep-rooted feelings of coherence; the various Arab "nations" are examples, as is the one, all-encompassing "Arab nation" propagated by Nasser; and in the case of still colonial Africa native nationalists themselves are sometimes unable to agree on the identity of the national units they so fervently hope to establish. Continual splintering into linguistic and other sub-groups threatens the coherence of India and Indonesia or leads to the production of one "-stan" after the other (from Afghanistan to Pakistan to "Pushtunistan") in demands for self-determination. This is not to brush aside the manifold

[41] See above, ch. 4.

grievances which cause movements of this sort to emerge; it is only to question the rationality of their objective, national self-determination, in an age when, contrary to conditions in the eighteenth and nineteenth centuries, traditional nation-statehood has become incapable of providing populations with two basic needs: economic well-being and military protection.

The fact that many of the newer units—and some of the older ones as well—survive only through economic and military assistance vividly illustrates the obsolescence in our times of national independence in the traditional sense. Perhaps it would not be too much to expect their experience in this respect to render some of these nations protagonists of a universalism which recognizes the need for world-wide planning and action in regard to the problems with which they are beset but with which they cannot cope singlehandedly. Today, their formal independence means little if they have to turn to one or the other power bloc for aid; it only results in exacerbating a nationalism unable to realize its fundamental objective. In turning toward universalist objectives, on the other hand, far from being "unfairly" deprived of that which older nations have, namely, a national independence, which today can only be a spurious one, the newer nations would emerge as pacemakers in bringing forth new developments from which they themselves, together with other nations, could only profit.

In the case of the older nations world-wide tasks undertaken in fields like conservation of resources or planning of population might likewise have an effect which would mitigate an exclusivist nationalism. The transition from medieval feudalism to the modern territorial state meant the consolidation in one territorial unit of all those influences which, under feudalism, had played upon the individual from different vantage points. He thus became a "nationalist." It is possible that in the future this process will be reversed and the exclusiveness of territorial jurisdiction over individuals and groups included in the nation-state will be broken by diverse influences emanating from supraterritorial agencies. This would constitute a new kind of "permeability from above": not penetrability by force—as under atomic conditions—but "peaceful penetration," a situation in which, alongside continuing territorial jurisdiction, a whole bundle of superterritorial or extraterritorial jurisdictions would take effect within national boundaries. This might be accompanied by similar developments in the field of international law and legal ideology. Where, formerly, the interests of the different territorial units were clearly separable, legal rules had for their primary objective the implementation of the separateness of nations by delimiting their respective jurisdictions as clearly and sharply as possible; with the intertwining of national interests new rules have become necessary, rules which give expression to the pursuance of common interests. Insistence on "exclusive national jurisdiction" over the air space above national territory is inconsistent with the requirements of civil aviation or weather research (not to speak of the new problems of outer space); claiming unlimited rights to exploit the treasures of the sea and its subsoil runs counter to a global interest in their common, and possibly planned and limited, use. With new concepts arising from new functions of supernational agencies and new standards of international law, the idea of the nation-state as the ultimate unit of control may, in the minds of people, yield to the more modest image of one unit among others. As we have seen in discussing "functionalism," intermingling of national and international tasks does not per se eliminate or solve the problems of power and power politics. Indirectly, however, it can affect the power sphere through a modification of attitudes resulting in an abatement of nationalist exclusivisms. But although, or perhaps because, so strengthened, a rising universalism is liable once more to clash with its most dangerous opponent, exclusivist national allegiance, proclaimed as the only valid political morality by all those who represent the partial and particular interests in the world against the mutual, common, world-wide ones.

We must not forget that the feeling of allegiance or loyalty, even in our age of "depolitization" and widespread indifference to matters that do not affect individual (personal) concerns directly, is one of the remaining—perhaps the most important among the remaining—idealistic sentiments which still arouse man's passion. And because it has for so long been connected with the most important among modern political units, the nation-states, "national" allegiance, loyalty to one's country, is frequently so strongly rooted in the emotions that any movement opposing it or seeking to replace it with another allegiance might seem to many to be doomed to failure. Feelings like loyalty to country appear to be "timeless," that is, permanent and beyond any change of historical circumstances and conditions. History shows that this is an "ideological" illusion. As in other instances, the concepts developed in this study for basic international relations and structures can be applied to national allegiance as one of those seemingly "eternal" phenomena, and it can be shown that there is a close connection between feelings and attitudes of allegiance on the one hand, and the development of units of international relations on the other. It may then appear that the opposition of nationalism to universalist trends partakes more of the nature of "last-ditch desperation" than of the strong conviction which the "higher" or "more timely cause" imparts.

"Loyalty" has usually been connected with "protection." The individual was supposed to owe "allegiance" to that unit, and its ruler or government, which offered protection for his life, goods and values from dangers arising within the protected unit as well as from without. In the Middle Ages this was a relationship of direct "give and take," with vassals owing fealty to their lords for the latter's protection, which was given in return for the help the vassals provided with their own might to make the lords strong enough to grant such protection. With the institution of the centralized territorial state, and the power of the state as such so much greater than that of the single individual citizen, the relationship became more one-sided, but with nationalism and the "nation in arms" the old principle of service in return for protection was restored. In the nation-state, the citizen was required, if need be, to lay down his life as token of the supreme loyalty due the protecting unit. This merely reflected the fact that the modern territorial state had emerged as the ultimate unit which could uphold and defend individual and group security within and without. In time, thus, national allegiance emerged as the prototype of loyalty. Indeed, because it might involve the "supreme sacrifice," it was made to appear as the overriding, if not the only valid kind, reflecting the tribalism of "My country right or wrong."

In reality, it was not, nor could it ever become, the only standard. The first mistake, or oversimplification, lay in assuming that its meaning was clear and unequivocal. That this was not so is apparent from the political-ethical problems that arose in those cases in which a ruler neglected the interests of the nation by condoning its subjection to another unit, perchance for reasons of personal gain or safety. In such an event, the very existence or continuance of the national unit might demand, not loyalty to the ruler, but resistance, and quite possibly "revolutionary" action. This was the problem with which Prussians like Yorck von Wartenburg were faced when their king refused to join the liberation forces against Napoleon, and perhaps this was the justification for Joan of Arc's forcing her king's hand against the English in France. In similar fashion, this was the problem with which the Resistance forces in Nazi-occupied Europe were confronted wherever a quisling regime had been installed, in so far as their action was directed against their own puppet rulers. In cases of this nature, the question inevitably arises: Who is to determine whether or not the—or a—"national interest" is being betrayed by the ruler? Even some quislings may have acted out of a subjectively sincere sentiment of duty and a belief that this was the way to serve their nation best. Neither law nor ethics here yield clear rules or standards of conduct; no positive "right"—right of resistance or right to revolution—has ever been validly demonstrated. Those acting act at their own risk, their consciences being their only guide. If they were lucky, the moral judgment of their fellow nationals, and of mankind, would sooner or later absolve them from guilt even when they failed to succeed and would recognize that theirs had been the more "genuine" loyalty to the nation.

Second, and beyond situations like these—which at base still involve "national" loyalty—there is the realm of certain higher-than-national loyalties which not even at the height of the nation-state and its nationalism were ever completely silenced. Protection afforded by the group to which one belonged was the barest minimum expected; what if the state or its ruler-ship turned tyrannical, suppressing the freedoms and liberties of all or most? What if it turned exploitatory, permitting a minority to live at the expense of a majority of slaves, or serfs, or "proletarians," groups which then were hardly even protected any more in any valid sense of the word? What if elementary humanitarian principles were neglected in respect to minorities, for instance, or a religious belief, or a religion as organized church, persecuted? Was it then to be deemed inconsistent with national allegiance to resist, or even to take up a fight against, the specific way in which the nation was organized? That is, to oppose its government, its ruling group or class, by force if need be, so long as the aim remained to provide one's country with a better form of government, or a better "way of life"? No immutable valid principle of "right" or "justice" can be established here either, centuries-old efforts to create natural law doctrines notwithstanding: Creed still stands against creed, "ideology" against "ideology"; but liberal democracy, the ruling ideology of the more advanced nation-states, has usually recognized at least the subjective "good faith," that is, the validity of the loyalty feelings, of those who sincerely have striven to remake their nation according to their ideal—whether they have been believers or atheists, liberals or socialists, communists or reactionaries. In this view, so long as they did not betray the image of the nation they carried in their minds, they were not "traitors," except, possibly, in a purely legalistic sense. Even if they were "internationalists," believing in a higher-than-national cause and promoting it through some "international" movement, they could hardly be considered "disloyal" so long as their internationalism was genuine, that is, conceived of as in the interest of all nations including their own, and not in the interest or service of a particular nation or group of nations.

In such cases, an extreme conflict situation might arise when it was necessary to ally oneself temporarily with one's country's enemies and to work against one's country in war in order to destroy a tyranny. Then, defeat and even loss of territory or similar sacrifices had to be endured as the price for making one's country a better country or, at least, a tolerably good one again. The price might look like "betrayal" to the more obtuse and primitive nationalists within the nation and abroad. In this lay the dilemma of the anti-Fascists in Fascist Italy, the anti-Nazis in Hitler-Germany, for the goal of their action did not appear so straightforwardly "national" as that of the resisters in the countries under Axis control. In a deeper sense however, they were not disloyal; indeed, under a liberal-democratic philosophy, even according to standards of an elementary humanitarianism, they were the only ones true to their nation when its image was most cruelly distorted.

The loyalty problem thus is not so simple as the "terrible simplifiers" of any problem—above all the self-appointed defenders of an allegedly self-explanatory "national allegiance"— would have it. As in the past, they are defending a status quo which is more likely to be that of the past than that of the future. In an age of bipolarity in particular they have a chance to distort the stand and attitude of those who would advocate an allegiance beyond, or broader than, the narrowly conceived national one, because, under conditions of such a power conflict, the broader stand becomes at once more complicated and more easily misinterpreted. We noted earlier that Communism, which was once conceivable as a bona fide movement toward what its adherents would consider a better economic and social system, is now outlawed as inconsistent with allegiance to a country included in the Western bloc of nations. And it is true that its advocacy now inevitably involves partisanship for that power and power bloc which is out to weaken if not to destroy the other one. The trouble is that under conditions of mutual and often exaggerated suspicion, any movement or attitude that deviates from the traditional pattern can be tainted with the stain of lending aid and assistance to "the enemy." And it must be admitted that there is actual danger of corruption through involuntary affiliation with the interests and policies of "the other side," especially of the high-minded but naive and voluble, and when it comes to the propagandistic exploitation, by Communists, of general humanitarian ideals.

Are we then, as an alternative, reduced to the narrowest kind of parochial and exclusivist loyalty as the only admissible standard of allegiance? Are we to forego advocacy of change altogether, whether domestic or international, and to tie loyalty entirely to the status quo? At this point we may recall universalism as the other alternative of the age. Universalists, first of all, may point out that, in a negative way, traditional national allegiance no longer possesses the meaning which it had at the time of the protective, impermeable nation-state. In those days it was the counterpart to genuine protection, itself guaranteeing that the protecting unit remained cohesive and strong enough to fulfill its protective function. Today, in major war, the nation can avail itself of national allegiance only as a means to marshal unquestioning readiness to suffer (as well as to inflict) annihilation. With the national unit no longer in a position to function as it used to, traditional loyalty likewise undergoes a transformation, and a loss, of function. Universalism, on the other hand, is in a position to draw the ultimate conclusion from the demise of the nation-state's protective function. As was pointed out before, working for universalism may well imply action to *restore* this protective function to the nation; to nations, to be sure, which will have foregone the use of the most destructive means of power and warfare but which, on account of this very renunciation, will have become territorial units in somewhat the older sense again. They will not, of course, revert to old-fashioned total "sovereignty" and self-sufficiency, but they will at least become defensible and thus identifiable units once again. Loyalty to a higher-than-national cause in this way reveals itself as national loyalty in a higher sense, indeed, as the only possible genuine national allegiance now. National allegiance in the parochial sense today points the way toward destruction, the doom of all nations—including one's own. Allegiance to universalist aims points the way to a better life, to a new security, to the survival of nations—including one's own. Old-type nationalism at best safeguards a temporary and precarious continuation of life for those presently living; universalism is concerned with the lives of our children and of theirs far into the dim ranges of the future.

Such new allegiance will arouse suspicion among those who are wedded to the narrower concept of national allegiance. They will not only indict its adherents as "starry-eyed idealists" who in effect betray the nation, but brand them as willful betrayers. And indeed, if universalists would be realists, they must be chary of the abuse which powers and power politics *can* make of universalist ideals; one latter-day example has been "peace" propaganda in the service of the Soviet bloc. Such a misuse, of course, does not rule out peace as an aim of genuine universalism, as little as use, or misuse, of anti-imperialism, anticolonialism, or technical and economic assistance on the part of one or the other bloc renders such policies and objectives less valid when pursued in the framework of universalism. But once universalists realize this and avoid being "used" by powers for power-political or ideological ends, any "disloyalty" charges would lose validity in the face of their higher and broader loyalty.

WHO WILL SPEAK FOR MAN?

From all that has been said it should now be clear that universalism, if it ever is to emerge as an important force in the world, will arise through a revolution in minds and attitudes rather than in the shape of a mass movement of the kind known to previous history. This, however, poses a serious problem to those who would be realist students of international affairs. Ideals, to be effective, have always had to align themselves with specific, concrete "bearers," or "carriers," that is, groups and forces organized for political action and strong enough to translate ideals into reality, whether they were nations, or social classes, or religious organizations. Universalism here finds itself in a real dilemma. For, as has been pointed out before, the marrying of a universal ideal to a "movement" has so far always meant its eventual transformation into something serving particular, power-political aims and purposes and hence its corruption, whatever the "universal" class or group carrying it originally. Ideals and ideas not so married to a "bearing" foundation, on the other hand, are usually destined to remain in the realm of utopias dreamed up by philosophers, theologians, or moralists alienated from reality. Ours, in particular, is an age when individuals are more and more lost among the masses of millions and billions, and where effective social action depends more than ever on those who man the key centers and control the "commanding heights" of large-scale, interlocking organization. How, then, can anything be expected to succeed in the face of opposition from those who make the vital decisions in and for those units which still are the primary ones in international politics, the "powers"? How helpful is it if some people in India and some in Germany, some in America and some maybe even in the Soviet Union become converted to universalist ideals, and if we find them scattered among any number of social groups, including the "international civil service"?

Their importance should not be underrated, because they might in time become the carriers of a massive trend exerting pressure on those in power. But it is also true that much will eventually depend on those in power positions. It is hardly conceivable that universalists will stage revolutions in which they themselves take over positions of power. The very idea of their doing this makes realists smile, for universalists are likely to be "peaceful" men of "good will," rather than hard-boiled organizers of political movements. Moreover, scattered as they necessarily are among diverse groups, they will not have any one group at their disposal to initiate and carry such a movement. Finally, revolutions in the traditional sense are not likely to succeed in an age of overwhelming counter-strength of centralized governments (whether totalitarian or democratic), particularly when, under bipolarity, any such effort can be discredited as "enemy"-inspired and "enemy"-directed.

May we then put our hope in a kind of Constantinian conversion of rulers into believers in and promoters of the right faith? If we do, does this not run counter to a basic assumption of international politics, that the compelling force of power concerns and security considerations which the individual statesman neglects, he neglects at the risk of disregarding his country's vital interests? Universalism would be a utopian instead of a realist approach to international affairs if it were blind to the security dilemma and all it involves. But it would also be unrealistic to neglect the potentialities which do exist within the framework and the limits of power politics, for, as we have remarked before, there are periods and constellations in which some "leeway" and "discretion" are left to the acting, when it is a matter of the more or the less that can be done, when what is actually done is a matter of choice between different policies, none of which is inconsistent with power and security interests. Especially if we assume that a period of "peaceful coexistence" will lessen tension—and this is the only assumption under which universalism has a chance—statesmen may find opportunities to plan in the interests of all and for the future of all—that is, to inaugurate policies which need not be antagonistic to their own countries' interests. And if they seemed to involve sacrifices according to narrow nationalist viewpoints, they would appear as beneficial in long-range, broader views.[42] Already

42 People have sometimes commented upon "the paradoxical situation that present-day foreign ministers enjoy considerable popularity in every country save their own" (see Henry A. Kissinger, "American Policy and Preventing War," *Yale Review* [Spring, 1955], p. 323); but this is nothing new, as witness Briand and Stresemann, and even earlier examples. Farsighted and, in a broad sense, "liberal" statesmen, who try to advance the "general" interest together with that of their own nation whenever the situation leaves leeway for such action, will always incur the suspicion and the wrath of self-appointed "guardians of the national interest." See Kenneth W. Thompson's recent remarks on the relation between national interest and liberal statesmanship in his article "The Limits of Principle in International Politics: Necessity and the New Balance of Power," *Journal of Politics*, 20: 437 ff. (1958), in particular pp. 464–67.

such policies as technical and economic assistance to under-developed countries appear justified to many under standards of "national interests" broadly conceived, although they may involve expenditure without immediate return in cash or even in political profit. This attitude, if generalized, might become a basis of universalist statesmanship. I say this, not in the expectation that it will materialize easily and in frequent instances, but rather in the sober hope that that which Raymond Aron has called for as "good will without illusions"[43] will guide leaders and nations wherever and whenever it is realistically justifiable, and that the accumulating effect of such action may consist in further mitigation of those power and security factors which under lessened tension will have lost some of their harsher implications anyhow.

Statesmen, or indeed all those who feel responsible to posterity and to mankind as a whole, will then act in a double capacity: as agents of the more particular units and, simultaneously, as representatives of the whole; they will try to avoid conflicts of interests between the larger and the smaller groups wherever possible; their greatest merit will be that they uphold the wider interest and maintain the broader view even when the opposite side provocatively clings to the pursuance of the narrower policy. Such a duplication of functions would not be as radically novel as it may appear; it would correspond to the well-known situation in domestic and international affairs in which broad-minded representatives of particular group interests (business, for instance, or labor) have been known to serve the interests of the larger entity, for instance, the nation, without neglecting or "betraying" those of the smaller one. This duplication is no innovation in international politics either, where countries and their statesmen have been known to act at times as "caretakers" of a larger group interest as well as of the interests of their own, as, for instance, when foregoing expansionist policies in favor

---

[43] "Bonne volonté sans illusions."

of a common balance of power or a concert of powers. There it constituted a parallel to that *dédoublement fonctionnel* which the French international lawyer, Georges Scelle, considers the characteristic trait of the behavior of legal representatives of nation-states in international affairs so long as international law is primarily a law whose legal subjects are nation-states.[44] Exactly as, legally speaking, such persons act as agents of a state and, simultaneously, as organs of the international community, whose law they implement, they would under universalism have to act, politically, as agents both of the partial and of the universal group.

Can we distingush, in the present-day world, some units (countries, powers, groupings of such) which are in a better position than others to promote global solutions along with the pursuance of their own interests? Whose leadership can afford universalist attitudes better than the leadership of others? In a general way it can perhaps be said that big powers, with their world-wide interests, have better opportunities to conceive of their interests as "responsibilities" to all than have lesser powers, considering the latters' natural preoccupation with their own, smaller sphere. Especially where the latter have gone down the scale of power, where they are partitioned, or where they have similar special reasons to be concerned about one overriding "national interest," do they tend to be "ego-centered" to a degree which may preclude any larger concern with broader, "common interest" problems. They are inclined to take notice of such problems more or less in the light of how they affect their own particular interests. Present-day France and West Germany offer examples of such attitudes. On the other hand, there are among the lesser powers some that—in regard to their security as well as to their economic and similar interests—are so dependent on international arrangements and alignments that global attitudes and universalist approaches might come more

44 See Georges Scelle, *Précis de Droit des gens* (Paris, 1932).

naturally to them. Those countries in particular which have not become used to considering themselves mere "clients" of powerful nations but which, despite actual dependencies, continue to foster a spirit of independence and to maintain a tradition of "making up their own minds" may be counted in this category. Norway,, or Switzerland, are more likely to stand for "internationalism" (as they have done traditionally) than others. Such attitudes may even be found among the countries which only recently have come into existence. Some of these, of course, are inclined to subordinate everything to the safeguarding of their newly found independence in potentially or actually hostile environments; they tend to be not only ego-centered but isolationist or ultranationalist; and they may be further handicapped by the emotionalism, parochialism, or, simply, the unfamiliarity of their new leadership personnel with the ways and possibilities of diplomacy. But some among the new countries, at least, have been as outstanding in their advocacy of universalist solutions as they have become important to the world in their capacity as "natural" mediators wherever mediation and similar activities have had a chance in the bipolar world. One should not expect too much by way of self-abnegation even from countries like India, which sometimes show extremely nationalistic inclinations when it comes to problems which are geographically or otherwise close to them. Still, they can afford to embrace the universalist cause at times when the other powers, and especially those powers which are arranged in blocs on opposite sides, tend to perceive everything in the light of their bloc interests.

But short of the emergence of, let us say, India as one of the really "big" powers on a par with the present superpowers, one can hardly bank on the world's being saved by the uncommitted nations. Can one expect more from those which actually determine world politics today? Despite, or perhaps because, of their world-wide interests and commitments, the two leading powers seem at present particularly unlikely to play the above-mentioned dual role of agents of the narrower and of the universal interest. In the instance of one of them this, paradoxically, is so exactly because it embraces a cause which it claims to be "universal." Since the non-Communist world cannot accept that cause as universal, it would have to be enforced upon the world if it ever were to become the universal solution in practice. Things would then be solved "globally," indeed, but under Soviet world-rulership. That the Communist bloc does not approach universal problems from any other but a power-political vantage point is demonstrated by the attitude of the Soviets to a problem like that of overpopulation. To them this problem appears exclusively in the light of their own military (manpower) and related interests, exactly as it did to powers like Nazi Germany or militarist Japan. The universalist concern with the problem is contemptuously rejected by these powers as being "neo-Malthusian," a trick of imperialist powers to disarm their opponents and the rising colonial world to which the Soviets direct their propaganda.[45]

For reasons mentioned previously, which are clear enough in a world split with respect to power and ideology, the United States of late has been and still is singularly preoccupied with its own problem of security. Universalist attitudes, indeed mere "internationalism" which was commonplace not so long ago, have become suspect in the eyes of many, to be ridiculed as idealist but ineffective "globaloney," or, worse, to be considered as part of the Communist "world conspiracy." Still, there is not that complete identification in America of narrower national or ideological cause with the

[45] Where, however, as in China now, population increase reaches a point which endangers the future of the nation in question, there is of course no hesitation to resort to "neo-Malthusian" remedies like birth control. Here, then, Communist policy and universalist interest may coincide, but not because of any universalist concern on the part of those in power.

"universal" cause which we find on the Soviet side. Western liberal-democratic and humanitarian ideology continues to conceive of universalism as something broader than and superior to the special and narrower interests of the groups into which mankind is divided. Liberal-democratic nations, therefore, can at least in principle distinguish between narrower and broader policies, the power approach and the universalist one. As has been pointed out, there is not always and necessarily a contradiction between the one and the other. In the case of powerful nations in particular a "surplus" of power may give them a chance to subordinate power considerations to the furtherance of the "general" interest; or an economic "surplus" may permit the same approach in the economic sphere. One can then be generous without being suicidal. As in former times the public, despite its separate group interests, could be concerned with "just" and "fair" solutions of the great domestic problems, now that international problems have come to loom so much larger than internal ones, it is, perhaps, not utopian to expect that enlightened nations may become concerned with "just" and "fair," that is, universalist, solutions in the field of international relations despite their own involvement.

So far as present attitudes and inclinations are concerned, Britain and some Commonwealth nations would seem readier than America to espouse the universal interests together with their own. But while they may play a restraining role in the Western alliance, they have less leeway, power-politically or economically, for decisive action otherwise. There remains the United States. Will it yet revert to its high tradition—sometimes ill-used and therefore often maligned—of moral leadership to save the world—not, as it was in the first "American dream," by isolating itself and building the heavenly city at home, nor either, as it dreamt later, through "crusading" for freedom and democracy abroad, but rather through setting an example of how, in a realistic, hard-boiled Yankee fashion, the objectives of one nation can, indeed have to be, interpreted and pursued so as to satisfy those of all nations? How, in other words, the long-range can take precedence over the short-range interest, that of future generations over the narrower one of those presently living, that of survival over immediate increase in power? Whether in the realm of nuclear armaments or as a matter of defining aggression, whether in regard to a problem of world population or to one of conservation of world resources, universalist approaches can be found which do not necessarily involve the sacrifice of vital national interests. Skeptics should remember that there was a time when, in the domestic affairs of the United States, the particular "interests" and the "general welfare" seemed to be irreconcilably opposed to each other. The "American way," as then commonly conceived, seemed to brook no interference with a predatory exploitation of wealth (natural as well as human resources) which threatened the future of the country as a whole. Then, far-sighted leadership established limits by taking measures which, while not sacrificing the particular interests involved, saved at least part of the public domain for future generations. This was genuine concern for the "widest group," at that time still the nation. On the global plane, to be sure, where action is required today, everything is a hundredfold more complicated, if only because the widest group is unorganized and particular ones have to act in its name. It may reflect the bias and the wishful thinking of someone living in one of these particular units to believe that this nation, great in the past and so often mankind's hope for the future, may yet show a spirit and produce a leadership commensurate with the tasks of universalism. It was America which fashioned and used the first atomic weapon, thereby writing finis to an age of territorial protection and safety. It should be America's prime endeavor to retrieve that minimum of security the world over without which lives cannot be lived in dignity.

Index of Personal Names